Sebastian Westcott, the Children of Paul's, and *The Marriage of Wit and Science*

TREVOR LENNAM

TREVOR LENNAM is a member of the Department of Drama at the University of Calgary.

The Children of Paul's was the most important chorister company of its time and the favourite of Queen Elizabeth I. Its stage performances entertained courtly and public audiences for the best part of a century, with the company under the direction of Sebastian Westcott for 35 of those years. In this volume Professor Lennam traces Westcott's career, records the history of the company, and places both in proper perspective.

Founding his work on *The Child Actor*, the pioneering study written by N.H. Hillebrand some fifty years ago, and on the more recent research of Arthur Brown, Professor Lennam contributes much new information about Westcott's life and career, the organization and personnel of the company, their repertoire, and the playhouse in the precinct of St Paul's Cathedral. He also provides an edition, with a critical introduction, of one of the two surviving plays presented by the company over four hundred years ago.

This study corrects misconceptions concerning Westcott and reveals him to be an unusually interesting man and a major figure in the history of pre-Shakespearean theatre. It is also valuable in providing a clear understanding of the place of the boy actor in adult troupes and school and chorister companies in the sixteenth century, an understanding essential to the assessment of his status in later times.

THE PUBLISHER

TREVOR LENNAM

Sebastian Westcott, the Children of Paul's, and *The Marriage of Wit and Science*

UNIVERSITY OF TORONTO PRESS
TORONTO AND BUFFALO

© University of Toronto Press 1975
Toronto and Buffalo
Printed in Canada

Library of Congress Cataloging in Publication Data

Lennam, Trevor N
 Sebastian Westcott, the Children of Paul's, and the
 Marriage of wit and science.

 Bibliography: p.
 Includes index.
 1. Westcott, Sebastian, 1524–1582.   2. Children of
 Paul's.   3. Marriage of Wit and Science.   4. Theater –
 London – History.   5. Children as actors.   I. Title.
 PN2598.W28L45   792'.0233'0924 [B]   75-5797
 ISBN 0-8020-5312-2

To G. R. Wilson Knight,
Richard Brooks, and David Galloway
with gratitude

Contents

Sebastian Westcott and the Children of Paul's

The Marriage of Wit and Science

Preface

THE COMPOSITION of the interludes, *Wit and Science* by John Redford, the anonymous *Marriage of Wit and Science* presented by Sebastian Westcott, and Francis Merbury's *Marriage between Wit and Wisdom*, together with the plays these influenced, span well over half a century. The bitter conflict over church worship that filled the intervening years, periodically lit by the fires of martyrs and resounding to the clamour of opposing convictions, left no traces upon these plays. Unlike so many contemporary dramas, they are free of religious propaganda or indignation. The earliest two appeal to the courtly pleasures of hearing the pipe of choristers' voices in graceful speech and song and of watching the spectacle of 'little eyasses' attempting the flight of eagles; the last play makes its appeal, no less entertainingly in its way, to college hall and perhaps to common stage. Yet, like so many others connected with the drama of the time, the men associated with the *Wit* plays were churchmen. Westcott and Redford were cathedral officials, Vicars Choral, Almoners, and Choirmasters of St Paul's; Merbury was ordained deacon not long after writing his play and leaving the University of Cambridge. Although strife between the old and the new worship was, fortunately, not reflected in their work, it came near to blighting the lives of two of them.

Westcott's stubborn papistry and his dogged resistance to the pressures of religious conformity are paralleled by the more vocal and belligerent protestant, Merbury. That fervid young deacon defied episcopal authority because, in his view, it had not reformed enough. At that time Merbury's oratorical gifts had not yet secured for him the protection of a patron, and there was no one to shield him from the consequences of his youthful zeal. He was imprisoned several times, fortunately never for long. Before the last of such confinements, he was brought before the Bishop of London in the Consistory Court of St Paul's – was Westcott among those 'standing by' one wonders? Merbury's keeper was instructed by the weary and irritated John Aylmer to 'have him to the Marshal Sea, there he shall cope with the Papistes.' The date was 5 November 1578. Had this incarceration taken place a few months earlier, Merbury would have had the opportunity of exercising his persuasive oratory upon Sebastian Westcott, who was committed to the Marshalsea 'for papistry' from 30 December 1577 to 19 March 1578. It is doubtful whether Merbury would have effected what so many others had failed to do; nevertheless, it is pleasant to speculate that the presenter of *The Marriage of Wit and Science* and the author of *The Marriage between Wit and Wisdom* would, perhaps, have found a common sympathy – a union of wit and wisdom, say – strong enough to overcome a mutual Marshalsea foe, the monster Tediousness.

As schoolmasters, all three men would have been fortunate to escape at least a passing acquaintance with tediousness. Redford and Westcott no doubt taught the choristers more than music. Merbury became a grammar school master after he left Christ's College. Although Merbury, to some extent, and Redford particularly, find place in this study, the main concern is the attempt to trace the career of Sebastian Westcott and record the history of the company of young actors with whom he was intimately associated for thirty-five years; it also hopes to offer students of the early Elizabethan drama an edition of one of the two surviving plays presented by him over four hundred years ago. Of all the men connected with the pre-Shakespearean drama, no one has a longer or more interesting record of theatrical activity than Sebastian Westcott, Redford's friend and successor at St Paul's. His career as a presenter of plays at court extends from at least 1551, when he collaborated with John Heywood in a presentation before Princess Elizabeth, until his death in 1582. This career might possibly have begun even earlier, since he was a Yeoman of the King's Chamber in 1545. For more than twenty years from Elizabeth's accession until the year of his death, the Paul's boys under his direction performed regularly at court; by the first decade of the young Queen's reign they were her favourite acting company.

It is almost fifty years since Harold Newcomb Hillebrand published his first study of Westcott, and over forty years since the appearance of his history of the Elizabethan chorister companies in which he incorporated his pioneer work on Westcott and the Paul's boys. *The Child Actors* continues to be an indispensable guide to the subject. Interpretation of the evidence about Westcott and the boys differs in several ways herein; nevertheless the debt to Hillebrand will be clearly apparent. Almost all the new information about Westcott, published in the interim between 1926 and this study, is contained in a series of articles by Arthur Brown, whose discoveries solved problems related to Westcott's employment at St Paul's and, building upon the researches of A.W. Reed, settled the question of his relationship with John Redford and John Heywood.

Notwithstanding all this, Westcott's contribution to the early stage continues to be misunderstood, and even more seriously, to be overlooked. Biographical errors such as those contained, for instance, in the *Dictionary of Catholic Biography* (1962) and speculative attempts to show that he wrote *The Marriage of Wit and Science* and, indeed, other plays, cloud our knowledge of him and obscure his true achievement. *Early English Stages* (1963–72), the most recent, comprehensive, and in many ways penetrating study of the early theatre, does not mention him; it also omits any discussion whatsoever of the playhouse at Paul's which Westcott founded and successfully operated before either Farrant or Burbage established their respective theatres. In placing him more clearly against his background in Devon and London, and in providing new information about the man, this study aims to correct lingering misconception. In offering a critical text of *The Marriage of Wit and Science* the principle hope is that the play will be recognized as a worthwhile addition to the small number of surviving early Elizabethan comedies. A major dislocation in the text of the unique edition has for too long obliterated its inherent merit and misled critics and editors alike.

Sebastian Westcott's resolute adherence to the old faith brought him alarmingly close to adversity. His ability to ride out the dangerous currents which disturbed, but which did not check, his long career, argues an unusual degree of resolve and resource and these qualities will be discernible in the attempt to follow his life from the use of known and the recovery of additional records. Harder to estimate are those other qualities, a creative talent and a personal charm among them, which secured for him the protection of the Queen and the respectful address of court and civic officials, even hostile ones, who refer to him by his first name.

Acknowledgments

I SHOULD LIKE to acknowledge the research grants I have received from the Canada Council in the summers of 1965 and 1966, and to express my thanks to the University of Calgary for a grant to cover my travel expenses when I journeyed to England in 1968.

Investigation of local records gave me the pleasant opportunity of working for brief periods at various County Record Offices and west country libraries. I acknowledge with pleasure the personal kindness as well as the material assistance received from the archivists and staffs of the Devon, Somerset, Buckingham, and Berkshire Record Offices, and from the librarians of the City of Exeter and the North Devon Athenaeum, Barnstaple.

Two sections of this book are based upon articles which have already been published. Chapter v is a briefly expanded version of a paper delivered at the Second International Conference on Elizabethan Theatre held at the University of Waterloo, Ontario, in July 1969 and published in *The Elizabethan Theatre 11* (Toronto 1970). The final portion of 'The Heirs of Wit and Science' which concludes the introduction to *The Marriage of Wit and Science* has appeared in a slightly different form as 'The Ventricle of Memory: Wit and Wisdom in *Love's Labour's Lost*,' in *Shakespeare Quarterly* xxiv (Winter 1973) 54–60.

I am also grateful to those institutions at which I worked in London – the Public Record Office, the British Museum, the Principal Probate Registry at Somerset House, and to the Bodleian Library for permission to include photographs of the recto and verso sides of the title-page from the unique quarto of *The Marriage of Wit and Science*. I am indebted to Mr J.G. Woodward, Assistant Keeper of Manuscripts at the Guildhall Library, for putting me in touch with sources of information, and to Miss M.B. Honeybourne of the London Topographical Society for advising me about the topography of Old St Paul's. I must also express thanks to the Dean and Chapter and to the Reverend Canon F. Hood, Canon-Residentiary and Chancellor of St Paul's Cathedral, for kindly permitting me to work in the Cathedral Library. To the Librarian, Mr A.R.B. Fuller, I owe very special thanks. It is a pleasure to record my obligation to him for many services generously and courteously offered over the past few years.

Finally, I wish to thank my wife, Una, and my colleagues Drs William Magee and Robert Tener for reading my manuscript and improving it with valuable corrections and suggestions.

This book has been published with the help of grants from the Humanities Research Council of Canada, using funds provided by the Canada Council, and from the Andrew W. Mellon Foundation.

TL
The Department of Drama
The University of Calgary

Illustrations

Abbreviations and Short Titles

Annals	*Annals of English Drama 975–1700* ed. A. Harbage, revised S. Schoenbaum 1964
BM	The British Museum Library
Chambers	E.K. Chambers *The Elizabethan Stage* Oxford 1923. 4 vols
Cal. LP For. & Dom.	*Calendar of the Letters and Papers Foreign and Domestic*
Cal. Pat. Rolls	*Calendar of the Patent Rolls*
Cath. Rec. Soc.	*Catholic Record Society Publications*
DCNQ	*Devon and Cornwall Notes and Queries*
DNB	*Dictionary of National Biography*
EETS	Early English Text Society
EHR	*English Historical Review*
ES	*English Studies*
ESRS	*Emporia State Research Studies*
Feuillerat, E & M	Albert Feuillerat *Documents Relating to the Revels at Court, King Edward VI and Queen Mary* Louvain 1914
Feuillerat, E	Albert Feuillerat *Documents Relating to the Office of the Revels in the Time of Elizabeth* Louvain 1908
Grove's	*Grove's Dictionary of Music and Musicians* Fifth Edition, ed. Eric Blom. London 1954

Hillebrand	H.N. Hillebrand *The Child Actors* Urbana, Ill. 1926
Hist. Man. Comm.	Historical Manuscripts Commission
JEGP	*Journal of English and Germanic Philology*
Milman	H.H. Milman *Annals of St Paul's Cathedral* London 1868
MA	*The Musical Antiquary*
MSR	Malone Society Reprint
MLN	*Modern Language Notes*
MLQ	*Modern Language Quarterly*
MLR	*Modern Language Review*
MP	*Modern Philology*
NQ	*Notes and Queries*
PCC	Prerogative Court of Canterbury Wills
PQ	*Philological Quarterly*
PRO	Public Record Office, London
Reed	A.W. Reed *Early Tudor Drama* London 1926
RD	*Renaissance Drama*
RES	*Review of English Studies*
SAB	*Shakespeare Association Bulletin*
SEL	*Studies in English Literature*
SP	*Studies in Philology*
SQ	*Shakespeare Quarterly*
SR	*A Transcript of the Registers of the Company of Stationers of London* ed. Edward Arber. London 1875–94. 5 vols
STC	*Short-Title Catalogue of English Books 1475–1640* Comp. by A.W. Pollard and G.R. Redgrave for The Bibliographical Society. London 1963
TDA	*Transactions of the Devon Association*
TFT	Tudor Facsimile Texts

Sebastian Westcott, the Children of Paul's,
and *The Marriage of Wit and Science*

BIBLIOGRAPHICAL NOTE

IN TRANSCRIPTION OF MANUSCRIPTS the original spelling has been preserved and no silent changes have been made. Contractions and abbreviations have been expanded and the expansions are printed in italics. Additions appear in square brackets and lost or indecipherable letters and words are denoted by the use of pointed brackets. A superscript is used for verso; no symbol indicates recto.

Sebastian Westcott and the Children of Paul's

I

Early Years

THE EARLIEST COMPREHENSIVE SOURCE of information about the Westcotts of Devon is to be found in Thomas Westcote's compilation, *A View of Devonshire* (c1630).[1] The antiquarian has nothing directly to tell us of Sebastian, since he was personally and principally concerned with the ancestry and fortunes of Shobrooke-Raddon Westcott gentry, and Sebastian is clearly of humbler yeoman stock. Nevertheless from him we do learn of the antiquity of the name and of the area in North Devon where the family had long established themselves. This was at Marwood, a few miles from Barnstaple. It is in the surrounding parishes, Tawstock, Bishop's Tawton, Swimbridge, Chittlehampton, Warkleigh, North and South Molton, and Chulmleigh where Westcott (Wescot, Wescote, Westcot, Westcote) tradesmen, husbandmen, and yeoman-farmers fare in the sixteenth century. Sebastian was born at Chulmleigh, and if a guess be permitted, in 1515 or thereabout.[2]

The little market town lies almost midway between Barnstaple and Exeter on high ground to the north of the Little Dart about a mile from its confluence with the Taw. The surrounding countryside is sylvan and undulating. By Westcott's day the town appears to have prospered from its

1 G. Oliver and P. Jones, eds (Exeter 1845); see also *The Visitations of the County of Devon* (Exeter 1895) and the file on the Westcott family in the Exeter City Library. The later historians of Devonshire, Prince, the Lysons, and Oliver all refer to and use Thomas Westcote's work.
2 To the poor 'of Chimley where I was borne' Westcott left the sum of three pounds. See will, PCC 14 Tirwhite, 3 April 1582, printed (with some minor inaccuracies) by H.N. Hillebrand in *The Child Actors* (New York 1964) App. 3.

connection with the wool trade and also by virtue of its location on the main highway linking the north and south coasts and at cross-roads leading to Devon hinterlands.

While a few surviving records enable us to piece together a fragmentary account of Westcott's brothers, William, George, Robert, Philip, and a sister, Jacquet, they tell us nothing about his parents or about the family property. The *Register* of St Mary Magdalene where, presumably, these persons were baptized perished by fire in 1803 and so we are barred from knowing the sequence of their births. The bombing of Exeter in 1942 destroyed a part of both the Devon and Somerset archival collections including several pertinent Westcott wills.[3] However, all the evidence we have suggests that Sebastian and his kindred passed their early years in the Chulmleigh neighbourhood.

George Westcott, yeoman, owned land and property in Chulmleigh, had some connection with Swimbridge, married and settled in North Molton where he raised his four children. He died in 1589.[4] Jacquet, after whom George named one of his daughters, married Robert Goodenough of Kingston, near Taunton, Somerset. Her husband died in 1579.[5] Widow Goodenough with her six children, four daughters of whom Sebastian remembered in his will, remained in Kingston.

The Westcott connection with Kingston is far older than this marriage, as a deed in 1356 between John Westekota and a Yeovil parson attests.[6] In our time the fine fifteenth-century Gothic tower of Kingston St Mary has provided evidence of the continuing association of the Westcotts with the parish. Not long ago repairs to the roof uncovered two memorials to former churchwardens and among the four names inscribed in the lead are those of Richard Westcott (1706) and I. Farthing (1777).[7] It is interesting to find these

3 See *Index of Wills and Administrations relating to the County of Devon*, John J. Beckerlegge, ed. Devonshire Association for the Advancement of Science, Literature and Art (1950). The wills of Anthony Westcott (20 Sept. 1592) and Robert Westcott (1587), both of Chulmleigh, were lost in the air-raid.
4 PCC 95 Nevell, 1 July 1589
5 PCC 18 Arundell, given probate 6 May 1580
6 PRO *Ancient Deeds*, B1643, Somerset: 'A Covenant between John of Rysyndon, parson of the Church of Ievele, and John Westekota and Matilda his wife, relative to a messuage and curtilage next Mileswardiswill in Kyngeston [Somerset], sixth of the Kalends of May, 30 Edward III'
7 I am indebted to Captain A.C. Pawson of Yarford Cottage, Kingston, for a photograph of these memorials which he was largely instrumental in saving from destruction, and I also wish to acknowledge his account of them in *The Parish Church of Kingston St Mary* (Taunton 1948).

two names side by side in eighteenth-century memorials because two hundred years earlier the two families had been on friendly terms. Sebastian remembered Elizabeth Farthing in his will, and she in hers remembered the poor of Kingston and left the church 'twoo shillinges for a knell to be rong for me.'[8] She died in Uffculme, Devon, less than fifteen miles from Taunton. Thomas Farthing of Kingston was an overseer of the will of Robert Goodenough, Sebastian's brother-in-law. A more prosperous Farthing was a Bartholomew of the parish of St James, Taunton, who owned considerable land scattered throughout the Vale of Taunton Deane, and who chose to be buried in Kingston Church.[9]

Adjoining Kingston and just outside the town of Taunton is Cheddon Fitzpaine. Here Sebastian's brother, William Westcott, eventually settled, married Margaret Hare in 1562, and raised his three sons, one of whom he named Sebastian.[10] William died in 1570 and his widow married a Riche.

The above identifications of George, Jacquet, and William are sure; it is not possible to be so certain about Robert, who was alive in 1582 to dispute Sebastian's will. The ruling of the Prerogative Court on that occasion offers us no help in locating him. The only clue provided by the will is that he had several children and that one, Andrew, was singled out for a much larger legacy. Robert Westcott may possibly be the one who lived at Chulmleigh and who died in 1587.[11] Another possibility is a Robert Westcott, yeoman of South Petherton which lies some twenty miles south-east of Taunton between the towns of Ilminster and Yeovil and where there was a small settlement of Westcotts. He had four sons, one named Andrew, and two daughters.[12] However, his death (between July 1609 and June 1611) was so much later than the deaths of Sebastian's other immediate kin that one is cautious about making this identification.[13]

Philip Westcott, Sebastian's remaining brother, became a merchant. An account of his marriage and other travail will be more appropriately related later. Like Sebastian, he left the west country for the greater opportunity London and even more beguilingly distant places offered. Unlike Sebastian, he was to know more of Fortune's buffets than rewards.[14]

We may now return to Sebastian and consider the implications of hitherto

8 PCC 121 Dorset, 5 February 1605/6
9 PCC 3 Rutland, 9 January 1587
10 See *Register* I (1558–1636) of St Mary the Virgin, Cheddon Fitzpaine, Somerset.
11 See n3.
12 See *Register* I (1594–1674) of Sts Peter and Paul, South Petherton, Somerset.
13 PCC 60 Wood, 20 July 1609
14 See pp 52–3.

SEBASTIAN WESTCOTT'S RELATIVES AND THEIR FAMILIES
mentioned or referred to in his will (PCC 14 Tirwhite) 1582

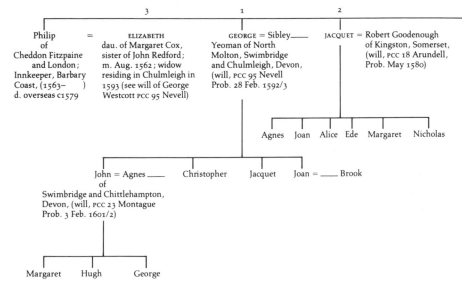

LEGACIES

1　'my brother George Westcote' – 40/-
　　'And to everie of his children' – 25/8

2　'my sister Jacquet Goodinowe' – £10
　　'the daughters of my sister Jacquet Goodinowe' – £3 'a
　　peece beinge fower of them'

3　'Elizabeth Westcote, widowe, my sister in law' – £20
　　'together with Lease of Westgrene ... all ye household
　　stuffe and kyene and cattel'

4　'my brother Robert Westcote' – £13-6-8ᵈ
　　'Andrewe Westcote his sonne' – £10
　　'And to everie of his other children' – 30/-

5　'Roger Westcote, Sebastian & Frances Westcote sonnes of my
　　late brother William Westcote, to everie of theme' – £10

6　'Margaret Riche my sister in lawe' – 40/-

　　'to Westcote that is blinde' – £3 (untraced)

　　'The Residue of all my good, cattell, monnye plate Jewell
　　　... I wholie geve and bequeathe porcion and porcion like
　　amongst thee children of my brethren and sisters'

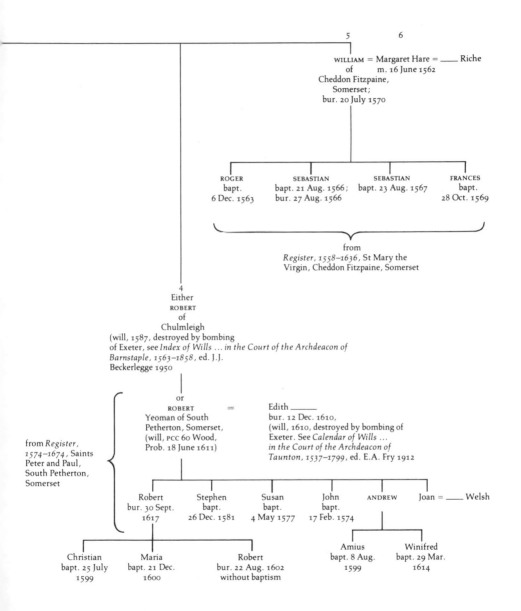

WILLIAM = Margaret Hare = ＿＿ Riche
of   m. 16 June 1562
Cheddon Fitzpaine,
Somerset;
bur. 20 July 1570

ROGER	SEBASTIAN	SEBASTIAN	FRANCES
bapt.	bapt. 21 Aug. 1566;	bapt. 23 Aug. 1567	bapt.
6 Dec. 1563	bur. 27 Aug. 1566		28 Oct. 1569

from
Register, 1558–1636, St Mary the
Virgin, Cheddon Fitzpaine, Somerset

4
Either
ROBERT
of
Chulmleigh
(will, 1587, destroyed by bombing
of Exeter, see *Index of Wills … in the Court of the Archdeacon of
Barnstaple, 1563–1858*, ed. J.J.
Beckerlegge 1950

or
ROBERT   =   Edith ＿＿＿＿
Yeoman of South   bur. 12 Dec. 1610,
Petherton, Somerset,   (will, 1610, destroyed by bombing of
(will, PCC 60 Wood,   Exeter. See *Calendar of Wills …
Prob. 18 June 1611)   in the Court of the Archdeacon of
                     Taunton, 1537–1799*, ed. E.A. Fry 1912

from *Register,
1574–1674*, Saints
Peter and Paul,
South Petherton,
Somerset

Robert	Stephen	Susan	John	ANDREW	Joan = ＿＿ Welsh
bur. 30 Sept.	bapt.	bapt.	bapt.		
1617	26 Dec. 1581	4 May 1577	17 Feb. 1574		

Amius	Winifred
bapt. 8 Aug.	bapt. 29 Mar.
1599	1614

Christian	Maria	Robert
bapt. 25 July	bapt. 21 Dec.	bur. 22 Aug. 1602
1599	1600	without baptism

overlooked but revealing records of his early life. Both Sebastian and his brother William (before the latter settled in Cheddon Fitzpaine) were in Holy Orders. William appears to have been ordained Deacon on 15 March 1521–2.[15] Unfortunately, the record of Sebastian's ordination has eluded search; it may possibly be concealed by a clerical error in Bishop Vesey's *Register*.[16] Whether or not this is so, Sebastian and William are listed as stipendiary priests receiving pensions in 1540; at that time Sebastian was employed by the churchwardens of Chulmleigh, and William was in the neighbouring parish of Warkleigh in the service of the Rector.[17]

After the dissolution, displaced and pensioned clergy frequently acted as curates of churches in the vicinity of their former religious houses.[18] It would seem likely, therefore, that Sebastian Westcott was either a monk or a member of a College in the neighbourhood of Chulmleigh before 1540. The church of St Mary Magdalene in Chulmleigh, an ancient and originally collegiate foundation, appears by Westcott's time to have had only a nominal collegiate status and it would seem to have been an unlikely location for him.[19] It is more likely that Westcott served in Crediton, which lies nine miles to the south of Chulmleigh where the church of St Mary and the Holy Cross had unquestionable collegiate status until at least 1545.[20] Crediton (or

15 List of Ordinations, *Register* of John Vesey I (1519–41), Chanter No. 14, Devon Record Office

16 Vesey's *Register* contains the names of several Westcotts, including a Thomas (priest, 4 March 1519), and a Richard (deacon, 7 April 1520: priest, 2 June 1520); a Walter Westcott was admitted *Tonsurati et Accolati* on 24 February 1531/2.

17 PRO *Valor Ecclesiasticus*, Portfolio I, 1540–1. These lists of Devon pensioners were found misplaced in the *Valor* by Frances Rose-Troup who published them in DCNQ XVII (1932) under the title 'Lists relating to Persons Ejected from Religious Houses' 285ff.

18 Cf. Rose-Troup, Lists, 81.

19 According to George Oliver, *Monasticon Dioecesis Exoniensis* (Exeter 1846–54) 291, the founder was a Lord of Okehampton and its six prebends were in the gift of the Courtenay family until the attainder of Henry, Marquis of Exeter in 1539; see also O.J. Reichel, 'The "Domesday" Hundreds of Devon,' TDA XXX (1898) 391-432: Hamilton Thompson, *The English Clergy* (Oxford 1947) 86–7 claims that the church had 'no corporate signs of a college, no capitular meetings, no common seal or fund' and his claim is supported by the remarks on the state of the church in 1547 by J.B. Pearson, 'The Church of Chulmleigh, North Devon,' TDA XXXIX (1907) 208–15.

20 See George Oliver, *Historic Collections relating to the Monasteries in Devon* (Exeter 1820), and *The Ancient Religious Houses of Devon*, Dom. John Stephan, ed. (Exeter 1935); also O.J. Reichel, 'The Manor and Hundred of Crediton,' TDA LIV (1923) 160–2. There is a conflict of opinion as to the exact date of dissolution. Authorities such as the Lysons, Oliver, Reichel, and G.H. Cook hold that the College was suppressed by Edward VI in 1547, while Beatrix Cresswell and Vivian Summers in their respective histories of the church claim 1546 was the date. The dissolution, however, may have begun earlier because Elizabeth, Countess

'Kyrton' as it is still locally pronounced) was an older, larger, and more important religious and trade centre than Sebastian's birthplace. Until the mid-eleventh century it was the See of the Bishop of Devon. Although the reports of Episcopal Visitors to the church in the early sixteenth century are a melancholy record of its decline, vestiges of its former organization remained.[21] The maintenance of the choir and of the choral tradition aroused the particular concern of successive bishops. In 1523 the 'clericus' who instructed the choristers and presided over the organ had a salary of £6-13-4ᵈ.[22] As late as 1535 Leland noted: 'There be XII good Prebends in Kyrton beside certen Bursaries, Ministers and Choristers.'[23] Was it here then in Crediton, the poor townsfolk of which he generously remembered in his will, where Sebastian Westcott acquired his musical knowledge and experience in training choristers, which were to make him acceptable first for court service and later for the position of Master of the Choristers of St Paul's Cathedral?

If, indeed, Westcott had been in charge of the Crediton choristers, his duties would doubtless have been similar to those of Thomas Haskewell of Durham, whose indenture, dated 4 December 1513, states that he was 'to teach [the boys] to play the organ and to acquire a knowledge of plain chant and harmonized chant by practising plain-song, prick-note, faburden, descant, swarenote and counterpoint.' Haskewell was also obliged 'to attend in person in the choir of the cathedral at all Masses, Vespers and anthems of Our Lady' and 'to play the organ and sing the tenor part or any other part that suits his voice,' for which service he received £10 a year and livery.[24]

We do not know how long Westcott remained at Chulmleigh in the employ of the churchwardens and drawing his small pension. Not long after 1541 one would guess. It will be evident from all that is hereafter recorded of Sebastian's career that adversity would not long subdue him. He was, in fact, both resilient and tenacious to a remarkable degree. If the great dissolution

of Bath, and Sir Thomas Darcye were granted 'all possessions, temporal and spiritual of the late college of Credyton, alias Kyrton, Devon, except Church, Churchyard and Vestry, Chapter House, Our Lady Chapel, leads, bells and glass, the vicarage and advowson as enjoyed by George Mason, clk. now near there,' on 22 September 1545 (*Cal. LP For. & Dom., Henry VIII* xx).

21 Visitations by Bishop Oldham (1511) and by Bishop Vesey (1522) drew attention to the bad state of the college (cf. R.J. King, *The Church of St Mary and of the Holy Cross*).
22 See Alfred Edwards, 'Crediton Musicians,' *TDA* XIV (1882) 321–8.
23 *Itinerary*, 3rd ed. (1768) III 68
24 See Dom. David Knowles, *The Religious Orders in England*, 3 vols. (Cambridge 1959) III 17–18, who cites *Historia Dunelmensis Ecclesiae Scriptores Tres*, J. Raine, ed., no. cccxxiii, p ccccxiii.

had deprived him of his original vocation, it is safe to suppose him riding the blow, recovering and redirecting his energy and resources toward a fresh objective. If Devon would no longer fulfil him, there was London beckoning, as it had to many a resolute west countryman. His journey thither would have inevitably taken him through the heart of Somerset where sister Jacquet and Goodenough relatives were settled at Kingston. Perhaps he travelled thus far with his brother, William, dispossessed like Sebastian, who would also have been seeking fresh pasture. William did indeed find one at Cheddon Fitzpaine close by Kingston. Sebastian's sojourn in Somerset before setting out for London might well have been of some duration: long enough, at any rate, to claim a final charity to 'the poore within the Towne of Tawnton' and to 'the poore of Kingstone near Tawnton.'

II

Court and Cathedral: 1545-58

BY 1545 SEBASTIAN WESTCOTT was in the King's service. He was paid his quarterly wage as a Yeoman of the Chamber at Christmas.[1] It is not possible to explain the translation from dispossessed priest to court official; nor can one answer the questions this advancement raises about the nature of his service and how and when he began it. There were several Westcotts in court employment in the early decades of the sixteenth century but no connection between any of them and Sebastian has so far come to light.[2] It has been suggested that Westcott made the acquaintance of John Redford, the Almoner and Master of the Choristers of St Paul's Cathedral at this time.[3] This seems most likely, and, if so, it is also likely that he met John Heywood who,

---

1 *Chamber Accounts*, BM MS ADD. 27, 404, fols 17 and 31; see also E.K. Chambers, *Elizabethan Stage*, 4 vols (Oxford 1923) II 12, and H.N. Hillebrand, 'Sebastian Westcote, Dramatist and Master of the Children of Paul's,' *JEGP* XIV (Oct. 1915) 569.

2 Edmond Westcott was a servant (1509, *Cal. LP For. & Dom., Henry VIII* I 17) and Thomas Westcott a chaplain (1526, *Cal. LP For. & Dom., Henry VIII* IV Pt 1, p 870) in the Royal Household. John Westcott, yeoman of New Windsor and Keeper of the Royal Park appears quite frequently in the records between 1529 and 1559 in connection with grants, payments, and disobediences (*Cal. LP For. & Dom., Henry VIII* XVIII Pt 2; XXI, Pt 2; *Cal. Pat. Rolls, 1 Mary*, Pt 4; *1 Elizabeth*, Pt 9). Henry Westcott appears to have jobbed land and property confiscated from the monasteries (*Cal. LP For. & Dom., Henry VIII* XXI Pt 1). Christopher Westcott, gentleman, a court messenger in 1530, later settled in Buckinghamshire as squire and magistrate and served as commissioner of the peace as late as 1554 (*Cal. LP For. & Dom.* V; *Cal. Pt. Rolls, 1 Edward VI* Pt 3; and *Cal. Pat. Rolls 4 & 5, Philip and Mary* Pt 4).

3 By Arthur Brown, 'Two Notes on John Redford,' *MLR* XLIII (Oct. 1948) 508–10

although retired from court service as singer and musician, retained his interest in occasional play presentation and was associated with Redford in other ways.[4] One further and admittedly flimsy possibility of a link between Westcott and Heywood might be thought scarcely worth mentioning were it not for a need to account for Sebastian's appearance in London and his unexpected position at court. In February 1521 Heywood received an annuity of ten marks. This annuity was formerly in the possession of Thomas Farthing, Gentleman of the Chapel, who was associated with Heywood in the revels at Greenwich on 9 December 1520.[5] One wonders if this Thomas was related to the Farthings who lived near the Westcotts at Kingston?

Sebastian Westcott's long, prosperous, and sometimes troubled association with St Paul's Cathedral began perhaps in 1546, certainly not later than 1547 when he was said to be 'oon of the vicars of poulis.'[6] John Redford died that same year, and in all likelihood Westcott assumed charge of the almonry and of the choristers. His official appointment, however, remained unconfirmed for six years.[7] Redford made Westcott his residual legatee and sole executor 'to do for me as he shall thinke best in his conscience.' He was survived by two brothers, William and Henry, and by a widowed sister, Margaret Cox, who had a daughter, Elizabeth. At the time of her brother's death Margaret Cox was living in premises adjacent to the almoner's house leased to her on 13 August 1528 by the Dean and Chapter. On 3 July 1555 a new lease was drawn, the terms of which permitted her to stay on the premises provided that she made available one chamber 'for the sycke chyldren' (presumably the choristers) and sufficient space for some stairs to lead from this chamber 'downe to the well house.'[8] The lease was to be void one year after the death of Margaret and the property was to revert to the use of the almoner. She died sometime between 1556 and 1558 and, like her brother, made Sebastian residual legatee and sole executor.[9] Her daughter,

4 Heywood 'with his children' presented an interlude before Princess Mary in 1537/8, see *Book of Expenses*, BM MS Royal, 178, xxviii, fol. 42. For more precise information on the links between Heywood and Redford cf. A.W. Reed, *Early Tudor Drama* (London 1926) 55ff.

5 Reed, *Tudor Drama*, 55

6 By John Redford in his will, PCC 50 Alen, 7 October 1547

7 See Arthur Brown, 'Two Notes,' MLR XLIII (Oct. 1948), and also his 'Three Notes on Sebastian Westcott,' MLR XLIV (April 1949) 229–32 wherein he has convincingly supported Reed's proposal that Westcott succeeded Redford as almoner in 1547.

8 Cf. *Chronicle of the Grey Friars* 65: 'Item the vij [day of Ja]nuary [1550] was vj men destroyed at the makynge of the welle within the howse that was some tyme the Peter College nexte the denes place in Powlles church yarde.'

9 Will, Dean, and Chapter of St Paul's, vol. A, fol. 117, dated 30 September 1556 and proved 3 April 1558. The witnesses were John Hayward, 'petycanon of poulis,' and Thomas Prideaux.

Elizabeth, passed into Sebastian's care and he employed her in his own household.

It is not surprising to find that Westcott's appointment was held in abeyance. The Dean, William May, was a reformer who appears to have welcomed the King's commissioners in September 1547 when they super-vised the destruction of images and insisted upon compliance with the new edicts aimed at ending Roman Catholic ceremonial. This was the first of several purges carried out at St Paul's during Edward VI's reign.[10] No matter how able an administrator or how competent a musician Westcott might have been, his firm adherence to the old faith must have caused his seniors to regard him as a doubtful prospect. Circumspection on his part and caution on theirs were only to be expected during the troubled period.[11] Fortunately for Westcott the accession of Mary in July 1553 arrested reforming zeal; her sovereignty during the next six years ensured for him the privileges and fruits of the office he had held without official recognition since 1547. The record of his appointment as almoner is dated 1 February 1553/4.[12] Not long after this John Feckenham replaced May as Dean, and the services and customs of the cathedral resumed their traditional ceremony. Indeed, St Paul's regained its place as the centre of national, religious, and civic pagean-try. Royal visits, state celebrations and funerals, mayoral installations, and certain guild anniversaries were marked with pomp and splendour within the cathedral. Outside in the great churchyard religious and civic processions mustered in preparation for their circumlocutory passage through London streets, and returned to the cathedral for divine service before dispersing. On many of these occasions throughout Mary's reign, the St Paul's choir played their part, and there can be no doubt that Westcott was kept busy supervising the activity of his boys both inside and outside the cathedral.[13] We can picture him, for instance, on the Eve of St Katherine, leading the choristers after evensong on their annual climb up the tower to the parapet at the base

---

10 See *A History of St Paul's Cathedral*, W.R. Matthews and W.M. Atkins eds (London 1964) ch. 2 ; also H.H. Milman, *Annals of St Paul's Cathedral* (London 1868), and *The Chronicle of the Grey Friars of London*, J.G. Nichols, ed. Camden Society LIII (1852) 54ff.

11 After the deprivation of Somerset and Bonner in 1549 and the translation of Ridley to London in 1550, Northumberland's tougher policy against catholicism made itself felt at St Paul's. In June 1550, the high altar was pulled down ; in September Dean May directed that use of the organ should be discontinued, and in November the new Prayer Book was introduced.

12 St Paul's *Registrum, 1536–1560*, fol. 276ᵛ ; cf. Arthur Brown, 'Three Notes,' MLR XLIV (April 1949).

13 See the numerous descriptions of these events between 1553 and 1559 in *The Diary of Henry Machyn*, J.G. Nichols, ed. (1848), and also in *Chronicle of the Grey Friars of London*.

of the steeple, and there, amid the lighted torches, which illuminated the effigy of the saint and perhaps warmed the celebrants of her feast, conducting the singing of anthems.[14] Another custom revived at this time and one in which the Paul's boys participated was the ancient ceremony of the Boy Bishop. On St Nicholas' day (6 December) 1554 'the chylde bysshope of Poules church with his company' appeared before Mary 'in her privie chamber at her manour of Saynt James.'[15]

During the years of his stewardship, Sebastian probably lived in the almonry situated in the north churchyard.[16] After his appointment, the six choral vicars including Westcott were permitted residence on 2 June 1554 in 'Curlowes howse adjoyning ... the office of pentencyarys,' and this house was formally leased to them on 18 November 1556.[17] Soon after that date Feckenham became Abbot of Westminster and he was succeeded in the deanery by Henry Cole. From the new Dean and the Chapter Westcott obtained the lease of Paul's Wickham Manor in Essex on 2 June 1557.[18] In return for the obligation of collecting for the cathedral the fines and perquisites of the Manor Court and maintaining the upkeep of the property, Westcott became the possessor of a considerable estate. This handsome source of income, however, had to be backed by a bond of £40 (to be void, if he met the terms of the lease), and two friends of Westcott added their signatures in support of it, 'Johenn Heywood de London generosus, et Thomas predioxe de medio Templo London generosus.'[19] It is worthwhile

14 Machyn observed and briefly described this ceremony on 24 November 1553 and again in 1556; another witness in 1553 was the Grey Friars' Chronicler.

15 See E.K. Chambers, *Medieval Stage*, 2 vols (Oxford 1903) I 366–7, who cites the full title of 'The song of the Chyldbysshop' composed for the occasion by Hugh Rhodes, a member of the Chapel Royal. The song of thirty-six octaves (now lost) was printed in black letter quarto and seen by Thomas Warton who described it as 'a fulsome panygyric of the queen's devotion' in his *History of English Poetry*, W.C. Hazlitt, ed. 4 vols (London 1871) IV 237. Feuillerat has a brief record that appears to refer to this performance: 'iij vestmentts for sayntnycolas' (E & M 190 and 292).

16 See M.E.C. Walcott, 'Old St Paul's,' *Transactions of the St Paul's Ecclesiological Society* I (1885) 177–87. Westcott is named in the Lay Subsidy Rolls of St Gregory's parish, Castle Baynard Ward, in 1550 (PRO E/179/145/174).

17 St Paul's *Registrum, 1536–1560*, fol. 343ᵛ; the vicars named are: 'Sebastyan Westcotte, Philip Apryse [Ap Rhys?], Robert Say, Thomas Martyn, Robert Bale and John Moore.'

18 Ibid., fol. 360. The Manor, for which Westcott paid annual rent of £20-6-8d, had over 200 acres under cultivation, some livestock, and farm implements; the place is now known as Wickham Bishop's.

19 Ibid., fol. 361ᵛ. Arthur Brown has drawn attention to this evidence of Westcott's continuing association with John Heywood and Thomas Prideaux, noting that Prideaux 'contributed to the collection of poems preserved, with Redford's interlude "Wit and Science," in ADD. MS 15233,' see 'Three Notes.'

noting that John Heywood was Lord of the Manor of Brokehall, near Tiptree, only a few miles away from Westcott's property.[20]

From a St Paul's account book it is possible to compute with fair accuracy Westcott's income as vicar choral and master of the almonry in 1554.[21] The sums are modest, but indicate that he was comfortably off, especially if it be remembered that they represent only a portion of his total earnings, because they do not include gratuities and fees that would have come his way for services performed on private occasions.

In the same year Westcott, acting for the choristers and the choral vicars, petitioned through the Court of Exchequer for the payment with arrears of a yearly revenue granted to them in 1549. His suit was successful and he obtained £27-2-10^d for the boys and £19-11-0$^{1/2d}$ for himself and his colleagues.[22]

Since Mary's accession he had much to be thankful for. He was now well established at St Paul's and in circumstances that must have been congenial after the precarious years of the regency. On New Year's day, 1557, he presented to the Queen 'a booke of ditties written.'[23] What exactly these compositions were, or whether they were Westcott's own or the works of others, we have no means of knowing. The gift, however, marks a crest in the rhythm of his existence. With the oncoming of Mary's decline, apprehension about his future security must have been renewed.

20 The lease was granted to Heywood on 21 Nov. 1540; see Robert W. Bolwell, *The Life and Works of John Heywood* (New York 1966) 33.

21 'Michael Shaller's Note-Book' in the Library of St Paul's Cathedral, see appendix, 75.

22 Exchequer K.R., Memoranda Roll, Michaelmas, 1 & 2 Philip & Mary, r. 238 *dors*, cited by Hillebrand 110. It was not possible to check this document (PRO E/159/334) because it could not be found by the Public Record Office (Sept. 1968).

23 John Nichols, *The Progresses and Public Processions of Queen Elizabeth*, 3 vols (London 1823) I xxv

III

St Paul's: 1558-75

THE MARIAN REGIME AT ST PAUL'S remained almost unchanged during the months immediately following the accession of Elizabeth. Alexander Nowell, writing to a friend in Strasbourg, noted that 'St Paul's and certain other churches still keep to popish service.'[1] In 1559, however, the reformers began to have their way, and by the end of the year the governance of the cathedral was in the hands of new men. Bonner was deprived in May. In August the Queen's commissioners pressed the depleted chapter – many of the principals having absented themselves – to subscribe to the injunctions and to purge the services of superstition.[2] William May was soon reinstated as Dean. The consecration of Parker as Primate and of Grindal as Bishop of London took place in December. In August 1560 Nowell succeeded May as Dean; with this appointment the way was paved for the Elizabethan religious settlement at St Paul's.

These changes appear to have been conducted with remarkably little fuss.[3] Officials like William Saxey, the treasurer, for example, quietly accepted the new order. As for Sebastian Westcott, he may have refused to subscribe and been bound over, but there is no evidence for Strype's claim

---

1 Letter, 28 May 1559, cited by Ralph Churton, *Life of Alexander Nowell* (Oxford 1809) 40–1
2 Milman, *Annals* 259
3 John Harpsfield, Archdeacon of London, his brother, Nicholas, and a few other prebendaries opposed and were deprived.

that he was either sequestered or deprived.[4] It is more likely that he remained non-committal and bided his time. Perhaps his behaviour was less
guileful than it may now seem, for the changes he witnessed, no doubt with
great uneasiness, were at first more administrative than theological. In
September 1559, for instance, the obsequies of Henry II of France were
'celebrated in the cathedral with much of its traditional splendour – with
"hearse, scutcheons, coats of arms and mantle of cloth of gold"' ;[5] and, at the
installation of Nowell a year later, the Dean was welcomed by the pealing of
the organ and the chanting of the choir.[6] Westcott, who had somehow
retained his position through the difficult period of the Edwardian regency,
may well have found the situation at this time less threatening. Indeed, the
confusion at St Paul's, between 1558 and 1560, caused by deprivation,
absenteeism, and tenurial uncertainty may not have been disadvantageous
to him; however this may be, Westcott was certainly not the first Minor
Canon and Subdean in 1560.[7] He must also have been heartened by the
renewal of his appointment as Almoner on 1 December, 1559[8] and by the
recognition of his services to the Queen for his successful theatrical presentations at court.

Westcott's staunch catholicism, however, could not for long be either
veiled by himself or ignored by his colleagues and superiors; his ambiguous
position was clarified when he was confronted by Edmund Grindal at the
Bishop's visitation to St Paul's in April 1561. During the next three-and-a-
half years the two men were periodically engaged, the one in a long-
suffering attempt to persuade and convert, the other in a stubborn resistance
to spiritual change by means of special pleading and procrastination. Grin-

4 *Annals of the Reformation*, 4 vols (London 1725–31) I 168–78 and his *Life of Edmund
  Grindal* (Oxford 1827) 88 ; also H.N. Birt, *The Elizabethan Religious Settlement* (London
  1907) 171
5 Matthews and Atkins, *History* 132 and Machyn's *Diary*
6 Milman, *Annals* 276
7 The claim was made by the Rev. George Hennessy, *Novum Repertorium Ecclesiasticum
  Parochiale Londinense* (London 1896) 6 and followed by Chambers, Hillebrand, et al.
  Hennessy cited volume two of the Pridden MSS. A search through the five volumes of
  Pridden Papers in the St Paul's Cathedral Library failed to reveal any record of the
  appointment. Furthermore on Grindal's several visits to St Paul's between 17 April 1561 and
  26 November 1562, William Whytebrook is repeatedly referred to as the first Minor Canon
  and Subdean (see *Liber Visitatum*, 1561, Guildhall Library, MS 9537/2, fols 4–19). Whytebrook had held these positions since at least 1554 (see 'Michael Shaller's Note-Book,' St
  Paul's Cathedral Library, MS W.D. 32, fol. 73ʳ). Westcott never belonged to the College of
  Minor Canons.
8 St Paul's *Registrum, 1536–60*, fol. 377ᵛ ; see Arthur Brown, 'Three Notes,' *MLR* XLIV (April
  1949) 229–30 for correct interpretation of the document.

dal, who must have known Westcott quite well since his time as Precentor at St Paul's (1551–4), proceeded with earnest goodwill and great patience – qualities which suggest his inherent friendliness towards his obstinate charge. Be that as it may, the Bishop's diplomatic perseverance was not, perhaps, wholly the product of his kindly disposition. He must have been fully aware that behind the tiresome and humble recalcitrant there waited an imperious patron.[9]

In these circumstances Grindal's decision in July 1563 to do his duty and excommunicate Westcott must have been as ticklish as it was resolute.[10] He could hardly have been unprepared for the immediate consequence. Writing to Sir William Cecil on 12 August 1563, ostensibly upon other business, the Bishop informed the Secretary that 'My L. Robert [Dudley] wrote to me earnestly for *Sebastiane*, to whom j have written a longe letter much like an Apologie, the copie wherof j sende to you herwith.'[11] Dudley's intervention on behalf of Westcott was, it would appear, an energetic appeal to Grindal either to rescind or to postpone the excommunication. Grindal's lengthy response, defensively detailing the protracted history of Westcott's case, coupled with his desire to keep Cecil informed of his handling of the affair, reinforces one's suspicion that Dudley's mediation was conducted on behalf of the Queen.[12]

At any rate the appeal won a reluctant reprieve from the Bishop, who told Dudley that he would give Westcott until 1 October to reform his conscience. 'I am contented,' wrote Grindal, 'bicause yoᵣ L. writeth so earnestly for him,

9 See 'Dr Nicholas Sander's Report to Cardinal Moroni, May, 1561,' J.H. Pollen, ed. *Miscellanea* I Catholic Record Society (London 1905) 21 and *Cal. SP Relative to English Affairs Preserved in Rome, Elizabeth 1558–1571*, J.M. Rigg, ed. (1916) I 67. Sanders lists ten schoolmasters who suffered for their faith; Westcott is fifth: 'Sebastian, Organist at St Paul's, London, did not shrink from ejectment; but Elizabeth was so loath to part with him, that without in any way complying with schism, he keeps his place in the church.' Chambers II 14 gives the Latin version.

10 *Libri Vicarii Generalis, Huick 1561–1574* III fol. 77, Records of the Consistory Court of London, Principal Probate Registry, cited by Hillebrand 120. The record is printed by Hillebrand in App. 3.

11 Letter to Cecil, BM MS Lansdowne, 6, no. 69; copy of Grindal's letter to Dudley, BM MS Lansdowne, 30, no. 55 in the hand of one of Cecil's clerks according to note on outer sheet.

12 Eleanor Rosenberg, *Leicester, Patron of Letters* (New York 1955), observes that Leicester 'was connected by blood and marriage with most of the more advanced Protestant nobility of his age' (p 197), and that his 'position as a champion of Protestantism was well established by 1572' (p 212). He was certainly not noted for his protection of recusants. There is no evidence to support Strype's conjecture (*Life of Grindal* 113–16), repeated by Birt (*Eliz. Relig. Settlement* 442) and by Grattan Flood, 'Master Sebastian,' MA III (1913) 155 that Westcott lived in London after his deprivation under the protection of Lord Dudley.

to forbeare *prosequntinge* ye penaltie of the lawes againste him till after *Mighelmasse* or *Hallowentyde*, prayenge godde in the meane tyme to open his eyes.' What happened after this is far from clear. One thing is certain however; Grindal's prayers went unanswered. We may surmise that the excommunication was never in fact imposed, since Westcott retained all his authority as Almoner and Master at St Paul's. There is no evidence to show that Westcott made any accommodation with the reformed view of the transubstantiation – the sticking point in his discussions with Grindal – and later events indicate that he continued steadfastly to adhere to this central doctrine of the old faith.

One year after the Bishop's correspondence with Cecil and Dudley, Westcott bound himself on surety of one hundred marks to Grindal.[13] The bond stipulates first that if he

shall not frame his consciens so as the same⟨ ⟩it self agreable to all and singler such poynt*es* and articles of Relligion as are nowe ... That then if the said Sebastian after⟨ ⟩feast [Easter,] 1565 and notice given that his consciens cannot agree vnto the same shall quietly⟨ ⟩the exercise and mynystery as well of all such Romes offices *pro*mocons chardges....

Thus Westcott's refusal to accept the reformed communion was permitted a further period of toleration. The second stipulation is more surprising:

And also if the said Sebastian⟨ ⟩all tymes on this side the said feast of Easter next comynge shalbe discreet and⟨ ⟩words and behavio^r towardes the Quenes maiestie That then this *prese*nte be voide and of none affect....

This clause raises some intriguing questions. Does it, in effect, exempt Westcott from the threat of ecclesiastical penalty? He had, after all, already proved himself a loyal and useful servant of the Queen, and was hardly likely to be indiscreet in word or action towards his royal patron. Is the whole bond, therefore, merely a temporizing formality which, while saving the face of Grindal, permitted Westcott to continue at St Paul's in the Queen's service? Such would seem to be the case. In the period between 1565 and 1575 the recusant appears to have been untroubled by opposition to his religious belief from either the Bishop or the Dean. Fortunately for Westcott, Nowell was of

---

13 Bond, dated 8 November 1564, St Paul's Cathedral Library MS A/77/2059. The document is much faded and the inner margin badly frayed; some words are lost and others illegible. Hillebrand transcribes and prints it in his App. 3 with minor inaccuracies.

a mild and conciliatory disposition and no persecutor. The meek and unlucky Dean twice suffered humiliating rebukes from the Queen, and these disconcerting experiences may well have encouraged his tolerance of the almoner.[14] It is surprising to find that no mention of Sebastian Westcott is made in the visitation to St Paul's made by Bishop Sandys in 1574. His name is not included among those in the list of choral vicars.[15] Is this, one wonders, an indication of the attitude ecclesiastical authority adopted towards him as the years went by? Did they, by closing their eyes to his embarrassing official presence, simply pretend he was not there?

Westcott continued to hold his place as one of the chief play presenters at court and to carry on with his duties at the cathedral. According to a contemporary witness, by the early 1570s the St Paul's choir was second to none: 'See whether we may get by the quier and we shall heare the fearest voyces of all the cathedrall churches in England.'[16] No doubt much of his life centred upon the almonry house within the precinct where the boys were dormered and perhaps schooled. It appears probable that John Redford's sister, Margaret Cox, supervised the domestic arrangements until her death. When her residence adjacent to the almonry was released to her in 1555, she agreed to reserve one room as a sanatorium for the children. After she died her daughter, Elizabeth, was there to replace her. Sebastian's brother, Philip, was also in London and, if not actually residing with Westcott, at least living close by.

Philip worked for the rich, influential cloth-merchant and alderman, Sir Thomas White, serving as Sir Thomas's Factor dealing with the north African coast.[17] He courted Elizabeth Cox, got her pregnant, and then married her in August 1562.[18] The following mid-summer he left London

14 On New Year's Day, 1561/2 when Elizabeth angrily rejected his gift of a Prayer Book containing engravings of saints and martyrs; and when she interrupted his Ash Wednesday sermon (1564/5) and bade him return to his text, see Ralph Churton, *Nowell* 70 and 111 and *DNB* XIV 688–95. In 1584 Nowell went to the aid of a recusant kinsman, John Townely, who had been imprisoned at Manchester; see P.M. Handover, *The Second Cecil* (London 1959) 89.

15 *Lib. Visit.* (1574), Guildhall Library MS 9537/3, fols 1–5

16 Claude Desainliens (Claudius Holybande), *The French Schoolmaster* (1573), cited by Morrison Comegys Boyd, *Elizabethan Music and Musical Criticism*, 2nd ed. (Philadelphia 1962)

17 *DNB* XXI 76–8. Born 1495; sheriff 1546; lord mayor 1553; founder of St John's College, Oxford, and principal benefactor of the Merchant Taylor's School; died February 1566/7. For White's catholic sympathies see W.H. Stevenson and H.E. Salter, *The Early History of St John's College, Oxford* (Oxford 1939), and also C.M. Clode, *The Early History of the Guild of Merchant Taylors* 2 vols (London 1888).

18 *London Marriage Licences, 1521–1869*, Joseph Foster, ed. (London 1887)

for the Barbary coast on a mercantile venture in which he was associated with several other merchants. By 1567 Philip was in serious difficulty abroad. The bankruptcy of one of his creditors, 'Isaac Cabessa,' who owed him 'a great peace of mony,' put Philip into severe financial straits and because of this he was unable to get a licence to leave Morocco. In an effort to restore his financial standing he remained and operated a 'Tabling or A Victualling house' for English merchants and travellers 'at a place callyd Cabo de Ghearra in the playe in the Country of Barbarye.'[19] He managed to free himself from debt by 1576, but civil disorder and the dangerous state of the country prevented him from returning home. He was able to keep in touch with his wife and brother through the services of seamen and merchants and wrote to Sebastian on 21 May 1575, authorising him to act on his behalf in a dispute over lands and tenements on the Manor of Cheddon Fitzpaine which will be discussed below.

Throughout this time Sebastian Westcott continued to pay rent for properties outside the churchyard in Paternoster Row, Carter Lane, and Sermon Lane, as well as to enjoy whatever came to him from the cathedral estate at Paul's Wickham in Essex, granted to him in 1557. It is not surprising to find that many of the persons mentioned in his will were either recusants or sympathetic to the old religion, and that several of them lived near him in London and in Essex. A fellow Devonian, the court musician John Boult, became a secular priest at Douai and ended his days at Louvain as organist at St Monica's convent.[20] John Heywood until his exile had a neighbouring estate in Essex. Another Chulmleigh contemporary and 'especiall good frende' was Sir John Southcott, Justice of the Queen's Bench. John and Elizabeth Southcott's London house was in Carter Lane and their country estate was at Witham only a few miles from Paul's Wickham.[21] Sebastian left him 'a guilte cuppe the cover havenge on the cover St Sebastian.' Dr James Good of the College of Physicians in Knightrider Street was

---

19 Possibly La Guera or Cape Blanco at the southern extremity of the Nocoya Peninsula, which is bisected by the boundary between Spanish Sahara and Mauritania and where Port Etienne stands today; see *Atlas Historico y Geografico de Africa Espanola*, Dirección General De Marruecos Y Colonias E Instituto De Estudios Africanos (Madrid 1955).
20 See *Grove's* I 799, and II 949–51.
21 DNB XVIII 685. Born in Chulmleigh 1511; died 1585. Southcott sat on the commission appointed in November 1577 to consider ways and means of dealing with recusants. He resigned from the bench in 1584, refusing to pass sentence of death on a recusant priest at Norwich; see Philip Caraman, *The Other Face* (London 1960) 229–30. Southcott's London residence is established from records of payments of Lay Subsidy, Guildhall Library, MS 2859/S.R. 21–6 and PRO 10/63, Transcript of Second Payment, 18 Elizabeth.

another friend. Good was imprisoned in 1573 for alleged secret correspondence with Mary, Queen of Scots, and in 1575, while in the Tower, fell
sick.[22] He died a year before Westcott, who bequeathed 'a ringe of golde with
a blew stone' to Joan, the Doctor's widow.

22 For some information about Dr James Good (1527–81) see *Roll of the Royal College of
    Physicians of London* I 1518–1700, compiled by William Munk (London 1878) 58 ; also Birt
    445, who cites BM MS Lansdowne, XXI, no. 60 for evidence of Good's illness in the Tower.

1 St Paul's Cathedral and Environs c1560

2 St Paul's, West Prospect 1656

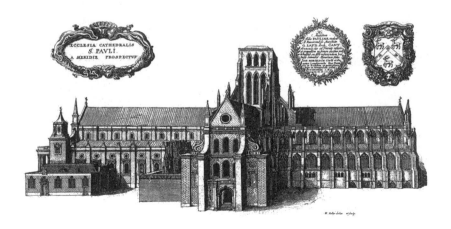

3 St Paul's, South Prospect 1656

4 St Paul's, The Nave 1656

5 St Paul's, The Choir 1656

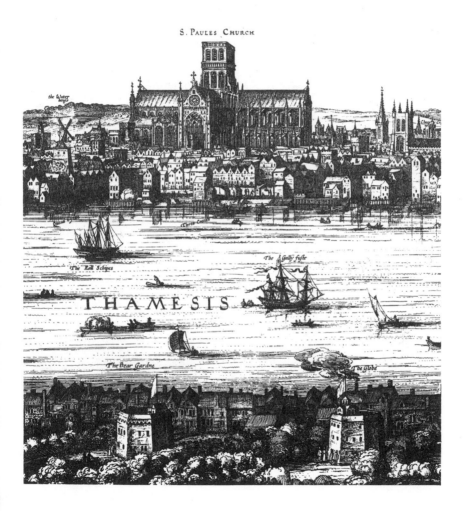

6 St Paul's Cathedral and South Bank 1616

IV

'Mr Sebastian'
and the Children of Paul's

IT IS NOT POSSIBLE TO SAY when Master Sebastian Westcott first presented boys in stage plays: his collegiate or perhaps monastic experience in Devon may well have fitted him to train, supervise, and educate choristers long before we find him at court in 1545. There is little doubt, however, that by the time Westcott was a vicar choral in 1547 he had become acquainted with the circle of writers and musicians associated with John Redford and John Heywood at St Paul's, and involved with the dramatic work of the two men. Redford was then nearing the end of his life and Westcott was soon to succeed him as Almoner and Master of the Choristers. Heywood, at fifty years of age, possibly no longer a singer of distinction and very likely no longer writing plays, was nevertheless still active as an instrumentalist, epigrammatist, poet, and court entertainer. His association with Redford's choristers may have begun as early as 1537/8 when he presented an interlude 'with his children' before the Princess Mary.[1] He continued to associate himself (in what precise way it is not clear) with stage presentations by Paul's boys in 1551/2, possibly at Easter 1553, and in 1559.[2] He was also a prominent contributor to the miscellany of music, verse, and fragments of Redford's plays, apparently an uncompleted collection of the work of a St Paul's literary and musical circle possibly gathered together after the death of

1 See p 14 n4. For further evidence of Heywood's connection with Redford and Westcott see Arthur Brown, 'Two Notes,' MLR XLIII (Oct. 1948) 508–10.
2 See Calendar of Presentations by the Children of Paul's, pp 55–7, nos 1, 2, and 5.

Redford.[3] Westcott's connection with this volume is *sub silentio*. In addition to his association with Redford and Heywood, he was on friendly terms with at least two other contributors, Thomas Prideaux and John Thorne.[4] *The Marriage of Wit and Science*, probably presented at court by Westcott in 1567/8, and recorded in the *Revels Accounts* as 'witte and will,' was an adaptation of Redford's *Wit and Science*, a substantial portion of which is in the manuscript.[5] Finally, there is A.W. Reed's plausible suggestion that the 'booke of ditties written' given by Westcott to Queen Mary on New Year's day 1557 may have been based upon the manuscript repertory of St Paul's songs.[6]

During the short reigns of Edward and of Mary the Paul's boys were not in demand, and their appearances in plays at court were as meagre as they are uncertain.[7] Most of the performances before Edward were either given by the Chapel or by the King's Players.[8] As soon as Mary came to the throne, she prohibited performances of interludes and plays without royal licence, fearing the controversy that might result from matters touching religious doctrine.[9] She was not occasionally averse to witnessing an approved play at court, but on the whole seems to have preferred masques and pastimes and, of course, musical entertainment for which she had a special aptitude and liking. Unlike Elizabeth, neither of these sovereigns was particularly impressed by the appeal of the children's companies. However, the Paul's boys found themselves welcome elsewhere. They were invited to entertain the Guild of Merchant Taylors on St John's day in 1549, 1551, and again in 1554. On all these occasions the choristers were paid for playing upon viols and singing, and upon the last visit they shared the program with the musicians of 'my Lord of Pembroke.'[10]

---

3 BM MS Add. 15233. The other contributors from St Paul's were Thomas Prideaux, John Thorne, Myles Huggard, and Master Knight; see Arthur Brown's brief description of the MS in *Grove's* VII 79–81.

4 Prideaux witnessed Margaret Cox's will, to which Westcott was residual legatee and executor (1556); Prideaux was also a co-signatory of the bond supporting Westcott's acquisition of the lease of Paul's Wickham in 1557, see p 16; for John Thorne, see p 37.

5 *Calendar*, no. 17

6 *Early Tudor Drama* 58

7 *Calendar*, nos 2, 3, and 4.

8 See Feuillerat, *E & M* xii–xv.

9 Proclamation dated 16 August 1533, printed by J.P. Collier, *The History of English Dramatic Poetry* 3 vols (London 1831) I 157–8

10 See C.M. Clode, *Memorials of the Guild of Merchant Taylors* (London 1875) 526 and 528–9. Perhaps this association with the Merchant Taylors was encouraged, if not inspired, by Sir Thomas White, who employed Sebastian's brother, Philip.

Westcott's boys played before the eighteen-year-old Princess Elizabeth at Hatfield House in 1551/2, and on that occasion Heywood was in attendance either as *entrepreneur* or as a musician.[11] This is the only unquestionable record of a performance by Paul's boys before Elizabeth prior to her coronation. In view of her immediate preference for Westcott's company after her accession, one suspects that her delight in them was founded upon a more substantial acquaintance than that merely afforded by a single presentation, however memorable. We may be inclined, therefore, to give some credence to the not unlikely possibility of a Paul's performance at Hatfield House in either 1554 or 1557.[12]

Elizabeth's notable predilection for the children's companies and, above all, for Westcott's boys has remained something of a mystery. Hillebrand suggests that Westcott 'was *persona grata* for being an old friend of Elizabeth's' but goes on to admit that it 'hardly enables us to understand why Westcote's company was so much more acceptable than the Chapel or indeed, we might add, than any other company.'[13] Sir Edmund Chambers discussed the problem in the light of the renaissance humanistic tradition and pointed out the long history of the Chapel entertainers, 'the decay of the royal interluders,' and the fact that the 'other professional companies had not yet found an economic basis in London.'[14] To these explanations another may be added. After Elizabeth's accession the boys of cathedral and chapel were no longer so busily engaged in the performance of duties, ceremonies, and rituals associated with the old faith. The reformed religious services must have increased the freedom of the choristers from daily ecclesiastical obligation. This is very likely the reason why the Paul's boys did not, so far as we know, appear in plays before the devout Mary during her reign, when the cathedral once more resumed its central place in the religious and civic life of London.[15]

Hillebrand's suggestion that Westcott enjoyed the special favour of Elizabeth because he was an old friend would certainly seem true by, say, 1570; there is little doubt that she indirectly but effectively protected him from clerical authority in the early sixties, and also that, although often capricious, she was unswervingly faithful to old friends. It does not, how-

11 Calendar, no. 1
12 Calendar, no. 4
13 Hillebrand, *Child Actors* 74
14 *Elizabethan Stage* II 4
15 It is significant that the only visit the Paul's choristers made to her court was in a ceremony of the Boy Bishop in 1554, see p 16.

ever, explain her patronage of his company at the very beginning of her reign; the records of only one, perhaps two, presentations by him before the young Princess are all we possess as evidence of their acquaintance. In pursuing the answer to this puzzling question, it is perhaps more fruitful to glance at Elizabeth's preference for the 'quality' of the Paul's boys, rather than at her patronage of her servant, Sebastian. The most important clue to this lies in the Queen's temperament. Throughout her life she rarely failed to respond to the appeal of intelligent and accomplished youth, particularly to handsome, audacious, and eloquent boys. Wherever she went the grace and ingenuousness of young men and boys charmed her and drew from her praise if not reward. Westcott's enduring success in pleasing the Queen was based, perhaps not altogether without conscious intent, upon an appeal to this deeply-rooted susceptibility within Elizabeth – the product of the conditioning factors of her early life and of her later circumstances.[16] After all, many others traded upon this partiality in other ways and to much greater profit than the almoner of St Paul's.

Two records early in the reign show that Westcott recognized and was willing to grasp the opportunity of consolidating his initial enterprise as a court entertainer. The first promotion, whether occurring fortuitously or achieved by foresight, gave him a new measure of freedom. Arthur Brown has drawn attention to the implications of the wording of Sebastian's re-appointment as almoner on 1 December 1559: 'Previously Westcott was to exercise his office "in persona sua propria." Now he may exercise it "per se vel sufficientem deputatem suam sive deputatos suos sufficientes".' Brown has observed that the appointment of a deputy or deputies would have given the almoner more time for his dramatic activities, and also would have permitted him to be absent from St Paul's.[17] The second record explains the use Westcott was to make of this contingency. Seven months later he was empowered by a royal warrant to 'take-up' boys from other collegiate and cathedral churches 'within our Reallme' for service at St Paul's, and ec-

16 See Elizabeth Jenkins, *Elizabeth the Great* (London 1958) passim, for one of the most perceptive studies of 'That long-preserved virginity,' and in which many instances of Elizabeth's delighted response to bright youngsters is recorded.
17 'Three Notes,' MLR XLIV (April 1949) 230, and 'Sebastian Westcott at York,' MLR XLVII (Jan. 1952) 49–50. Were Gyles Clothier and John Boult, the musician (see p 27), who were beneficiaries of Westcott's will, and who were mentioned immediately after the bequest to the 'tenne choristers' and in the middle of a list of bequests to cathedral officials, Sebastian Westcott's deputy almoners in 1582?

clesiastical authorities were advised to co-operate 'whereof ffail ye nott as ye tender our favour and will answere for the contrary.'[18] Westcott's commission is similar to the one granted to St George's Chapel on 8 March 1560, and shows that the Queen intended to have not only excellent choral establishments at Windsor and at St Paul's but also worthy acting companies, since the boys taken up for service 'would be chosen as much for their histrionic as for their singing ability.'[19] In the spring of 1571 Westcott visited York in search of singing boys, and since his commission was transcribed in the Minute Book of the city, he may have succeeded in persuading John Thorne, the cathedral organist, to part with a promising lad.[20] It would appear that Sebastian's customary search for new boys was made not long after the festive season at court ended. In the spring of 1580 he took up a boy from Christ's Hospital.[21]

By 1560 Sebastian Westcott was well prepared for future service to the Queen. As successor to John Redford he had gained considerable experience at St Paul's since 1547; he had also inherited Redford's repertory of plays. He was already familiar with the Queen's theatrical taste as a result of several successful presentations, at least two of them in association with the elderly and very experienced musician and dramatist, John Heywood. He had lately acquired extended power as Almoner and Master of the Choristers for the improvement of his company. Ahead of him lay over twenty years of almost uninterrupted dramatic presentation.

Fortunately the names of many of Westcott's boys have been preserved. A comparison of the lists in which their names appear is instructive.

18 Minutes of the City Council of York, xxiv fol. 241, first printed in *York Civic Records* VII, Yorkshire Archeological Society, Record Series, 125 (1950), and reprinted by Arthur Brown, *MLR* XLVII (Jan. 1952) 49–50. The warrant is dated 'the last of June in the second yere of our Reigne' and appears to have been copied into the Minute Book in May 1571.
19 Brown, 'Westcott at York,' *MLR* XLVII (Jan. 1952) 50. The chief difference between the Windsor and the St Paul's commissions is that the former was expressly forbidden to take men and boys from either the Chapel Royal or St Paul's (see Chambers II 62), whereas Westcott was left quite unrestricted.
20 Friendly co-operation from Thorne would seem likely, if he were the same Thorne whose compositions appeared with Redford's and Heywood's in BM MS Add. 15233 and with Redford's in BM MS Add. 29996.
21 'Mr Sebastian of Paulls is appointed to have Hallawaie the younger out of this House to be one of the singing children of the Cathedral Church of Paulls in this Citie' (Court Minute 5, March 1579/80), cited by 'Dotted Crochet,' in 'The Children of St Paul's and the Plays They Acted,' *The Musical Times*, 1 Jan. 1907.

1554[22]	1561–2[23]	1574[24]
John Burde	[John Halcocke]	George Bowring
Simon Burde	[Richard Prince]	Thomas Morley
Richard Hewse	John Rainoldes	Peter Phillipp
George More	Anthony Pickeringe	Henry Nation
John Alkok	William Foxe	Robert Knight
Gilbert Maxsey	Richard Priddam	Thomas Brande
Roger Stakhouse	Samuel Bushe	Edward Pattmie
Richard Prynce	Richard/Robert Boker	Robert Baker
John Farmer	Thomas Wilkingson	Thomas Johnson
Robert Chofe	John Marshall	
	John Whalye	

1580[25]

Hallawaie the younger

Presumably Halcock or Alcock and Prince who were in the choir in 1554 had by 1561 recently departed. It is possible that the Robert Boker of 1561–2 was the Robert Baker of 1574, but in view of the time span perhaps not very likely. To these names may be added those ex-choristers mentioned in Westcott's will.

Peter Phillipps and (possibly) Thomas Venge

Bromeham
Richard Huse
Robert Knight
Nicholas Carleton } 'sometymes children of the
Bayle   saide Almenry howse'
[Henry?] Nasion
Gregorye Bowringe

22 Given by Hillebrand 110 from suit in the Court of Exchequer. The John Farmer in the list may very well be the composer and instrumentalist. See *Grove's* III 30–1.
23 From Bishop Grindal's Visitation, see p 20. There are two lists: the first (April 1561) on fol. 7 contains the names of Halcock and Prince at the head crossed through, and Boker's first name is given as Richard; the second (November 1562) on fol. 19 omits Halcock and Prince and includes Robert Boker.
24 Given by Hillebrand 111 from Bishop Sandys' Visitation. See p 24. Robert Knight in the list may possibly be the musician. See *Grove's* IV 780.
25 See p 37.

Whether or not the Thomas Morley in the 1574 list was the great composer is still uncertain.[26] Peter Phillips in the 1574 and 1582 lists has been identified as the recusant composer and organist.[27] He was living with Westcott in 1582 and after his master's death went abroad.[28] He might well have been Sebastian's assistant music master after leaving the choir. Nicholas Carleton, like John Farmer, was a later composer of vocal and instrumental music.[29] Of no renown but of great interest to us are Bowring, Nasion, Knight in the 1582 list and Richard Hughes in the earliest one, since these persons were, like Phillips, living with Westcott in 1582, not, one supposes, in the almonry house, but quite possibly in the Sermon Lane property which was originally left to the cathedral for the express purpose of maintaining senior choristers after they had left the choir.[30] Hughes, if indeed he is the 'Hewse' of the first list, must have been about thirty years of age at the time of Westcott's death; the others may have been between sixteen and twenty-one years of age. Why was Westcott harbouring these seven former choristers? Could the answer be that they were still useful to his theatrical enterprise, perhaps aiding, and some of them even augmenting, the ten choristers in the more spectacular and demanding presentations of classical legend and history which are a prominent feature of the Paul's repertory from 1571 onwards? The number of performers in the court plays may perhaps be estimated by the numbers of pairs of gloves the Revels Office supplied to the various companies, both men's and boys'. There is a marked increase in the quantity given to the Paul's boys.[31] They were issued with a dozen pairs for *Titus and Gesippus* in 1577, and eighteen pairs for their respective presentations of *Scipio Africanus* in 1580 and of *Pompey* in 1581.[32]

Glancing over the list of choir boys in 1574 we are reminded that one of

26 *DNB* XIV 981–2, claims the identification; *Grove's* V 895–8 makes no mention of Morley's possible association with the St Paul's choir. The composer was organist at the cathedral for a brief period in 1591.
27 See *Grove's* VI 712–15.
28 'I geve to Peter Phillipe likewise remanyning withe me sixe poundes thirtene shillinges and fower pence'; see also A.G. Petti, 'Peter Phillips, Composer and Organist 1561–1628,' *Recusant History* IV (1957–58) 45–60.
29 See *Grove's* II and also Gustave Reese, *Music in the Renaissance* (London 1954) 855.
30 See p 47.
31 The plays performed by the schools, Eton, Merchant Taylors, and Westminster invariably required more gloves than those of the chorister companies in the late sixties and early seventies. It may be that their greater resources of personnel and their more ambitious plays forced the choristers to compete with presentations of greater scope by the mid-seventies; cf. Feuillerat, *E*, passim.
32 See Feuillerat, *E*, fols 276, 321, and 336.

them 'being one of his principall plaiers' was abducted from Westcott's *ménage* in December 1575. This affair became a matter for immediate Privy Council action and a letter was sent to the Master of the Rolls and to one of the Masters of Requests instructing them to 'examine such persons as Sebastian holdeth suspected and to proceade with such as be founde faultie according to Lawe....'[33] It is not known if Westcott recovered his boy; however, the loss of a star must have been a serious inconvenience coming as it did shortly before his appointment to present a play at court.[34]

Among the exciting and arduous undertakings the choristers were called upon to endure, once they were established as regular visitors to court, were the journeys by cart and barge to the royal palaces at Richmond, Whitehall, Greenwich, and Hampton Court. Earlier in their history there were dusty perambulations to such places as Hatfield House in Hertfordshire and Nonsuch in Surrey.[35] Later there were miserable mid-winter journeys by river, and one wonders at the resilience of the boys, since they gave their performances on the same night. The serpentine trip to Hampton Court was certainly the most tedious and perhaps the least to their liking. All arrangements for travel were made by the officers of the Queen's Revels, at first from the Blackfriars, after 1560 from their accommodation at St John's Hospital, Clerkenwell. The Paul's party – the boys, the attendant tirewoman and dressers, the stage assistants, and the master – gathered at Blackfriar's wharf and boarded a wherry loaded with their playing stuff, usually returning in the early hours of the following morning.

One wonders how the choristers felt about their master. No commendatory statement about Westcott, such as Thomas Tusser's affectionate appraisal of John Redford, exists to show how he treated the fifty or so boys who must have passed through his hands during his long career. From the evidence of Westcott's bounty to the boys in his will – each chorister received £5 and seven former choristers 'Twentye shilling*e*s a peece' – domestic life in the almonry would appear to have been comfortable. The lads slept in pairs in their dormitory and were fed from a well-equipped kitchen.[36] The house was furnished with much of Sebastian's own stuff, hangings, tables, chests,

33 *Acts of the Privy Council* IX 156. Hillebrand, citing *Privy Council Registers, Elizabeth* II 408, prints the document in full (p 124).
34 Calendar, no. 26
35 J.T. Murray, *The English Dramatic Companies, 1558–1642*, 2 vols (New York 1963) II 206 notes payment 'to the pawlle plaiers – ii^s' at Hedon (a few miles east of Hull), Yorkshire, 'after 1 Edw. VI, year uncertain.'
36 'fyve bedsteads, fyve mattresses, fyve paire of blanckett*e*s, fyve bolsters of floxe, fyve coverled*e*s suche as are accustomablie vsed for the Tenne Choresters'

cupboards, and the like, all of which he bequeathed 'to the use of the Al-
menary.' That he must have been as kindly regarded as his predecessor is
to some extent borne out by the fact that some of his former boys remained
with him after their service in the choir had ended. Certainly to the officials
at court and cathedral, to the clerks at the Office of the Revels and to the city
authorities, he seems to have been regarded as something of a 'character' by
the early sixties. Thereafter and until his death most of them referred to him
simply as 'Master Sebastian.'

v

The Playhouse
and the Repertory

THE EARLIEST SURVIVING RECORD of the existence of Westcott's playhouse belongs to December 1575 when the Court of Aldermen were 'enformed that one Sebastian that will not comvnycate with the Church of England kepethe playes and resorte of the people to great gaine and peryll of the Corruptinge of the Chyldren with papistrie,' and instructed the City Remembrancer, Thomas Norton, to ask Dean Nowell to remedy the situation 'within his iurysdyccion, as he shall see meete for Christian Relygion and good order.'[1] Aldermanic indignation is directed expressly against Westcott's contumacy; however, it follows immediately after an instruction to the governors of Christ's Hospital to collect 'all such somez of monye as by an Acte of Common Counsell lately made' from innkeepers and householders on whose premises interludes or plays took place. Perhaps the aldermen were equally upset that Westcott's 'great gaine' was exempt from the dues they felt should have been surrendered by him to the sick and poor as laid down in their Act of 6 December 1574.[2] It is safe to infer from all this that Westcott's playhouse, whether located within the walls of the churchyard or in some cathedral property just outside, was, in fact, immune from civic ordinance and that it was operating successfully, drawing crowds and making profit.

Sebastian's theatre may have started a few years earlier; indeed, it is quite

1 Hillebrand 123, prints the passage from *Repertories of the Court of Common Council* XIX fol. 18; see also the Malone Society, *Collections* II Pt 3, 309.
2 See Chambers IV 273–6.

possible that small audiences had watched the final rehearsals of plays commissioned for the Queen's entertainment for over a decade or more before his 'exercise' of plays became the kind of fully-fledged commercial venture which so disturbed the aldermen in 1575. Nothing seems to have come from this protest; in December 1578 the Privy Council required the Lord Mayor to suffer six companies, among them the children of Paul's, 'to exercise playeng within the Cittie.'[3] The only other reference to the Paul's playhouse made in Westcott's lifetime was Stephen Gosson's brief allusion to it in 1581/2.[4]

The precise location of the Paul's playhouse remains obscure. Among the places within the precinct so far proposed, we need to consider the almonry house, the hall of the college of Minor Canons, St Gregory's Church, and the Chapter or Convocation House.[5] In one way or another none of these proposed buildings appears to be a convincing site. The petty canons' hall may be ruled out. Westcott was not a Minor Canon and so would have had no privileges within the college premises; it is also most unlikely that the canons would have tolerated a playhouse in their midst.[6] Not far from the petty canons in the north churchyard was the almoner's house. Westcott lived there, residing with the choristers and the household staff. He gives the impression in his will that the almonry (in which he died) was merely a residence and a refectory, perhaps also a school.[7] As for the parish church of St Gregory, it had been appropriated by the college of Minor Canons and may well have been the song-school of the almonry boys in earlier times when the almoner was a member of the college.[8] There is no evidence to

3 For Privy Council Minutes see Chambers IV 278.

4 See Calendar, no. 33.

5 The fullest discussions of the playhouse are by W.J. Lawrence, *The Elizabethan Playhouse and Other Studies*, 1913 (re-issued, New York 1963), passim, J.Q. Adams, *Shakespearean Playhouses* 1917 (reprinted, Gloucester, Mass. 1960) 111–18, Hillebrand 112–14, and by Chambers II 10–11, and II 134–45.

6 In medieval times the almoner was a minor canon; the last of such was Thomas Hickman who seemingly relinquished his post to become subdean probably between 1528 and 1530. He died in 1534. John Redford, who succeeded Hickman, and Sebastian Westcott, who followed Redford, were both only vicars. By 1574 Westcott was simply the almoner; his name was omitted from the list of vicars choral (supra 23). He designates himself only as almoner in his will.

7 W.A. Armstrong, *The Elizabethan Private Theatres: Facts and Problems* (London 1958) 3, places the theatre 'in a small hall in the Almonry House.' In his 'The Audience of the Elizabethan Private Theatres,' RES x (1959) 233, the 'Almonry House' is described as 'a small building behind Convocation House'; in fact, however, these two buildings were quite distinct, the former in the north churchyard, the latter in the south churchyard.

8 Chambers claims that Stow (*Survey* II 19) said that the song-school was housed in St Gregory's by the twelfth century, but as Hillebrand points out, such is not Stow's claim.

show that either Redford or Westcott continued to use the church for their choir practices. Nevertheless Howe's continuation of Stow's *Annals* (1631) says that the playhouse was the 'singing-school.'[9] Richard Flecknoe in *A Short Discourse of the English Stage* (1664) locates the playhouse 'behind the Convocation-house,' which J.Q. Adams incorrectly places 'in or near Paternoster Row.'[10] Had the song-school been transferred from the parish church to the Chapter House by Westcott's time?[11] Although it was only a short distance to the east of St Gregory's in the south churchyard, it seems very doubtful that the great upper room where the Dean and Canons met, situated over the open eight-sided undercroft, was used as a singing-school. Convocation House seems to be a most unlikely site for a playhouse. The building was octagonal in shape, entirely surrounded by a square, two-storeyed cloister and completely enclosed from the churchyard by a high wall. The only entrance to it was situated in the middle of the south transept.[12] Thus, of the possibilities within the churchyard, St Gregory's church appears to be the most likely, and, furthermore, Hillebrand has shown that in 1598 the church was being used as a schoolhouse, presumably for the education of parish boys.[13] Yet there is reason to be sceptical about this location. Howes alludes to the 'singing-school,' not to St Gregory's. Burbage and Heminges refer to Paul's playhouse as 'the said house near St Paul's Church'; they do not mention St Gregory's,[14] and neither does Stephen Gosson in 1581. If the song-school had been in the church, and if the song-school had been the playhouse, it is odd that a building so venerable, central, and well known as St Gregory's church should remain unassociated by name with the playhouse it supposedly housed. Perhaps we should look elsewhere for Westcott's playhouse.

As almoner, Westcott leased from the Dean and Chapter, at least as early as 1554, three properties immediately outside the walls of the churchyard.[15] Two of these, in Carter Lane and in Sermon Lane, lay scarcely more than fifty yards from the south gate known as Paul's Chain. The four tenements

9 *Annales, or A Generall Chronicle of England*, 1631, sig. iiii, cited by Adams 111 and also by Hillebrand 112

10 *Shakespearean Playhouses* 111 n3

11 W.J. Lawrence, *The Elizabethan Playhouse* 25, perhaps in an attempt to reconcile the views of Flecknoe and the *Annales*, describes Paul's playhouse as 'in the Choir Singing School, near the Convocation House.'

12 See the ground plan of Old St Paul's in *A History of St Paul's Cathedral* 344.

13 *The Child Actors* 112–13

14 In the suit *Keysar and Burbadge and Others* (Court of Requests 1610), privately printed in full by C.W. Wallace, 1910 and included in his *Shakespeare and his London Associates* (1910) 95

15 See map, p 46.

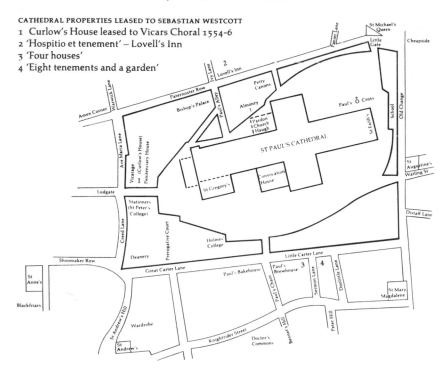

CATHEDRAL PROPERTIES LEASED TO SEBASTIAN WESTCOTT
1 Curlow's House leased to Vicars Choral 1554-6
2 'Hospitio et tenement' – Lovell's Inn
3 'Four houses'
4 'Eight tenements and a garden'

ST PAUL'S CATHEDRAL PRECINCT 1550-1600

Based upon 'An Exact Surveigh of the Streets, Lanes, and Churches . . . 10 Dec. A°. Dom^i. 1666 . . .
John Leake, John Jennings [et al.] Surveyors.'   BM King's Topographical Collection, xx, no. 17

on the corner of Sermon and Carter Lanes possibly housed the ex-choristers who remained with Westcott, since this property was left to the cathedral as a maintenance for senior choristers whose future, after their service in the choir, was not yet settled. The eight tenements and a garden in Carter Lane were situated between Sermon and Dolittle Lanes and such a property seems large enough to have housed a small playhouse, especially if we accept Maria Hackett's authority that it was used as a schoolhouse for St Paul's boys until the nineteenth century. The third property in Westcott's hands was immediately outside the north churchyard in Lovell's Inn fronting Paternoster Row at the entrance to Paul's Alley, which divided the press of buildings in the churchyard and opened to the northwest of the cathedral. Here the almoner had at his disposal a 'hospitio and tenement.' Was there a hall here and was this property the site of the playhouse? At any rate the Carter Lane and Paternoster Row locations appear to fit Burbage's and Heminges' descriptions of the playhouse 'the said house near St Paul's' more aptly than St Gregory's church, and they were both near enough to the almonry to have been conveniently used as a song-school.[16]

Westcott made no direct references to the Paul's playhouse in his will; he did, however, leave small sums of money to 'Shep^d [Sheppard?] that kepeth the doore at playes' and to 'Pole the keper of the gate.'[17] Earlier in the document he had listed bequests to seven or eight ex-choristers, and to Peter Phillips the musician and former chorister who, it has been suggested above, may have been acting as his assistant music master. Included in this section of the will are bequests to 'Thomas Bluet, Thomas Barsey and Robert and John Aunderson nowe remayninge in my house.'[18] Were these men associated with Sebastian's theatre? The house referred to need not necessarily be taken to be the almonry; it could have been one of the properties outside the churchyard. Certainly the scale of the St Paul's dramatic activity in the

16 Hillebrand (p 113) draws attention to a statement in J.P. Malcolm's *Londinium Redivivum* (London 1803) 7, which reads: 'The house of John Gyles was partly formed by St Paul's and was lately used for a playhouse.' Malcolm gives the impression of obtaining the information from ms presentments on visitations at St Paul's in 1598. Hillebrand's effort to check the accuracy of the claim by a thorough search of the relevant ms in St Paul's Library was unsuccessful and he offers the conjecture that Malcolm may have misread 'John' for 'Thomas' and thus perhaps refers to the incumbent Master of the Choristers, Thomas Giles. If Hillebrand is right, Giles would have been administering the same properties belonging to the almonry as his predecessor, Westcott, and the 'house' referred to may well have been one of the properties discussed above.
17 See the codicils. Pole, presumably, kept one of the gates of the churchyard, perhaps the one leading to the playhouse.
18 They received 'fyve poundes a pece.'

last decade of Westcott's career would suggest that he was unlikely to be operating the company and the playhouse single-handedly.

Of the thirty-two performances of St Paul's plays under the direction of Westcott the titles of no more than ten are known, and of these only two moralities, *The Marriage of Wit and Science* and *The Contention between Liberality and Prodigality*, survive in print. At the beginning of his career, Westcott perhaps had in stock for revival the plays written by his friend and predecessor at St Paul's, John Redford.[19] And since there is evidence of a close association between John Heywood and Westcott up to at least 1559, perhaps Heywood also supplied him with plays. Aside from the performances of the two above-mentioned moral interludes, nothing is known of the plays presented before 1571. There is not a shred of evidence to show that Westcott himself either composed music or wrote plays.[20] Fortunately, we are better informed about the presentations in the last ten years of his career. We may surmise from the description of the plays in the records, inadequate though they are, that his repertory included moralities (*Liberality and Prodigality*, revived, and *The Marriage of Mind and Measure*), tragedies (*Iphigenia* and *Alcmeon*), possibly an adaptation of a Plautine comedy (*Error*), romances from classical pseudo-history and from myth (*Titus and Gessipus* and *Cupid and Psyche*), and plays from classical history (*Scipio Africanus* and *Pompey*).[21]

From this list it seems clear that the Paul's boys were able to meet the changing demands of courtly taste in the seventies, replacing moral interludes with the more spectacular plays based upon classical sources. Whether or not Westcott was innovator of this trend, he was its most successful exploiter. No rival company offered so varied a repertory, and this despite the school companies having greater resources of material and personnel.

His success may well have been founded upon the establishment of his playhouse at Paul's during the fiercely competitive years between 1570 and

19 In addition to *Wit and Science* small fragments of two other interludes by Redford are contained in BM MS Add. 15233, the concluding ten lines of possibly a farce, and eight lines of another morality.

20 Cf. Arthur Brown, 'A Note on Sebastian Westcott and the Plays Presented by the Children of Paul's,' *MLQ* XII (June 1951) 134–6. There is, of course, much speculation to the contrary: Hillebrand, *JEGP* XIV (Oct. 1915); C.W. Roberts, 'The Authorship of *Gammer Gurton's Needle*,' *PQ* XIX (April 1940); J.P. Brawner, 'Early Classical Narrative Plays by Sebastian Westcott and Richard Mulcaster,' *MLQ* IV (Dec. 1943) 455–64; Roma Ball, 'The Choirboy Actors of St. Paul's Cathedral,' *ESRS* X (June 1962); and M.C. Bradbrook, ' "Silk? Satin? Kersey? Rags?": The Choristers' Theatre under Elizabeth and James,' *SEL* I (Spring 1961) 53–64.

21 See Calendar.

1575, when the number of companies appearing at court increased from three to nine, and when Hunnis (Chapel Royal), Farrant (Windsor), Elderton (Eton and Westminster), and Mulcaster (Merchant Taylors), to mention only the choir and school masters, must have gone before Benger and then Blagrave at the Revels Office in the keenest rivalry. It should also be remembered that it is precisely this period, up to the end of 1575, when Westcott, unembarrassed by civic disapprobation and apparently ignored by his church superiors, was free to enlarge his scope in peace. The expansion of his theatrical enterprise from 'exercises' followed by court performances at Christmas and Shrovetide to the operation of a company advantageously based in his own 'house,' however small its capacity and stage, immune from city jurisdiction and yet so immediately accessible to a densely populated area of residence and trade, would have offset whatever advantages his competitors possessed. The Paul's boys would have been able to play continuously between say November and March and hence acquire a greater polish and consistency in performance, aside from contributing 'great gaine' to their Master. There were experienced ex-choristers at hand to supplement the ten choir boys, and as we have noticed in the will, a number of men and women available to aid his thriving enterprise.[22]

Although Westcott's playhouse was older, perhaps by a few years, than Farrant's at Blackfriars, the records of the City of London should caution us against advancing the claim that it was the first 'private' theatre. There exist too many proclamations and admonitions addressed not only to tavern keepers and innholders, but also to householders forbidding performances of plays in their mansions, courts, and gardens.[23] Nevertheless, for the moment and so far as we know, the playhouse at Paul's was the first theatre to be settled in a privileged location, to have a permanent acting company, and to be patronized by a fee-paying public. Claims made on behalf of Richard Farrant that his 'Blackfriars was England's first indoor playhouse' must be dismissed.[24]

It has been fancifully suggested that Farrant was inspired to acquire the lease of the Blackfriar's premises in order to convert them into a theatre after his hearing of James Burbage's intention to build The Theatre.[25] If anybody

22 'vnto ffrydiswide Clunye widowe nowe beinge in house withe me ... mother Smalye ... mother Alyce ... mother Walker...'
23 See 'Dramatic Records of the City of London,' the Malone Society, *Collections* II Pt 3 (1931) 285–320, particularly nos 20 (1558), 22 (1564), 25 (1566), 29 (1569), and 35 (1573).
24 See Irwin Smith, *Shakespeare's Blackfriars Theatre* (New York 1964) 132, and Glynne Wickham, *Early English Stages* 3 vols (London 1972) II Pt 2, p 129.
25 Smith 133–4 and Wickham 126

inspired Farrant, it was indeed Sebastian Westcott. In the span of twenty-three years before Farrant made his bid to Sir William More for the lease in 1576, he and Westcott must have been well acquainted; after all Farrant was a Gentleman of the Chapel long before he became Master of the Choristers at Windsor. Their common vocations (particularly after 1567 when the Windsor boys first came to court and no doubt challenged the security of the old rivals, Chapel and Paul's) must have surely brought Westcott and Farrant together, if not at court, then at the Office of the Revels in the Blackfriars itself and only a few hundred yards away from the precinct of Paul's.

But it is not as bitter rivals one wishes to represent them here, whatever the existing records may be directed to suggest. One would rather take account of their respective contributions to the development of the Elizabethan theatre, the fruits of which, with sweet irony, followed quickly upon their deaths, Farrant's in 1580 and Westcott's about sixteen months later. Shortly after Sebastian died, his overseer and 'deere frende,' Henry Evans, took in hand the task of promoting the company Westcott had nurtured and directed in the theatre Farrant had built, and in association with a new luminary gave brilliant life to a second Paul's company. Under John Lyly's tutelage another generation of boys lit the way to the last and most splendid decade of theatre in the sixteenth century – and who shall deny that the two Masters with their choristers shared in making all that possible?

VI
Last Years

THE IMMUNITY FROM PERSECUTION enjoyed by Sebastian Westcott for over a decade ended in 1575. His position at St Paul's had long been precarious; yet, with good luck and by tactful management, and by pleasing the Queen year after year with entertaining plays, he had preserved himself. Times were changing, however. By the mid-seventies the more tolerant spirit of the early years of the reign had been eroded by a succession of events – the arrival in England of the Queen of Scots (1568), the northern rebellion (1569), the excommunication of Elizabeth (1570), and the massacre in Paris (1572). Anti-papal feeling became both more general and more intense as protestantism became increasingly reactionary and militant. In the early sixties Westcott had defied Grindal and also, presumably, Grindal's successor, Edwin Sandys (confirmed, July 1570), by abstaining from the communion. After 1577 he had to face a much less gentle episcopal authority in John Aylmer.

In 1564 Grindal, justifying his intention to excommunicate Sebastian, had urged the danger of permitting choristers to remain under his instruction:

And therefore I am affrayed I have an accompte to geve to godde for all those corrupte lessons of false Religion which he the space of 2. or 3. yeares hathe instilled into the eares and myndes of those children comitted vnto him; wherein (no doubte) he hathe bene to diligente as hathe appeared by his frutes.[1]

1 BM MS Lansdowne, 30, no. 55

One interprets the allusion in the last clause in a double sense as referring to the profit Sebastian made from his use of the choristers in stage presentations and also to those choristers under his guidance who, like Peter Phillips, grew up to be staunch catholics.[2] This charge was revived, as we have already noticed, in the complaint before Common Council on 8 December 1575. There is no further record of the matter and one must assume that Westcott was not affected by Thomas Norton's redress to Dean Nowell. A little more than a year later, in 1577, Sebastian was still described 'Master of the Children of Paules church' and valued at £100 in goods.[3]

Towards the close of 1576 Sebastian was engaged on behalf of his absent brother, Philip, in a legal action to save family property in Cheddon Fitzpaine, Somerset.[4] He initiated proceedings and the interrogatory was answered by Westcott deponents in February 1577. The defendants, a widow, Elizabeth Clifton, and a William Edwards and his wife, asserted that Philip 'maye not enjoye the benefytt of his customary tenement wythin the said manor' because he was either imprisoned or absent abroad, circumstances which, according to the custom of the manor, disbarred right of possession. They further alleged him to be a 'notorious and arrogant papiste,' to be in debt and to have deserted his wife, Elizabeth, who was accused of immorality. Sebastian was charged with acting improperly in bringing suit.

Four deponents responded on behalf of the Westcotts: Nicholas Bristow, aged sixty, of Ayot St Lawrence, Hertfordshire, who claimed to have known Sebastian forty years and must therefore have met him in either Devon or Somerset; Anthony Morris, aged fifty-six, merchant of Knightsbridge and Philip's business partner between 1563 and 1567; Thomas Cock, aged twenty-five, servant to Arthur Dawbney, a merchant tailor; and Robert Smith, aged thirty-six, a seafaring man. Although their testimonies deny all the allegations and exonerate Philip and Sebastian from the imputations, none of them has anything to say about the chief contention concerning the Cheddon Fitzpaine property. The outcome of this dispute is not known. Philip must have died abroad in the next year or two. Elizabeth, mentioned as a widow in Sebastian's will, received a legacy of £20 'together withe the

---

2 Hillebrand 122 seeks elucidation of Grindal's reference to 'frutes.'

3 Cal. SP Dom., Eliz. 118, 73

4 Chancery Suit, PRO C24/127, Westcote v Clifton, discovered by C.J. Sisson and briefly summarised by him in 'A Note on Sebastian Westcott,' RES xix (April 1943) 204–5. See also Arthur Brown, 'Two Notes,' MLR xliii (Oct. 1948) 508–10. Sisson, aware that Westcott was born in Chulmleigh, concluded that the land in dispute was in Devon at Cheriton Fitzpaine; however, 'Cheddon Fitzpaine' is clearly stated in the suit and our knowledge of Westcott's relatives in Taunton and adjacent parishes rules out any other locality.

lease of Westgrene ... and all the howshold stuffe and kyene and catell there.'[5]

Whether or not Sebastian was successful on Philip's behalf, he was unable to save himself some months later from imprisonment 'for papistry.' He appeared before the Privy Council at Hampton Court on 20 December 1577 and was ordered to be confined to the Marshalsea the following day. The date of his entrance to prison was postponed, however, to 'the last of December' when it was discovered that he was due to present a play before the Queen on the 29 December.[6] The Marshalsea was one of several prisons reserved for religious delinquents to which Aylmer confined both recusants and protestant non-conformists with a fine impartiality. Westcott spent nearly three months there and was 'discharged by my said Lords of the Counsell the 19 daye of Marche, 1577 [1578].'[7] This incarceration did not inhibit him from continuing to present plays at court nor indeed did it change his position at St Paul's in the few years that remained to him.

'Beinge greued in the sickenes' Sebastian made his will in the almoner's house on 3 April 1582. It is an orderly and quite lengthy document and from its main components – bequests concerned with his funeral, charities, almonry possessions, family, friends, and servants – one senses both the dispensatory mind of the cathedral official and the generous spirit of a prosperous man. One beneficiary, however, his brother Robert, did not take kindly to it. He challenged the will on two grounds: the questionable sanity of the testator and the maladministration of the executor; both complaints were dismissed by the court on 3 July 1582.[8] Perhaps it was this incident, or it may have been simply the hard task of meeting Westcott's rather carelessly expressed wishes regarding the disposal of the residue of the estate, which haunted the mind of his friend and executor, Justinian Kidd, sixteen years later when he came to make his own last earthly account.[9] The reasons for Robert's objections are not easily deducible from the will itself.

5 It has not been possible to identify Westcott's Westgreen property.
6 John Roche Dasent, ed. *Acts of the Privy Council of England*, 32 vols (London 1890–1907) x 127. Neither Hillebrand nor Chambers seems to have noticed this postponement. Chambers II 15 has 'They [the children of Paul's] played on 29 December, 1577, and one wonders whether it was anything amiss with that performance which led to an entry in the Acts of the Privy Council for the same day that "Sebastian was committed to the Marshalsea".'
7 *Cal. SP Dom., Eliz.* 140, 40. 'Certificate of prisoners remaining in the Marshalsea for papistry.' Westcott's name appears in a list of 'Papists at Liberty.'
8 PCC 31 Tirwhite
9 PCC 1 Kidd, 23 June 1598. 'And wheras also Sebastian Westcot late Almoner of Sancte Pawles in London deceased made his laste will and testament and therof made me ... his sole

The legacies which he and his children received are not singularly discrepant with those bestowed upon other surviving kin. Perhaps he took exception to the special favour shown to his son, Andrew, who was given ten pounds, whereas his other children received only thirty shillings each. Or, one is tempted to ask, was it because Sebastian's avuncular benevolence was mainly directed towards the younger generation, for it was the children of his immediate kin who not only benefited by substantial sums, but who were also to gain from the residue of the estate.

Sebastian Westcott died shortly after making his will, lingering long enough to order the insertion of a final codicil adding 'fortie shillinges' to the gift to Catherine, his maid, 'for that she toke greate paines withe him in his sycknes.' Probate was granted on 14 April 1582. If his last wishes were obeyed, the funeral and interment were dignified by the attendance of many of the clerical and lay officials of the great cathedral he had served as Vicar Choral, Almoner, and Master of the Choristers for about thirty-five years.

> Executor I protest before god that accordinge to the trust by him likewise reposed in me I have to the uttermoste of my power performed the same ... in all points and have not lefte any thinge unperformed as by my bookes of accompts made and orderly kepte concerninge his state and my playne and faithfull dealinge therin more playnly may appere.'

VII

A Calendar of Presentations
by the Children of St Paul's
under Sebastian Westcott 1551-81

Note: This compilation is based upon 'A Court Calendar' and 'Abstract of Payments' (Appendices A and B, *The Elizabethan Stage* 4), an independent search of the *Documents Relating to the Revels at Court*, also of *The Acts of the Privy Council of England* and with reference to *Annals of English Drama*, ed. A. Harbage, revised by S. Schoenbaum (1964), and *Supplement* (1966). Entries below marked with an asterisk are *not* recorded in the *Annals*.

1* WINTER 1551/2

A play (unknown) presented before Princess Elizabeth at Hatfield House:

Paid in rewarde to the Kinges Maiesties drommer and phiphe the xij[th] of Februarie, xx.s. Mr. Heywood, xxx[s]. and to Sebastian, towardes the charge of the children with the carriage of the plaiers garmentes, iiij[li].xix[s]. In thole as by warrante appereth vij[li].ix[s]. *Household Accounts of Princess Elizabeth 1551–2* Camden Miscellany, 2 (1853) 37

2* EASTER OR MAY 1553

A play (unknown) presented before King Edward VI:

... A playe of the state of Ierland by [William Baldwin] and another of childerne sett owt by M[r] haywood....

...for xxiiij^{ti} ells of lockeram for the making of xij cotes for the boyes in heywood*es* playe at xij^d ye ell (Feuillerat, *E & M* 142 and 145)

C.W. Wallace, *Evolution of the English Drama* (Berlin 1912) 84, and Reed, 59, suggest that the boys were the Children of the Chapel. Feuillerat, 288, supports Chambers' view that Heywood 'was put in charge of the singing-school of St Paul's, the boys of which probably performed his plays' (*Medieval Stage* 2, pp 203 and 444) ; see also *Elizabethan Stage* 2, pp 11–12.

Was the play presented on this occasion *Nice Wanton*? See no. 5.

3* JULY 1553

A pageant shown before Queen Mary at St Paul's on her progress through the city from the Tower to Westminster:

There was a pageant made against the Dean of Paul's Gate (on the s.w. side of the Cathedral) where the choristers of Paul's played on vialls and sung. (John Stowe *Annals* 1615)

...in Powlles chyrchyerde ij pagants; and ij scaffolds on Powlles stepull with stremars.... (Machyn's *Diary* 30 Sept. 1553)

4* DECEMBER 1554 OR APRIL 1557

A play (unknown) presented before Princess Elizabeth and Queen Mary at Hatfield House, see Thomas Warton, *History of English Poetry* 1871, 3, p 312.

As Chambers (*Medieval Stage* 2, p 196) and Hillebrand, 124, note, Warton's evidence for a performance in 1554 is confused and doubtful. The authenticity of the record has been questioned by H.E.D. Blakiston, 'Thomas Warton and Machyn's Diary,' *EHR* 11 (April 1896). However, neither Chambers nor Hillebrand mentions the alternative date in 1557 cited by Nichols, *Progresses* (1823) 1, p 17. J.T. Murray, who does, has: '1557. April. Princess Elizabeth was visited by the Queen in April. The great chamber was adorned with a sumptuous suit of tapestry called the "Hangings of the Seige of Antioch," and after supper a play was performed by the Choir boys of Saint Paul's,' *English Dramatic Companies 1558–1642* (2 vols, New York 1963) I 286.

5* 7 AUGUST 1559

A play (unknown) presented before the Queen at Nonsuch House, Surrey:

...and a play of the chylderyn of Powlles and ther master Se[bastian], master phelypes, and master Haywood, and after a grett bankett.... (Machyn's *Diary* 5 August 1559)

F.G. Fleay, *A Chronicle History of the London Stage 1559–1642* (London 1890) 57–8, conjectures the play was *Nice Wanton* (SR, 10 June 1560; 1560, John King; STC, 25016). Hillebrand, 125–6, discusses Fleay's suggestion at some length and is reluctant to confirm it. Nevertheless he concludes, 'We may assume that this was the play presented before Elizabeth, and, for all we know, the King in 1551–2, by the children of Paul's; it was kept in the possession of the owner, Westcote, possibly too the author; until it seemed advisable to use it at the revels in 1559.' Chambers dismissed Fleay's conjecture, and notes that 'Mr Philip' was organist of Paul's in 1557 and that if he 'was the John Phillip or Phillips who wrote *Patient Grissell* (*c.* 1560), this play may also belong to the Paul's repertory.'

There is nothing to support either Fleay's conjecture or Hillebrand's curious affirmation of it. *Nice Wanton* is erroneously described as 'Anti-Catholic' in *Annals of English Drama 975–1700* (1964) 30–1. It appears to have been written for boys, perhaps choristers, although only its final song, 'It is good to be merry,' printed after the 'Finis' can be compared favourably with the songs in proven chorister plays. The first two are duet-snatches covering the entrances of Ismael and Dalilah, and the third, a duet between Iniquity and Dalilah, scarcely anything better. The final song stands apart from these and has a distant affinity with the poem, 'Now you will be merry' attributed to John Redford in the collection of ballads and poems which accompanied the text of Redford's play *Wit and Science* (BM MS Add. 15233). *Nice Wanton* seems to have been presented at court first before a King and later before a Queen, but whether by Paul's or some other boys, it is impossible to say.

Patient Grissell (SR, 1565–6; nd [1569] Thomas Colwell; STC, 19865) has a cast list of twenty-four arranged for doubling by eight persons. This omits some minor speaking female roles, ie, Grissell's maid and Court Ladies (2 or 3 according to sd sig. D1) and, as Greg and McKerrow have pointed out (MSR, *Patient Grissell* 1910, xiii), is unworkable. If Patience and Constancy were female, over half the roles would be so. There are five songs, three solos by Grissell, a duet between Gautier and Grissell, and a lullaby by the nurse. The 'Commodye' is solemn, decorated with classical references, and repeatedly admonitory about the obedience of children to parents. For all these reasons Phillip's play appears to be written for boys to perform, perhaps by a chorister company.

COURT PERFORMANCES, WINTER 1559/60

Chambers lists only one play, performed probably by the Children of the Chapel on 31 December 1559, and this presentation is supported by a record in the *Revels Accounts* (Feuillerat, E 34), '...in ffurnishinge of a play by the children of the chapple.' However, two plays seem to have been presented to the Queen, the second on 6 January 1560. Machyn alludes to the first as displeasing Elizabeth, 'the wyche the plaiers plad shuche matter that they were commondyd to leyff off and contenent the maske cam in dansynge' (*Diary* 221), and to the second, 'the same night [6 Jan.] was sett up a skaffold for the play in the halle, and after a play was done ther was a goodlye maske....' (*Diary* 222). The payments in the *Declared Accounts*, 'to players of enterludes £13-6-8ᵈ' appears to confirm Machyn, since the customary payment for a single play until 1574 was £6-13-4ᵈ. The *Revels Accounts* (Feuillerat, E 79), also has 'playes and other pastymes sett forthe....' The Children of the Chapel may have been the offenders; they did not present again until the winter of 1564.

6 CHRISTMAS 1560

A play (unknown) presented before the Queen at Greenwich:

Sebastian Westcott Mʳ of the Children of Polles ... £6-13-4ᵈ (*Declared Accounts* 541, m. 28)

The Paul's boys and Dudley's men performed plays at Christmas. Chambers notes, 'one of the plays was Preston's *Cambyses*,' supposedly the 'huff-suff-and ruff' mentioned in a contemporary letter (4, App. A, 79). Despite Chambers' caution (cf. 3, pp 469–70), it is widely assumed that this identification is correct, that the author was Thomas Preston, scholar, Fellow and Vice-Chancellor at Cambridge, and that the play was presented by Dudley's men. The extant versions of *Cambises* (SR, 1569–70; nd [cOct. 1569] J. Allde; nd [1585?] E. Allde; STC, 20287) contain no evidence to support these assumptions. On the title pages of both editions appears a cast list of thirty-eight characters arranged for doubling by eight persons. What is often overlooked, however, is that the list omits two minor female roles – Hob's wife, Marian, and a Maid; that the roles of Commons Cry and Commons Complaint are undifferentiated and were probably originally conceived as a single character; that there is some confusion in the listing of the exact number of Lords; and that the cast contains in all seven women, two small boys (Cupid and Praxaspe's son), and another older boy (Otian) who describes himself (c2ᵛ) 'as tender childe.' *Cambises* does not appear to have been written for an adult company, certainly not in the early sixties. If the Thomas Preston of Cambridge was the author, then it may originally have been a college play.

Annals records Tom Tyler and His Wife (1558–63) as offered to the court by possibly either Chapel's or Paul's boys. Certainly this piece has characteristics of a chorister presentation: a cast of seven, seven songs (a solo, a duet, three trios, a concluding song by all, and finally an epilogue in the form of a song sung by one who 'cometh out ... and following all alone with instruments, and all the rest within sing between every staffe, the first two lines'). Would this be sung perhaps by the presenter? The play is a domestic farce of a fabliau kind with allegoric and morality elements, reminding one so strongly of the work of John Heywood that one wonders whether the play might not be earlier than the date proposed.

7* CHRISTMAS 1561
A play (unknown) presented before the Queen at Whitehall:

Sebastiane Westcote M^r of the Children of Powles ... £6-13-4^d (Declared Accounts 541, m. 37)

8* FEBRUARY 1562
A play (unknown) presented before the Queen at Whitehall:

Sebastiane Westcote M^r of the Children of Powles ... £6-13-4^d (Declared Accounts 541, m. 37)

9* CHRISTMAS 1562
A play (unknown) presented before the Queen at Whitehall:

M. of the children of Poles ... £6-13-4^d (Declared Accounts 541, m. 47)

...and to Sebastian Westcotte, Master of the Children of Polles for a like play presented by him before her Hyhnes ... vj^{li}.xiij^s.iiij^d (Acts of Privy Council 7, p 134)

COURT PERFORMANCES, WINTER 1563/4
Owing to an outbreak of plague in London, the Queen remained at Windsor where two plays were presented before her, one at Christmas and another at Shrovetide (see Chambers, 2, p 14; 3, p 214; 4, App. A, pp 81–2 and Feuillerat, E 116). The names of the plays and their auspices are unknown.

10* CHRISTMAS 1564
A play (unknown) presented before the Queen at Whitehall:

Sebastian Westcote M^r of the Children of Powles ... £6-13-4^d (*Declared Accounts* 541, m. 67)

Westminster, xviij of Januarye ... The Like letter for Sebastian Westcote, Master of the Children of Powles, for presenting a play this Christmas last before the Queen's Majestie ... vij^{li}.xiij^s.viij^d (*Acts of Privy Council* 7, p 87)

Eyrringe in Jenevary ffor cayrtene playes by the gramar skolle of westmynster and the childerne of powles.... (Feuillerat, E 117)

Chambers notes the discrepancy between the payments recorded in the DA and APC and thinks the latter is 'an obvious error' (4, App. B, 143).

11* 2 FEBRUARY 1565
A play (unknown) presented before the Queen at Whitehall:

Sebastian Westcott M^r of the Children of Poles ... £6-13-4^d (*Declared Accounts* 541, m. 67)

Westminster, ix of Marche ... to pay Sebastian Westcote, Master of the Children of Powles for presenting a play before the Quenes Majestie on Candlemas day laste ... vij^{li}.xiij^s.iiij^d (*Acts of Privy Council* 7, p 204)

Chambers, in error, states that this performance was given on 2 January (cf. 2, 14).

12,* 13,* 14* WINTER 1565/6
Three plays (all unknown), two at Christmas before the Queen at Whitehall, and the third before the Queen and Princess Cecilia of Sweden at Durham House in the Strand:

Sebastian Westcote M^r of the Children of Powles ... for two seūall playes ... at the Courte ... and one other also before her Matie at the Ladye Cecilias Lodgyng at the Savoye ... £20 (*Declared Accounts* 541, m. 76)

Cecilia, Margravine of Baden, sister of King Eric of Sweden, made an extended visit to England in 1565.

15,* 16* CHRISTMAS 1566

Two plays (both unknown) presented before the Queen at Whitehall:

Sebastian Westcote M^r of the Children of Powles ... £13-6-8^d (*Declared Accounts* 541, m. 92)

Westminster, vij Januarye ... to Sebastian Westcote, Master of the Children of Powles, for presenting two plaies before her Highnes at Christmas last past ... xiij^{li}.vjs.viij^d (*Acts of Privy Council* 7, 322).

17,* 18* CHRISTMAS-SHROVETIDE, 1567/8

Two playes 'witte and will' and 'prodigallitie' presented before the Queen at Whitehall:

Sebastian Westcote M^r of the Children of Powles ... £13-6-8^d (*Declared Accounts* 541, mm. 102 3)

Inprimis for seven playes, the firste namede as playne as Canne be, The second the paynfull plillgrimage, The tthirde Iacke and Iyll, The forthe six fooles, The fyvethe callede witte and will, The sixte callede prodigallitie, The sevoenth of Orestes and a Tragedie of the kinge of Scottes, to ye whiche belonged diuers howses, for the settinge forthe of the same as Stratoes howse, Gobbyns howse, Orestioes howse Rome, the Pallace of prosperitie Scotlande and a gret Castell one the othere side Likewise.... (Feuillerat, E 119)

Wit & Will not recorded, *Prodigality* ascribed to 'Rich's or Boys' in *Annals*.

The identification of 'witte and will' with *The Marriage of Wit and Science* (1569–70), Thomas Marshe; SR, Aug. 1569; STC, 17466) extant in a unique, undated quarto in the Bodleian Library (Malone 231.1) was first suggested by F.G. Fleay, *Chronicle History of the London Stage* (London 1890) 64 and restated in his *Biographical Chronicle of the English Drama* (London 1891) 2, pp 287–8 and 294. J.P. Collier was the first to point out that 'prodigallitie' was in all likelihood *The Contention between Liberality and Prodigality* (1602, S. Stafford f. G. Vincent; STC, 5593) in *History of English Dramatic Poetry* 1, p 194. Fleay agreed (*Biog. Chron.* 2, p 323) and Hillebrand confirmed the identification offering substantial evidence in 'Sebastian Westcote, Dramatist and Master of the Children of Paul's' *JEGP* 14 (October 1915). Hillebrand summarised his evidence in *The Child Actors* (1926) 128–30. Additional evidence from the *Revels Accounts* reinforcing Hillebrand is offered in the note to no. 25, a revival of the play in 1575.

A play (unknown) presented before the Queen at Hampton Court:

Sebastian Westecote m^r of the Children of Powles ... £6-13-4^d (*Declared Accounts*, 541, m. 113)

...that theris growne due vnto certayne credditou*r*s for stuffe by them deliu*er*ed unto the saied office, for the furnisshinge of suche playes, Tragedies, and Maskes as hath byn shewed before vs at Christmas, and Shrovtide Last past in the eleventh year of out Raigne.... (Feuillerat, *E* 124)

COURT PERFORMANCES, WINTER 1569/70

Chambers notes, 'During the winter of 1569–70 the company [ie, Westcott's] was exceptionally absent from Court.' Plays were performed by the Windsor boys (27 Dec. 1569), the Chapel boys (6 Jan. 1570), and Rich's men (5 Feb. 1570).

20* 28 DECEMBER 1570
A play (unknown) presented before the Queen at Hampton Court:

Sebastian Westecote M^r of the Children of Powles ... £6-13-4^d (*Declared Accounts*, 541, m. 115)

...And for Wagies due ... for working and attending theron, especially about the new making furnishing and setting furth of soundrie Comodies Tragedies Maskes and Showes wh*i*ch were showen before vs this Last C*hris*tmas and Shroftyde.... (Feuillerat, *E* 126)

21* 25–7 FEBRUARY 1571
A play (unknown) presented before the Queen at Whitehall:

Will͞m Honnyes, Richarde Farraunte and Sebastian Westcote M^{rs} of the Children of the Q ma ^{ties} Chapple Royall Windsore and Powles ... £20 (*Declared Accounts* 541, m. 127)

For a brief *Revels Accounts* record of these presentations see above no. 20.

22 28 DECEMBER OR 1 JANUARY 1571/2
'Effiginia A Tragedye' presented before the Queen at Whitehall:

Sebastian Westcott M^r of the Children of Powles ... £6-13-4^d (*Declared Accounts* 541, m. 137)

Westminster xij of Januarye, 1571 ... to deliver to Sebastian Westcote, Master of the Children of Powles, for presenting of a playe upon Newe Yeare's Day at night last past before her Majestie ... vj^{li}.xiij^s.iiij^d (*Acts of Privy Council* 8, p 62)

Effiginia A Tragedye showen on the Innosentes daie at night by the Children of powles (Feuillerat, ε 145)

...for the Apparalling, Disgyzing, ffurnishing ffitting, Garnishing & orderly setting foorthe of men, woomen and children in sundrie Tragedies, Playes, Masks and sportes with theier apte howses of peynted Canvas & properties.... (Feuillerat, ε 129)

Chambers (4, App. B) notes the discrepancy between the APC & *Revels Accounts* of the date of the performance and elects 28 December 1571. Among the six plays presented were *Paris and Vienna* by the Westminster boys and *Narcissus* by the Chapel boys, both spectacular to judge from entries in the *Revels Accounts*, and the former company received a double payment. Chambers convincingly dismisses Wallace's suggestion (*Evolution* 104) that Westcott's presentation was *The Bugbears* (BM MS Lansdowne, 807, fols 57 et seq.).

23* CHRISTMAS–TWELFTH NIGHT 1572/3
A play (unknown) presented before the Queen at Hampton Court:

Sebastian Westecote M^r of the Children of Polles ... £6-13-4^d (*Declared Accounts* 541, m. 150)

ij squirtes for the playe of the children of powles – viij^s (Feuillerat, ε 180)

24 27 DECEMBER 1573
'Alkmeon' presented before the Queen at Whitehall:

Sebastian Westcote M^r of the Children of Powles ... £6-13-4^d (*Declared Accounts* 541, mm. 165–6)

Alkmeon, playde by the Children of Powles on Saint Iohns daye at nighte there' (Feuillerat, ε 193)

Westminster xth of January, 1573 ... to Sebastian Wescote, vj^{li}.xiij^s.iiij^d.... (*Acts of Privy Council* 8, p 178)

Westcott's presentation was one of six plays given between Christmas and Twelfth Night, and, although there are a number of entries in the *Revels Accounts* concerning the other plays, there is nothing that appears certainly to relate to *Alcmeon*.

25* 2 FEBRUARY 1575

A revival of *Prodigality* (see no. 18) presented before the Queen at Hampton Court:

Sebastian Westcote M^r of the Children of Powles ... £13-6-8^d (*Declared Accounts* 541, m. 178)

Hillebrand (pp 128–31) offers evidence from the *Revels Accounts* to show that the play Westcott presented was essentially the surviving version called *A pleasant comedie shewing the contention betweene Liberalitie and Prodigalitie* printed in 1602 after possibly another revival. The entries he notices are:

A Cote, A hatt, & Buskins all ou*er* covered with ffethers of cvllers for vanytie in Sebastians playe... (p 241)

skynnes to furr the hoode in sebastians playe ffor making of ij sarcenet hood*des* for Cyttyzens in the same play (p 244)

A ffelt y^t was covered wi*th* mony (p 244)

Cownters to cast awaye by players (p 237)

Hillebrand has shown how these items are related to costumes, characters and scenes in the extant text. To these it is possible to add other entries which in all likelihood concern Westcott's presentation:

...ffor styching A Cote and a payer of Buskyns with a hatt made all ouer with sylver coyne and for sylk for the same... (p 234; cf. *L & P*, Mal. Soc. Rep., III.iii.615 s.d.)

Corde and a halter for an asse (p 234; cf. I.iv.199 and II.ii.326)

A planck & Beeche for a ladder (p 235 ; cf. IV.iv.903–5)

sylver paper to make mony (p 246)

Cariage of Stuffe for Candlemas Nighte to the watersyde. Barge hier to hampton Coorte then ... (p 244)

The boy companies especially seem to have pleased the Queen this season; Westcott, Farrant, Hunnis, and Mulcaster all received a bonus of ten marks.

26* 6 JANUARY 1576
A play (unknown) presented before the Queen at Hampton Court:

Sebasten Westcott M^r of the Children of Powles ... £10 (*Declared Accounts* 541, mm. 195–6)

Hampton Courte, the vijth of January, 1575 ... to Sebastian, Master of the Children of Powles, for presenting of a play before her Majestie upon Twelfe Day at night last past ... x^{li} (*Acts of Privy Council* 9, p 71)

The rewards to the companies increased from ten to fifteen marks (£10) from this year.

27 1 JANUARY 1577
'The historie of Error' presented before the Queen at Hampton Court:

Sebastian Westcote m^r of the Children of Powles ... £16-13-8^d (*Declared Accounts* Roll xv, Bundle 382)

The historie of Error showen at Hampton Court on Newyere's daie at night, enacted by the children of Powles (Feuillerat, E 256)

Edward Buggyn ... ffor the hier of a horse the 29: of December for 2: daies last before at xx^d the daie, to the Court and back for the plaie of Powles on Newyeres daie ... (Feuillerat, E 266–7)

The reward is exceptionally high; four of the five companies presenting benefited from an equally large sum.
Edward Buggyn was clerk-controller of the Tents and Revels from 30

December 1570 until 9 October 1584. In a series of entries in the *Revels Accounts* 266, payments were made to him for arranging the road and river transport for all the companies that winter, save Westcott's.

Feuillerat raises the question as to whether Westcott's presentation was adapted from Plautus' *Menaechmi* ; Quiller Couch and Dover Wilson, *The Comedy of Errors* (1922) xii–xiii, favour the idea 'that Shakespeare worked upon some older play based on Plautus' comedy. If so, it was probably the lost play *The Historie of Error* ... enacted by the children of ... (St Paul's): which same play seems to turn up again in 1583 as the "History of Ferrar" (!) in the Revels Accounts as having been produced at Windsor.' Chambers dismisses the idea, *William Shakespeare* (2 vols, Oxford 1930) 1 308–9.

28 19 FEBRUARY 1577

'The historye of Titus and Gesippus' presented before the Queen at Whitehall:

Sebastian Westcote ... £10 (*Declared Accounts* Roll xv, Bundle 382)

Westminster, xx[th] of Februarie, 1576 ... to paye to ... and the Master of the Children of Powles ... presented before her Majestie on Shrove Sunday, Monday and Tuesday last past, to eche of them the sum of vj[li]. xiij[s]. iiij[d], and besides by way of rewarde to eche of them v markes (*Acts of Privy Council* 9, p 293)

The historye of Titus and Gisippus showen at Whitehall on Shrovetuyesdai at night, enacted by the Children of Pawles (Feuillerat, E 270)

Hillebrand has noticed properties from the *Revels Accounts* 276; 'two formes for the Senatours,' to which may be added the following:

...for making of vj: Senatours Cappes of Crymsen Taffita

...ffor a dozen of Childrens gloves

ffor two Carres to Cary stuff for the Mask and for the Children of Powles from the Courte to S[t] John's (Feuillerat, E 277)

Paul's was the only children's company performing at Shrovetide with Howard's and Warwick's men; all three companies appear to have rehearsed before the Revels Office on the 16, 17 and 18 of February 1577, (cf. Feuillerat, E 277).

Feuillerat (p 461) notes possible sources: '... Boccacio, *Decam.*, Giorn. Decima, Nov. viii. The story had already been told by Sir Thomas Elyot in Bk. II, ch. 12, of his *Governour*. In 1562, Edwarde Lewicke brought out a translation in verse, the title of which was: "the most wonderful and pleasant History of Titus and Gisippus, whereby is fully declared the figure of a perfect frendshyp drawen into English metre by Edwarde Lewicke. Anno 1562" [not listed in STC (1963)]. Wynkyn de Worde had also printed another metrical version entitled "The History of Titus and Gesyppus, translated out of Latyn into englyshe by Willyam Walter" [not listed in STC (1963)]. A play founded on this tale is stated to have existed amongst those seen by him in the library of their author, Ralph Radcliffe (Warton III 308).' Chambers prints Bale's list of Radcliffe's plays including 'De titi & Gisippi, amicitia, Com ...' (*Medieval Stage* II 196–7).

29* 29 DECEMBER 1577

A play (unknown) presented before the Queen at Hampton Court:

Sebastian Westcott ... £10 (*Declared Accounts* 541, mm. 209–12)

It was after this presentation that Westcott was sent to the Marshalsea for almost three months. Chambers (II p 15) wondered if there had been anything amiss with the performance, but see ch. 6, p 53.

Towards the end of 1578 a series of Privy Council instructions restricted theatrical activity because of plague in the London area (see Chambers, 4, App. D, pp 277–8, who prints the PC Minutes). However, certain companies, including the Paul's boys, were exempted from restraint 'by reason that the companies aforenamed are appointed to playe this tyme of Christmas before her Majestie.'

Possibly *Cupid and Psyche* was presented on this occasion (see no. 33).

30 1 JANUARY 1579

'A Morrall of the marryage of Mynde and Measure' presented before the Queen at Richmond:

ye Mr of ye Children at Pawles ... £10 (*Declared Accounts* 541, m. 222)

Richmond, xvj of January, 1578 ... Six seuerall warrantes to the Thresurer of her Majesties Chamber for plaies presented before her Majestie, viz: by the Children of Poules one... (*Acts of Privy Council* 11, p 21)

A Morrall of the marryage of Mynde and Measure shewen at Richmond on the sundaie next after Newe yeares daie enacted by the Children of Pawles furnished somethinges in this office (Feuillerat, E 286)

Chambers and Feuillerat note that the date of performance given in the *Revels Accounts* is in error. As Feuillerat points out, the presentation took place on New Year's day: 'The ffirste of Januarie for a cariage of A frame for master Sabastian to the courte' (Feuillerat, E 299 and 462).

There seems to be a lingering suspicion (cf. *Annals of English Drama 975–1700* 46 and Chambers III 437) that Westcott's presentation might have been the play *The Marriage between Wit and Wisdom* by Francis Merbury (BM MS Add. 26782, dated 1579). Fleay first suggested the idea (*Biog. Chron.* II 287) without offering any worthwhile evidence. From what is known of Merbury (see SP, 65 [April 1968] 207–22) and of his play, it is more likely that Feuillerat is correct in rejecting this identification and in asking, 'But is it not more natural to admit that we have here another specimen of "marriage" moralities, which seem to have been favourites with the public?' (p 462) The early scenes in Merbury's play derive from the two earlier 'Wit' moralities: John Redford's *Wit and Science* (fragment, BM MS Add. 15233; ed. A. Brown for the Malone Society, 1951) and *The Marriage of Wit and Science*, 1569/70, Westcott's presentation at Court in 1567/8 (see no. 17). The latter part of Merbury's play eschews the educational morality and offers episodical antics of the Vice derived from *Gammer Gurton's Needle*, *Cambises*, and *Misogonus*.

31 3 JANUARY 1580
'Scipio Africanus' before the Queen at Whitehall:

Sebastian Westcote master of the children of the Churche of St Paules ... £10 (*Declared Accounts* 542, m. 8)

vj seuerall warrantes to the Tresurer of the Chamber to pay vnto the persons following; to everyone, the somme of x^{li} viz: ... to the Master and Children of St Powle in like sort, for having presented their playes before her Majestie (*Acts of Privy Council* 11, p 377)

The histor[y] of Cipio Africanus shewen at whitehall the sundaie night after newe yeares daie enacted by the Children of Pawles furnyshed in This Offyce with sondrie garmentes and tryumphant ensignes & banners newe made and their head peeces of white sarcenett scarfes and garters whereon was ymploied ... ells of sarcenett A Citie a Battlement and $xviij^{ne}$ payre of gloves (Feuillerat, E 321)

A play about Publius Cornelius (236–184/3 BC) surnamed Africanus, son of Publius Scipio the opposer of Hannibal, could hardly have failed to attempt heroic proportion when such feats as the saving of his father's life at the Battle of Ticinus, the capture of New Carthage, the defeat of Hannibal at the Battle of Zama and conquest of Carthage, the successful campaign against Antiochus III of Syria, and finally the defiance against his detractors in Rome were at hand to dramatize. In several ways the events of his life and essentials of his character parallel those of Coriolanus. The brief list of costumes and scenes supplied by the Revels' Office suggests a spectacular production; presumably the 'Citie' is Rome and the 'Battlement' is Carthage.

32 6 JANUARY 1581
'A storie of Pompey' presented before the Queen at Whitehall:

Sebastian Wastcote m^r of the children of Powles ... £10 (*Declared Accounts* 542, m. 21)

30 January, Westminster ... to the Master of the Children of Powles for a playe on Twelfte Daye at night ... £10 (*Acts of Privy Council* 12, p 321)

A storie of Pompey enacted in the hall on twelf nighte wheron was ymploied newe one great citty, a senate howse and eight ells of dobble sarcenet for curtens and xviij paire of gloves (Feuillerat, E 336)

*The duble sarcenett maid into Curtyns and Implowid about Storie of pompey plad by the Childring of powles/ The single sarcenett was im plowid for fasinges bandes scarfes & Girdles whan the Childring of the Chappell plaid before her Majestie.	*Thomas Skinner Orange taffeta sarcenet at x^s the ell viij ells } iiij^{li} Single sarcenet of diuerse cullors at vj^s viij^d the ell. xx. ells } vj^{li} xiij^s iiij^d (Feuillerat, E 338)

No clue remains for what purpose Westcott used the expensive orange coloured double-silk curtains; if he used all ten yards bought by the Revels' Office, it would have been sufficient to enclose the senate house.

As Feuillerat (p 465) notes, there are two possible allusions to this play: 'And if they [contemporary playwrights] write of histories that are knowen, as the life of Pompeie, the martial affaires of Caesar, and other worthies, they give them a newe face, and turne them out like counterfeites to showe themselves on the stage,' citing *A Second and third blast of retrait from plaies.* ... (1580; SR, 18 Oct. 1580), Hazlitt's edition, *The English Drama and Stage under the Tudor and Stuart Princes* (1869) 145; 'So was the history of Caesar and Pompey, and the Playe of the Fabii at the Theater, both amplified there, where the Drummers mighte walke or the pen ruffle; when the history swelled and ran to hye for the numbers of persons that should playe it. ...' (citing Stephen Gosson, *Playes Confuted in fiue Actions.* ... nd, SR, 6 Apr. 1582, Hazlitt's ed., *op. cit.* 188). However, both statements are too vague to take seriously as references to the St Paul's play; the second connects 'Caesar and Pompey' with the Theatre where an adult company would have performed it.

Eleven days earlier than Westcott's presentation of *Pompey*, Leicester's men performed 'A comodie called delyght' before the Queen on the 26 December 1580 (Feuillerat, E 336). This play may well be the 'playe of playes & pastimes' referred to and synopsized by Stephen Gosson in his *Plays Confuted.* We learn from Gosson (Hazlitt's ed., p 188) that it was 'showen at the Theatre, the three and twentieth of Februarie last' (possibly 1580 or 1581), and that it was an allegoric morality with such characters as Life, Delight, Glut, Zeal, Tediousness, and Recreation. It will also be noticed from Gosson's summary of the action that the play derives characters and situations from John Redford's *Wit and Science* and from *The Marriage of Wit and Science* which as 'Witte and Will' was presented by Sebastian Westcott at court in 1567/8.

33* 26 DECEMBER 1581
A play (unknown) presented before the Queen at Whitehall:

the M[r] of the Children of Powles ... £10 (*Declared Accounts* 542, mm. 32–3)

14 April, at Grenewiche, 1582 ... to paye to the Children of Powles, for a play presented before her Majestye on St Stephens Daye laste paste, the somme of tenne poundes (*Acts of Privy Council* 13, p 393)

The *Revels Accounts* are brief and, although there are a number of properties and settings mentioned, including an artificial lion, a wooden horse, a mount with a castle upon it, a Dragon, and an artificial tree, none of these items may be certainly connected with any of the companies presenting plays. By the time the warrant was made out Westcott was dead; hence his name does not appear there.

Chambers suggests that this final presentation of Westcott's 'may possibly be the *Cupid and Psyche*' mentioned by Gosson. The reference to it occurs in *Plays Confuted* 187: 'In Playes either those thinges are fained that never were, as Cupid and Psyche plaid at Paules.' Alternatively, and, from the context of the mention of the play in Gosson's book, perhaps more likely it might have been presented by Westcott somewhat earlier either on January 1576 or December 1577. The Admiral's Men appear to have performed a version of the story in the spring of 1600, but whether or not Chettle, Day and Dekker, the authors of the book bought by Henslowe (see *Diary*, eds. Foakes and Rickert (1961) 132 and 134–5), based their version upon the St Paul's play cannot be ascertained.

List of plays performed by the Children of St Paul's, 1551–81

	DATE	TITLE	AUSPICES	PRESENTERS	TEXTS
1.	Winter 1551/2	unknown	Princess Elizabeth	Heywood Westcott	
2.	Easter or May 1553?	*Nice Wanton?*	King Edward VI	Heywood (Westcott?)	i) 1560, John King ii) nd [1565?], John Allde
3.	December 1554 or April 1557	unknown	Princess Elizabeth and Queen Mary	Westcott?	
4.	7 August 1559	unknown	Queen Elizabeth	Heywood, Westcott, Phillips	
5.	Christmas 1560	unknown	Queen Elizabeth	Westcott	
6.	Christmas 1561	unknown	Queen Elizabeth	Westcott	
7.	February 1562	unknown	Queen Elizabeth	Westcott	
8.	Christmas 1562	unknown	Queen Elizabeth	Westcott	
9.	Christmas 1564	unknown	Queen Elizabeth	Westcott	
10.	2 February 1565	unknown	Queen Elizabeth	Westcott	
11.	Winter 1565/6	unknown	Queen Elizabeth	Westcott	
12.		unknown	Queen Elizabeth	Westcott	
13.		unknown	Queen Elizabeth and Cecilia of Sweden	Westcott	
14.	Christmas 1565	unknown	Queen Elizabeth	Westcott	
15.					

List of plays performed by the Children of St Paul's, 1551–81

	DATE	TITLE	AUSPICES	PRESENTERS	TEXTS
16.	Christmas–Shrovetide 1567/8	Wit and Will (*The Marriage of Wit & Science*)	Queen Elizabeth	Westcott	nd [1569–70], Thomas Marshe
17.		Prodigality (*Liberality and Prodigality*)	Queen Elizabeth	Westcott	1602, Simon Stafford
18.	1 January 1569	unknown	Queen Elizabeth	Westcott	
19.	28 December 1570	unknown	Queen Elizabeth	Westcott	
20.	25–7 February 1571	unknown	Queen Elizabeth	Westcott	
21.	28 December 1571 or 1 January 1572	*Iphiginia*, 'A Tragedie'	Queen Elizabeth	Westcott	lost
22.	Christmas – Twelfth Night 1572/3	unknown	Queen Elizabeth	Westcott	
23.	27 December 1573	*Alcmeon*	Queen Elizabeth	Westcott	lost
24.	2 February 1575	*Liberality and Prodigality* (revival, see no. 17)	Queen Elizabeth	Westcott	1602, Simon Stafford
25.	6 January 1576	unknown	Queen Elizabeth	Westcott	
26.	1 January 1577	*Error*	Queen Elizabeth	Westcott	lost
27.	19 February 1577	*Titus and Gesippus*	Queen Elizabeth	Westcott	lost
28.	29 December 1577	*Cupid and Psyche?*	Queen Elizabeth	Westcott	lost
29.	1 January 1579	*The Marriage of Mind and Measure*	Queen Elizabeth	Westcott	lost
30.	3 January 1580	*Scipio Africanus*	Queen Elizabeth	Westcott	lost
31.	6 January 1581	*Pompey*	Queen Elizabeth	Westcott	lost
32.	21 December 1581	unknown	Queen Elizabeth	Westcott	

Paul's plays and their connections or possible connections with later plays

John Redford's *Wit and Science* (c1540)	*The Marriage of Wit and Science* (1569/70), performed at court 1567/8	i) Francis Merbury's *The Marriage between Wit and Wisdom* (1579), possibly first performed at the University of Cambridge and surviving in MS
		ii) *Delight* (*Play of Plays and Pastimes*) performed by Leicester's Men at court, Dec. 1580, and at the Theatre on 23 Feb. 1580 or 1581
		iii) 'The Marriage of Wit and Wisdom,' the play within the play of *Sir Thomas More* (c1590–3); Munday, Dekker, Chettle, Heywood? Shakespeare?
	The History of Error, performed at court 1577	William Shakespeare's *Comedy of Errors* (c1592)?
	Cupid and Psyche, performed at court Dec. 1577 or Dec. 1581	Revised by Chettle, Day, and Dekker for Admiral's Men in 1600?
	Pompey, performed at court Jan. 1581 and at Paul's Theatre	*Caesar and Pompey* performed by Leicester's Men at the Theatre before 1582?

'Michael Shaller's Notebook'

IN THE LIBRARY of St Paul's Cathedral there is a MS notebook which at one time was used by Michael Shaller (or Shawler), a verger acting as under-chamberlain between 1566 and 1584.[1] H.C. Maxwell Lyte's description of this volume in the Report of the Historical Manuscripts Commission is misleading.[2] Although most of the memoranda and accounts do belong to the period 1566–88, and some of these are presumably in Shaller's writing, the notebook contains fragmentary records of earlier times in other hands, including miscellaneous accounts of the late fifteenth century, of the reign of Henry VIII, and of the year 1554. The volume probably belonged to the office of the chamberlain and passed into Shaller's keeping during his term as under-chamberlain.[3] From this document it is possible to set out in some

1 Press Mark, W.D. 32. Shaller was one of four vergers listed in the record of Grindal's Visitation in 1561.
2 'Michael Shaller's notebook of such "thinges as past in his time in the church," a volume of 92 pages, of which the first three are missing,' Hist. Man. Comm., Ninth Report Pt 1 (London 1883) 71. The accounts of the year 1554 are at the end of the volume between fols 67 and 88; 'The Rentall of all Rentes fermes And pensons belongynge to the charge of the collectyone of the chamberlayne of the cathedrall churche of saynt pawle in London the yere of our lord god. A thousand fyve hundred fyfty and ffower / A°. 1554./'
3 The notebook was noticed by W. Sparrow Simpson in Gleanings from Old St Paul's (London 1889) 82 ; apparently he accepted Maxwell Lyte's interpretation of its contents. It is also referred to by Hillebrand 108–9, who prints a list of payments made to the Master of the Almonry, citing fol. 71 which he believed 'belongs some time after 1571.' In fact these payments, which are summarised in this appendix, belong to 1554. Hillebrand has been confused by the mixed contents of the volume and has failed to observe that the entries are not in chronological sequence.

detail the property, emoluments, and perquisites enjoyed by Westcott as Vicar Choral and Amoner shortly after his official appointment to that office.

In 1554 Westcott paid a rent of fifty-two shillings for 'tentes somtyme the lord louelle lying in paternoster rowe And the landes in sermon lane And carter lane.'[4] Similar payments of rent were recorded in 1566 and in the years between 1568 and 1572; there is no entry for 1567.[5] In these later records, Westcott is mentioned, the rent and localities remain the same, but he is charged for tenements in all of them. At first glance it would appear that buildings were erected on the lands in Sermon Lane and Carter Lane some time between 1554 and 1566. This, however, is unlikely to be the case, and it is more probable that the 1554 record was an error. In fact, from the first Westcott paid rent for tenements on all three sites, because all these properties were formerly bequeathed to the cathedral for the maintenance of either the almonry boys or for the upkeep of the office of the Almoner. This is confirmed by a *Redditus* dated 1526 in which the revenues from various almonry properties are listed.[6] With the aid of this and other documents it is possible to identify their locations with some precision.[7]

The property in Paternoster Row was bequeathed by 'magistro Compton' and consisted of a 'hospitio and tenement' at one time belonging to 'magistro Wm Lovell' – or Lovell's Inn as Stow calls it.[8] The Carter Lane property was situated between Dolittle Lane and Sermon Lane and was bequeathed by a former almoner, William Tolleshunt, in 1329.[9] According to Maria Hackett it was described in the cathedral accounts of 1675 as comprising 'eight tenements and a garden in Carter Lane' and was known in her time (1826) as Knowles' Court.[10] The Sermon Lane property was the gift of Richard Newport, Bishop of London (1317–18); it consisted of four houses on the corner of Sermon Lane and Little Carter Lane and was originally intended by the donor as a maintenance for the senior choristers who, after leaving the choir, had yet to secure their future. In the year that Westcott died Shaller's record reads:

4 Fol. 67
5 See fols 35^v, 37^v, 39, 41^v, 43^v, and 45^v. On fol. 49 the record is for the year 1582 and the rent is charged to 'the Almoner of this Churche for the time beinge,' Westcott having died that April.
6 *Reddit. Elemosinaria ... cath sancti pauli*, London, Anno Dm^i M^{lmo} quinget^o vice^o sexto, St Paul's Cathedral Library, A/52/15
7 See map, p 46.
8 'Of old time was one great house, sometimes belonging to the Earles of Britaine, since that to the Louels and was called Louels Inne: for Mathild wife of John Louell held it in the first H the 6,' *A Survey of London* (1603), C.L. Kingsford, ed. 2 vols (Oxford 1908) II 343
9 See *Registrum Eleemosynariae, D. Pauli, Londinensis*, BM MS Harl, 1080.
10 *Correspondences and Evidences Respecting the Ancient Collegiate School Attached to Saint*

> Item of the Almoner of This Church for
> the time being for a yearely Rent due of
> Landes & tenements in Pater n^r Row Carter
> lane & Sermon laine in London....[11]
> } lij^s

Among the accounts preserved in the notebook are quarterly payments to minor clergy, officers, and employees of the cathedral on the reckoning of feast days of Christmas, Annunciation of Our Lady (25 March), Nativity of Saint John the Baptist (24 June), and Saint Michael the Archangel (29 September) of the year 1554.[12] The records concerning Westcott may be conveniently grouped into three categories: payments to him as Vicar Choral including his commons, refections, and annuities amounting to £3-18-8^d; pittances for particular performances at divine services totalling £1-3-0^d; payments to him for the maintenance of the ten choristers amounting to £20-3-6^d.[13] The main source of Westcott's income, like that of the other clerical and lay officers of the cathedral, was provided by the Manors of St Paul's – the two Caddingtons, major and minor, Belchamp Paul's, and Worboys. Secondary sources were derived from the annuity of John Reston[14] and the rents of the college founded by Roger Holmes in 1400 and suppressed in the reign of Edward VI. The pittances, one notices, are occasioned by performances of ritual and one wonders if this minor source of income, which must have ceased after the accession of Elizabeth, was thereafter provided by other means. If the amounts in the first two categories constituting his personal income appear to be modest, it should be remembered that they were doubtless supplemented by gifts and fees for professional services at state and civic ceremonies, and by payments for the service of the choir on private occasions.[15]

Paul's Cathedral (London 1832) xxviii Miss Hackett also stated that the buildings and garden 'was, within memory, used as a schoolhouse for the S. Paul's boys,' (appendix xiii).

11 Chamberlain's Receipts, St Paul's Cathedral Library, A/53/20

12 See fols 73 and 88.

13 See abstract of these payments.

14 Dr John Reston was Canon Residentiary in the reigns of Henry VIII, Edward VI, and Mary; in his will dated 17 August 1551 he left houses in Fleet Street, Bread Street, and Thames Street for this and other payments to the choir.

15 For example, the notebook records 'ffees due to all the officers and members of Poules for the buriall of the Lo: Keeper [Sir Nicholas Bacon, died 20 Feb. 1578/9]:
> xii Peticanons to eueri one v^s in all ... iij^{li}
> vj vicars to eueri one iiij^s in all ... xxiiij^s
> x choristers to eueri one ij^s vj^d in all.xxv^s.'

In August 1557 the choir of St Paul's sang the dirges at the funeral of the Duchess of Norfolk at St Clement Dane's Church, see Neville Williams, *Thomas Howard, Fourth Duke of Norfolk* (London 1964) 34. The great occasions at St Paul's during Mary's reign were the visits by King Philip (October 1554) and by Cardinal Pole (December 1554).

AN ABSTRACT OF QUARTERLY PAYMENTS TO SEBASTIAN WESTCOTT,
VICAR CHORAL AND MASTER OF THE ALMONRY AT ST PAUL'S CATHEDRAL
IN THE YEAR 1554, COMPUTED FROM ST PAUL'S MS W.D. 32. FOLS 67 TO 88

1 *vj vicars chorall* (fols 75^v, 80, 83^v, and 87^v)

In each of the quarterly payments to Westcott and to the five other vicars there are four items. Of these the three entries referring to their annuities and commons are constant; the other payment is for refections which varied in accordance with the particular number of days he and his colleagues were entitled to receive the extra 6^d.

Thus we have:

	Quarterly	Yearly
		£-s-d
for his com̄ons at x^d the weeke	x^s-x^d	2-3-4
to hym for the Annyte of Mr Reston		
at xiij^s iiij^d by yere	xiij^s–iiij^d	13-4
It out of the Rent*es* of Holmes colledge		
at vs by yere	xv^d	5-0
for Refecons Dec. – v dayes ii^{s}vj^d		
Mar. – ix dayes iiij^{s}vj^d		
Jun. – xv dayes vij^{s}vj^d		
Sept. – fyve dayes ij^{s}vj^d		17-0

£3-18-8

2 *Pitencyarye of the Vicars* (fols 75^v, 80, 84, and 88)

The pittances paid to the vicars choral varied from quarter to quarter depending upon the number of special anthems and masses sung by them. Among the invariable items are the following:

	Quarterly	Yearly £-s-d
for the stagiaryes	xxx^s iiij^d	6-1-4
for the pencone of Cadington	iij^s iiij^d	13-4
for the werynge of copies at x^d the weeke	x^s x^d	2-3-4
for the psalme of De profundis	iij^s iiij^d	13-4

To these must be added the payments for special anthems in the first quarter:

for the Messe & Anthem of S. Katheryne	xj^s viij^d	11-8
for the Anthem of O Sapientia	xv^s	15-0
		£10-18-0

From this total the sum of 20^s per quarter was 'deducted out for the tenthes of Certayne benyfices at iiij^{li} by yeare.' Thus the final sum to be divided among the six vicars was £6-18-0, giving them £1-3-0 each.

3 *Mr of the Almerye* (fols 76, 80, 84, and 88)

	Quarterly	*Yearly* £-s-d
The fixed items include payments:		
for the Comm ons of the tenn Querysters		
at vij the weeke	vij^s vij^d	1-10-4
to hym for the pencone of saynt pancras	xvj^s viij^d	3-6-8
to hym for the Annuyte of Mr Reston	viij^s iiij^d	1-13-4
to hym out of the Rent*es* of holmes colledge	v^s	1-0-0
to hym for the psalme of de profundis	ii^s vj^d	10-0

In the first quarter two additional sources of
annual revenue are listed:

		Yearly
to hym for the pencone of the Mannor of belchampe pawle xxvj^s viij^d		1-6-8
to hym for the pencone for the yeare of worboy xxvj^s viij^d		1-6-8

For the refections of the choristers he was paid
4^d a day per boy and the quarterly sums varied.

		Yearly
Dec. – v dayes xvj^s viij^d		
Mar. – ix dayes xxx^s		
Jun. – xv dayes 1^s		
Sept. – v dayes xvj^s viij^d		5-3-4

The other special payments were:

	Quarterly	*Yearly*
Dec. – for the Anthem of O Sapientia	xij^d	1-0
Mar. – for Maundy thursdaye	v^s	5-0
for the lyverie of the sayd Queristers	iiij^{li}	4-0-0
Sept. – to hym for Apples on Saynt James Daye	vj^d	6
		——————
		£20-3-6

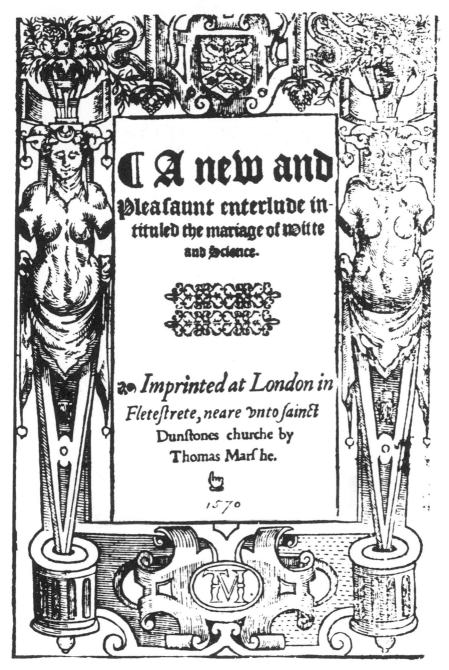

¶ A new and pleasaunt enterlude intituled the mariage of witte and Science.

Imprinted at London in Fleteſtrete, neare vnto ſainct Dunſtones churche by Thomas Marſhe.

1570

7 Original Title-Page, *The Marriage of Wit and Science*

❡The players names.

Nature	Science,	Shame,
Witte.	Reason,	Idelnes,
Will,	Experience,	Ignoraunce
Studie,	Recreation,	Tediousnes.
Diligence,	with thre o-	
Instruction,	ther women	
	singers.	

8 Original List of Characters, *The Marriage of Wit and Science*

The Marriage of Wit and Science

The Marriage of Wit and Science

Introduction

THE PRINTER'S COPY

The anonymous play, *The Marriage of Wit and Science*, is extant in a single, undated quarto in the Bodleian Library (Malone 231.1). This unique copy was in a volume of the collection bequeathed by Edmund Malone on his death (25 May 1812) to his brother, Lord Sunderlin, on condition that if it were not retained in the family, it should be deposited in some public library. The collection was then entrusted to James Boswell for his preparation of a new edition of Malone's *Shakespeare*, and, upon the completion of this work in 1821, it was at once deposited at Oxford. Nothing is known of the provenance of the play before it came into Malone's possession.[1]

The play was entered in the *Register* of the Stationers' Company in about August of the year 1569:[2]

Recevyd of Thomas marshe for his lycense for pryntinge of a play intituled the mariage of Wytt and Science ... iiij^d

(Register A, fol. 184^a)[3]

---

1 I am indebted to the Department of Printed Books, Bodleian Library, for this information.
2 See W.W. Greg, *A Bibliography of The English Printed Drama*, 4 vols (London 1939) I 133.
3 Edward Arber, *A Transcript of the Registers of the Stationers' Company* 4 vols (London 1875) I

In all probablility Thomas Marshe printed it shortly afterwards. If the *Register* faithfully reflects Marshe's activities as a stationer, the printing of a play was a new adventure for his establishment: indeed, it may have been the only native drama to issue from his press.[4] After his death, however, his name was indirectly connected with one other play title. It appears that Marshe's son, Edward, inherited the rights to his father's copies.[5] Although a freeman of the Stationers' Company in 1591, Edward Marshe does not seem to have followed his father's trade, for, on 23 June (?) in the same year, he transferred these rights to Thomas Orwin. Among the ninety or so titles of books listed in the transfer entry, the first is 'The mariage of wyt and wisdome.'[6] There are very good grounds for thinking that in this title 'wisdome' is a slip for 'science.' In the first place, as Greg has observed, there are a number of other errors of fact in the entry: *The Marriage of Wit and Science*, entered to Thomas Marshe in 1569 and issued by him soon after under his imprint, is not included in this list of Marshe's copies; the only extant copy of *The Marriage between Wit and Wisdom* is a private transcript which gives many indications of having been copied from a printed version that came from the press of either John or Edward Allde. It seems likely, therefore, that *The Marriage of Wit and Science* was the only native play printed by Thomas Marshe in a career that extended from 1554 to 1587 and during which 'he issued a very large number of books.'[7]

The next owner of the copy, Thomas Orwin, did not exercise his right to reprint the play in the two years of life that remained to him after its acquisition; nor, so far as is known, did his widow, Joan, who continued in business until 1597.[8] By that date, any interest in the thirty-year-old play for boys must have been mainly antiquarian. No doubt it was valued thus, when, almost a century after its composition and with its anonymity still inviolate, *The Marriage of Wit and Science*, an Interlude, appeared in Francis Kirkman's *A True, Perfect and Exact Catalogue* (1661, 1671).[9] Thereafter, its modest music apparently incapable of 'measuring out the steps of Time – the shocks of Chance,' the play, rescued from oblivion by Edmund Malone, survives in a single copy in the great Oxford Library.

4 In 1581 Marshe printed Seneca's *Ten Tragedies* (see Greg, III 1527). For some brief facts about Thomas Marshe see E. Gordon Duff, *A Century of The English Book Trade* (London 1905) 100.
5 See R.B. McKerrow et al., *A Dictionary of Printers and Booksellers* (London 1910) 186.
6 Arber II 586; Greg I 7 and 133
7 Duff 100
8 McKerrow 207–8
9 Greg III 1347

The collation is 4°, A-E4 F2: signed [BL] #3(-F2). The title within a compartment (McKerrow, *Printers' and Publishers' Devices, 1485–1640*, No. 154) appears on A1ʳ, the players' names on A1ᵛ, and the text, printed in black letter, begins on A2ʳ. Beneath the players' names is an ornament which reappears inverted at the conclusion of the play on F2. Catchwords appear throughout, though the use of type for these is inconsistent; eleven of them which prefigure speech headings are printed in black letter. The running titles employ two forms of the 'M' (*Mariage*), an ordinary italic capital and a swash, as well as two forms of the final 'e' (*Science*), the common and the swash *e* incorporating the full point: the regular appearance of these throughout, except for the variants on F1 recto and verso, indicate the use of a single skeleton-forme. Act and scene headings, stage-directions, speech headings, and a small number of characters' names within the body of the text are printed in roman. The scenes (except II.3 and III.2) are headed by a list of characters printed in roman; in the final scene this list is incomplete. Speech headings are mostly centred; a number, however, appear towards the inner margin and two are placed at the beginning of a single line of speech.

The text of the play is defective in a number of ways. Many lines have been wrongly assigned: 159 (to Will for Wit), 688–9 (to Will for Science), 745–6 (to Will for Wit), 924–5 (to Wit for Diligence), 1021–2 (to Will for Wit), 1101–2 (to Wit for Recreation), 1359–64 (to Wit for Reason), and 1498–1500 (to Instruction for Tediousness). The stage-directions 'Rub and chafe him' (983), 'Let him practise in daunsing al things to make himselfe brethles' (1121–2), and 'Say all at once, Tediousnes is slaine' (1536), are all printed in black letter and incorporated in the text as speech. The second of these is also misplaced. Exits are omitted at ll. 361 (Wit), 514 (Will), 772 (Experience and Science), 852 (Reason), 862 (Wit, Will, Instruction, Study, and Diligence), 938 (Study and Instruction), 970 (Diligence), 972 (Will), 980 (Tediousness), 1115 (Recreation and her companions), 1128 (Will), 1193 (Idleness and Ignorance), 1388 (Wit, Reason, Science, and Shame), and 1440 (Science). Act III, scene 2 is erroneously marked 'sena 1.' Act IV, scenes 3 and 4 contain an unusual number of errors, misattributed lines, at least one misplaced stage-direction and omissions of others. The most serious fault, however, is the dislocation of the text between C1ʳ and D1ᵛ in the original (ie, between ll. 556 and 926 in this edition). A concise and accurate analysis of this disturbance is given by Professor Brown, who was the first to notice what two previous editors and a host of historians and commentators had missed.[10] This textual situation may be stated thus:

10 MSR (1960) 1961, vii–ix

	This Edition	MSR	Marshe's Edition	Acts and Scenes Affected
A	548–56	545–53	$C1^r(5–13)$	Beginning of III.2 (wrongly marked as scene 1)
B	729–925	748–917	$C1^r(14)–C3^v(13)$	Final portion of III.2, whole of III.3, and first portion of IV.1
C	557–728	554–747	$C3^v(14)–D1^v(28)$	Middle portion of III.2
D	926–	918–	$D1^v(29)$	Text resumes with remainder of IV.1 and continues normally

It will be seen that section B of the text is out of order, and that a transposition of sections B and C restores the continuity. The wrongly placed section (B) consists of the remaining 26 lines ($C1^r$), $C1^v$ (39 lines), $C2^r$ (39 lines), $C2^v$ (39 lines), and 13 lines ($C3^r$) – a total of 194 lines, an equivalent of the number of lines in five pages. All the catchwords throughout the dislocations are quite correct.

The oversight of this mistake is much easier to explain than the cause of it. The erroneous link between A (556) and B (729) is masked to some extent by the rhymes of these lines, 'feare' and 'speare' respectively, though it should be noticed that both these words have their appropriate mates at 555 and 730. Further, the apparent sense of the dialogue at this join also partially obscures the error. Wit's boastful threat (730), given in error at this point to Will, may be taken, superficially at any rate, to refer to the rival suitor, who is imagined as closeted with Science, whereas, in their proper context, the lines refer to Wit's antagonist, the monster, Tediousness. Discussing this mistake, Professor Brown advances the possibility 'that the error was already present in the misplacing of pages in the copy from which the quarto was printed,' and he cautiously refrains from speculating further 'on the available evidence.' Nevertheless, another possibility – which one hopes will not be considered too speculative – should be considered.

There are abundant signs throughout the text that the printing was very carelessly, and possibly even hastily, performed. This is indicated by the evidence already presented, and confirmed by the footnotes to this edition, as well as by the more detailed notation supplied in the explanatory notes. There is also evidence, yet to be discussed, to confirm what Professor Brown himself has stated, 'that there may have been some kind of playhouse manuscript behind the printed copy,' though, admittedly, he has not pressed this identification as strongly as it will be pressed here. These two facts, and also a third, that analysis reveals a single compositor at work, indicate that the mistake might possibly be the result of a wrong imposition. If the composed lines of type were not immediately tied up in pages by the compositor, but, to save time, simply placed in the galleys to await imposition, a confusion of galleys by a careless imposer, whether pressman, compositor, or some assistant, would have led to the hasty matching of lines which appeared to make sense, and the rhymes of which appeared to be in order. The regularity with which the RTV's occur, the indications that there was only one compositor, and that pages were being made up from standing galleys all suggest that the forme was left on the bed of the press throughout. If it had been moved, it was put back with exemplary care. This explanation is offered because there are reasons, other than the stage-directions noted by Professor Brown, for thinking that the copy from which the quarto was printed was a playhouse manuscript, and, furthermore, one that had undergone some hasty revision.

The section of the text between lines 981 and 1128 (ie, IV.3 and the beginning of IV.4) takes us to the root of the matter. A full discussion of the errors, omissions, discrepancies, and misplaced, as well as misprinted, stage-directions is offered in the notes to the text. Here a brief recapitulation of only the major points needs to be made.

1 In the players' names listed on the verso of the title-page, Recreation is accompanied by 'thre other women singers,' yet the text has several references to only one companion.
2 The song (987) is somewhat tentatively arranged for two voices, yet it is not made clear precisely who sings. The song itself could very well be a rearrangement for two voices of an original set for four.
3 The dances that follow are also uncertainly indicated. The stage-directions which govern them raise problems: one appears to be ambiguous and perhaps misplaced (1093), and the other is misprinted and misplaced (1121).
4 Will's dismissal from the scene is abrupt, and his mute acceptance of it is quite uncharacteristic (1128). A later statement of his, referring to this exit, seems to be at variance with the facts (1416).
5 There are two wrongly assigned speeches (1020–40 and 1101–2).

It is hard to resist the conclusion that ambiguities and errors on these pages of the text result from the compositor's inability to interpret the revisions accurately and that the revisions were aimed at reducing the number of supernumerary women players.

Almost all the stage-directions are in those scenes in which Wit fights

Tediousness (IV.2 and V.5), and in which Wit is revived and entertained by Recreation and seduced by Idleness (IV.3) – in short, in scenes requiring the most physical action. Several directions are addressed to a particular character and indicate their source to be either author or producer: *Fight, strike at will* (Tediousness, 962), 'Rub and chafe him' (Will, 983), *Falle doune in to her lapp* (Wit, 1147), *Lul hym* (Idleness, 1152), *Let will trippe you downe* (Tediousness, 1508). The scantiness of stage-directions elsewhere, particularly of crucial exits, is puzzling, but it should be noted that these are generally omitted throughout the play, including those scenes in which other directions do appear. Perhaps these omissions are evidence of the printer's inexperience with a dramatic text. As has already been pointed out, *The Marriage of Wit and Science* appears to be the first play Marshe printed.

The next appearance of the play was in 1874 when W. Carew Hazlitt printed it in the second volume of *Dodsley's Old English Plays*. John S. Farmer included it in *Five Anonymous Plays* (Fourth Series) in 1908 and issued the original in the Tudor Facsimile Texts series in 1911. Both these editors may be said to have had only a nodding acquaintance with Thomas Marshe's copy.

THE SOURCES

The Marriage of Wit and Science is an adaptation of John Redford's interlude *Wit and Science* written for performance by the Paul's boys during the term of Redford's appointment as Almoner, Organist and Master of the Choristers between about 1534 and his death in the autumn of 1547. *Wit and Science* has survived in part in manuscript;[11] there is no contemporary reference to indicate that it was printed.

The two most notable features of Redford's play are the carefully articulated allegory which is simple, distinct, coherent, and spectacular, and the strict economy of the dramatic structure. Language and action vividly reinforced by the allegory display the conflict and the resolution with a striking clarity and charm. The homiletic purpose of the pursuit and attainment of the educational ideal is unobtrusive yet firmly in the forefront of the design. The expression of this ideal in terms of chivalrous endeavour is unemphatic yet precise. The comedy is robust, chiefly pedagogic, and, like other elements, depends for full effectiveness upon one's response to the function of allegory.

11 BM MS Add. 15233, edited by J.O. Halliwell [-Phillips] for the Shakespeare Society (London 1848). The play has been reprinted by the Malone Society (1951). References are to this edition.

So nicely poised are these elements in the play it would seem that any adaptation would inevitably lead to an emphasis of one or more of the finely balanced components. Such is the case with *The Marriage of Wit and Science*. It is clear that comic and romantic elements have been strengthened at the expense of allegoric form. What remains of the allegory is little more than the *personae*, and even some of these, Comfort, Quickness, and Strength, for instance, are listed merely as 'three other women.' Redford's Honest Recreation becomes simply Recreation, diminished not only in name, but also in function; she is no longer distinguished as the moral and pedagogical opponent of Idleness. The debate between them has been entirely omitted as has also the spelling lesson Idleness gives her half-witted son, Ignorance.[12] Riches, Fame, Favour, and Worship, who are rejected by Science, thereby clarifying her ideal nature as uncontaminated by worldly attributes, have been abandoned by the adaptor. Reason's two addresses to the audience have also gone. Allegoric costumes and properties such as the garment of Science, the gown of knowledge, the heart of gold, and the sword of comfort are either rejected or are no longer a visual reinforcement to the allegory. Finally, Wit's ascent to Mount Parnassus, vaguely alluded to early in *The Marriage*, is never given prominence, and in the climactic scene of Wit's triumph over his foe, the mountain is no longer a stage location as it appears to be in the original play.

The diminution of the allegoric structure has permitted the adaptor to give greater display to the courtship of Wit and Science, and, as a result, the part of Science has been expanded. Aside from the wooing perhaps the clearest illustration of the development of the romantic element may be seen in Science's intercession with her father, Reason, on her lover's behalf when Wit's transgression is chastised by Shame. The more important place given to the courtship has also necessitated a more fully developed relationship between the lover and the parents of his lady, especially with Science's mother, Experience. The chivalric status of Wit, lightly delineated by Redford, is more strongly emphasized in *The Marriage*, notably in the young squire's combats with the giant, the ultimate one of which, as has been noted, is something of a tournament.[13]

The most important difference between the two plays, though, lies in the change of a single character. Confidence, Wit's messenger, a minor figure in

12 F.P. Wilson and G.K. Hunter, *The English Drama 1485–1585* (Oxford 1969) err in thinking Ignorance to be a girl.
13 See Werner Habicht, 'The *Wit*-Interludes and the Form of Pre-Shakespearean "Romantic Comedy",' *RD* VIII (1965) 73–88.

Redford's allegory, has undergone a metamorphosis in the hands of the adaptor, who has brilliantly recreated him as Will. As Wit's impudent and often imprudent page, Will gives a new direction and vigour to the residual allegory. He appears to exemplify impulse, the contrary influence among Wit's helpmeets. His ambivalent feelings toward his master's love affair – a desire to serve Wit expeditiously is modified by his reluctance to see him married – are the source of a succession of amusing scenes.[14]

The missing leaves of *Wit and Science* (estimated to total between 130 and 190 lines) give us no chance to compare the respective dramatist's treatment of the part of Nature. In *The Marriage* Nature clearly derives from the goddess depicted in two earlier interludes which, as we shall see, were also influential upon Redford's play.

Notwithstanding this close connection of substance and structure there are surprisingly few parallels and correspondences of dialogue in the two plays. The versification also offers a complete contrast. The prevailing measure of *Wit and Science* is tetrameter couplet; there are also passages of dimeter ranted by Tediousness and an unclassifiable exchange between Idleness and Ignorance – all these forms are innocent of the poetic strain (see p 101) which seeks to elevate and quicken the shuffling fourteeners in *The Marriage*. As for the songs, Redford's three songs (the words of the final song *Remembrance* are not given) are superior in lyrical grace and complexity; nevertheless, we may note that the two songs in *The Marriage*, 'Give a leg,' which has echoes of its correspondent in the original, and 'Come, come lie down,' neatly reflect the opposing natures and actions of the singers, Recreation and Idleness respectively, the one to upraise, the other to degrade.

Before considering the antecedents of *Wit and Science* and *The Marriage* one further dramatic element shared by them should be noted. Redford's Wit, at his first assault upon Tediousness, is killed by the fiend and afterwards revived by Honest Recreation and her companions, Comfort, Quickness, and Strength. A stage-direction 'here wyt fallyth downe & dyeth' and the comment by Reason 'thowgh tedyousnes had kyld ye' suggest that the traditional renouveau of the Mummer's and kindred folk plays was here incorporated into the allegory.[15]

14 R.S. Varma, 'Philosophical and Moral Ideas in *The Marriage of Wit and Science*,' PQ XLIV (Jan. 1965) 120–2 briefly but pertinently discusses the relationship between Wit, Will, and Nature.

15 This incident in *Wit and Science* is briefly referred to by E.K. Chambers, *The English Folk Play* (Oxford 1933) 163, and by C.R. Baskerville, 'Mummers' Wooing Plays in England,' MP XXI (1924) 225–72. Redford's play has other vestigial traces of the Mummers, eg, the dance that follows the Mock Death and Cure; Wit is garbed like a fool and his face is blackened; Tediousness swears by 'mahowndes nose' and vaunts in the manner of Slasher, the Turkish Knight.

Wit and Science and the redaction *The Marriage of Wit and Science* derive from the late medieval dramatic conflictus represented in such plays as *The Castle of Perseverance* (1404–35), *Mankind* (1465–70), and *Mundus et Infans* (1500–22) wherein wayward man strays from the path of good, falls subject to vice, sins, repents, and hopefully redeems himself under the reasserted influence of faith and virtue. Once the term of mankind's corrupting worldly journey was contracted from a life pilgrimage to a youthful travail, three dramatic variations of the archetypal pattern emerge: plays treating the upbringing of children and parental responsibility, *Youth* (1513–29), *The Disobedient Child* (c1559), *Nice Wanton* (1547–53), *Lusty Juventus* (1547–53): plays thematically grounded upon St Luke's parable (15: 11–32) of the prodigal son which, like *Acolastus* (c1540), have their origins on the continent and which fertilize native drama as in *Misogonus* (1560–77): and plays influenced by humanist educational theory and ideals which stress secular knowledge rather than Divine Grace as the goal of the youthful pilgrim's quest. It is to the last of these sub-species of the broad morality pattern that *Wit and Science* and *The Marriage* belong, although it will be recognized that these categories are not mutually exclusive. Young Wit is reckless; he disobeys his symbolic mother, Dame Nature; he resists the authority of his surrogate parents, Reason and Experience; he suffers and repents. His travail concludes happily in a union with Science; his spiritual salvation is *implicit*. We may now turn to consider two plays – the second clearly illustrating the evolution of this third type of morality – which are influential upon Redford.

Henry Medwall's two-part interlude *Nature*, written before 1500 and printed without date by William Rastell, probably between 1530 and 1534, has several allegoric characters and a morality plot familiar to *Wit and Science*. Man, first instructed and encouraged by Nature, then aided by Reason and hindered by Sensuality, errs; he is brought back to the path of virtue by Shamefacedness and the renewed effort of Reason. Two passages prefigure Redford's conception of Man as Wit and of Sensuality as Will. Nature advises Man,

> I let thee wit thou art a passanger
> That hast to do a great and long vyage
> and through the world most be thy passage (sig. A.ii^v).

Later Reason admonishes Sensuality,

> Thou takyst a selfe well [*sic*] and wrong opynyon
> Whyche shalbe thyn and others confusyon (sig. A.iv^v).

The other play is *The Nature of The Four Elements* written by John Rastell after 1517 and printed by him about 1527. Rastell preserves the morality plot of *Nature* but his chief concern is to propagate an interest in secular learning, especially in natural science:

> And that it is a com̄yn good act to brynge
> people from vyce and vse good lyuinge
> Like wyse for a com̄yn welth occupyed is he
> That bryngyth them to knowledge ẙ yngnorāt be (sig. A.iii^v).

Rastell's Humanity, counselled by Nature and later subject to the opposing influences of Studious Desire aided by Experience, and of Sensual Appetite, is no longer confronted by the traditional moral enemies of man, the vices, but by a foe to intellect, Ignorance. In short, the theme reflects a movement away from Medwall towards Redford, who in *Wit and Science* confronts Wit with Tediousness, Idleness, and Ignorance. The scholarly content of much of the play contained in long speeches by the Messenger, Nature, and Experience expounding natural philosophy and cosmology make the play the first surviving example of the educational morality. There are other correspondences between Rastell and Redford. Nature gives Humanity a globe ('figure') for his 'instruccyon.' In *Wit and Science* and in *The Marriage*, Reason gives Wit 'a glas'/'glasse of Christal cleare' by which he is to make self-appraisal. The spelling test given by Experience to Sensual Appetite may well have suggested to Redford the more elaborate spelling lesson Idleness gives to Ignorance. Our single surviving copy of *The Four Elements*, lacking signature D (8 leaves) and also the last section of the play, make it impossible to show with certainty other correspondences with *Wit and Science*, but if we look at the action after the *lacuna* a further comparison is hard to resist. The break occurs at a point when Experience is demonstrating, no doubt using the globe Nature has left on stage, the spherical nature of earth, a lesson Humanity assimilates with difficulty. The play resumes with Ignorance in dialogue with Sensual Appetite. He is denigrating the study of cosmology and extolling his own power and influence. Sensual Appetite declares that he has just participated 'at a shrewd fray' and claims to have perpetrated some acts of violence. He then enquires 'where becam my maister'? Ignorance tells him that Humanity is 'Hyd here in some corner.' Sensual Appetite sees the recumbent figure, 'For yonder lo beholde ye may/Se where the mad fole doth ly.' Sensuality again describes Humanity as 'In manner of a fole' and together they persuade him to rise to his feet.

SEN. Now ryse vp maister huddy peke
      your tayle totyth out be hynde
      fere not man stande vp by and by
      I warrant you to ryse vp boldly
      Here is non but is your frynde
HU.   I cry you mercy maister dere
yng. Why what is cause thou hydest the here
HU.   For I was almost for fere
      Euyn clene out of my mynde
SEN. Nay it is the study that ye have had
      In this folyshe losophy hath made you mad.

A little later Humanity is persuaded to revel in singing and dancing with fresh company brought in by Sensual Appetite. The stage direction is

    Than he syngeth this song and daun[c]yth with all
    And euermore maketh countenance accordying
    To the matter & also other aunswer lyke wyse.

Whatever action has occurred in the missing leaves of the copy the above lines indicate that Humanity is degraded as a fool, that he is raised and joins a dance revel. This scene has its parallels in *Wit and Science* and *The Marriage*.

John Redford has long been known as a musician of merit. Thomas Morley in his 'Plaine and Easie Introduction to Practicall Music' (1597) lists Redford among those specially distinguished for composing plainsong. His *Organ Works* has been published in a modern edition (Cassell 1934). Recognition of Redford's literary achievement is, however, comparatively recent. A.W. Reed was the first to suggest that Redford was a member of a group of artists – musicians, poets, dramatists – centred around St Paul's towards the end of the reign of Henry VIII. [16] Reed also showed that the lives and works of some of these men were connected with the more distinguished group of humanists – artists, scholars, divines, and lawyers – associated with Sir Thomas More. John Heywood, for instance, who collaborated with Sebastian Westcott and very likely also with John Redford in the presentation of plays at court, and who contributed to the manuscript verse anthology which included *Wit and Science*, married the daughter of John Rastell, lawyer,

16 *Early Tudor Drama*

printer, dramatist, and brother-in-law of Sir Thomas More.[17] Dr Pearl Hogrefe has analysed the theories and programmes of education advocated by the More circle including those of Erasmus in *De Ratione Studii* (1511) and in *De Pueris Instituendis* (1529) and of Jean Luis Vives in *De Tradendis Disciplinis* (1531). She has shown how these two men, More himself, and some lesser figures of the group contributed to the drama and to its secularisation.[18]

While acknowledging the influence of the humanist educational theorists we should not exaggerate it. *Wit and Science* is a masterly compound of elements long familiar to medieval literature stretching back to a seminal source, *De Nuptiis Philologiae et Mercurii* by Martianus Capella, the fifth century treatise on the seven liberal arts which became a 'text book in the Middle Ages' and wherein '*sapientia*, the goal of all intellectual activity, and *ratio* as the means of acquiring it are repeatedly emphasized.'[19] Pilgrim man in quest of Wisdom and Grace, initiated by Nature into the mysteries of the universe, subject to the counsels of Reason and to the seductions of Sensuality are prominent themes in Deguileville's *Pèlerinage de la vie humaine* (c1330) and in *Les Échecs amoureux* (c1375) both translated by Lydgate in the early fifteenth century.[20] In one way or another homiletic and courtly allegories such as *A Pageant of Knowledge* (c1430),[21] *The Court of Sapience* (c1470),[22] *The Castell of Labour* (1503),[23] and Stephen Hawes' *The Pastime of Pleasure* (c1505)[24] all combine various moral and pedagogical elements found in Martianus' allegorical marriage between Eloquence and Learning.

17 See p 16 n19. Aside from Redford and Heywood the other contributors to the verse were Myles Huggard, John Thorne, Thomas Prideaux, and a Master Knight; eleven of the poems are unattributed, one of these is 'In youthful years when first my young desire began' by Richard Edwards and appears in *The Paradise of Dainty Devices* (1576); another, 'Let not the sluggish sleep' may be a version of George Gascoigne's 'Goodnight' printed in the *Hundred Sundrie Flowers* (1573). F.P. Wilson and G.K. Hunter (*The English Drama* 43) are mistaken in making the claim that Sebastian Westcott was also a contributor. It is quite likely that he became acquainted with the St Paul's circle of writers soon after his arrival in London. For his association with Prideaux and Thorne see p 14 and p 37.
18 See *The Sir Thomas More Circle* (Urbana 1959). The author is, however, confused about the relationship of the 'Wit' plays and is also mistaken about them individually.
19 C.S. Lewis, *The Allegory of Love* (Oxford 1936) 81
20 *The Pilgrimage of the Life of Man*, F.J. Furnivall and K.B. Locock eds. EETS (1899–1904). *Reason and Sensuality*, E. Sieper, ed. EETS (1901–3) was suggested as a source for Medwall's *Nature* by W. Roy Mackenzie, PMLA XXIX (1914) 189–99.
21 *The Minor Poems of John Lydgate*, H.N. MacCracken, ed. 2 vols EETS (1911–34) II 724–34
22 *English Verse between Chaucer and Surrey*, E.P. Hammond, ed. (New York 1965)
23 A.W. Pollard, ed. Roxburghe Club (1905)
24 W.E. Mead, ed. EETS (1928)

The Pastime of Pleasure, printed in 1509 and reprinted in 1517, 1554, and twice in 1555, is a courtly defence of scholastic training. It is the *trivium* and *quadrivium* which provide Hawes' hero, Graunde Amour, with the means of perfecting himself to win his lady, La Bel Pucell. There are close correspondences between it and *Wit and Science*. Both heroes fall in love before they first meet their ladies. Both attain their goals through exercise of academic virtues. Both have to overcome a monstrous creature before fulfilling their quests. In both works a punitive scene is depicted. Correction whips False Report masquerading as Godfrey Gobilive, who has escaped prison and is clothed in a fool's garment. In *Wit and Science* it is the hero himself who is whipped, after he has fallen from grace and been dressed as a fool by Idleness.

These poems are by no means an exhaustive list of allegories pertinent to the respective plays of Medwall, Rastell, and Redford. They merely serve to remind us that the material given such brilliant dramatic form in *Wit and Science* stems more from the late medieval allegoric poets than from the humanist educators, and that all Redford's characters save perhaps Tediousness (ironically enough) and Honest Recreation are quite familiar by the early sixteenth century. Sensuality or Sensual Appetite, of course, does not appear in Redford's play. However, the pilgrim-scholar, Wit, as his name implies, embodies *l'homme sensual* of the five outward wits or senses, just as Reason embodies one of the attributes of the inner wits. Hence when Wit is slugged insensible by Tediousness, Honest Recreation and her companions revive him with a song 'best phisycke' for his stricken senses 'When travell*es* grete in matters thycke/haue duld yor wytt*es* & made them sycke,' and he is invited in sequential stanzas to give ear, hand, and eye to his ministering angels in order to regain his feet.

The educational theory underlying the concept of Honest Recreation derives from Humanist approbation of classical authorities on the matter. Ascham's charming and extensive plea for the principle in *The Schoolmaster* (1570) is too well known to need quotation here. An earlier work of his, *Toxophilus* (1545), states his pedagogical aim more succinctly as 'intending none other purpose but that youth might be stirred to labour, honest pastime and virtue, and as much as lay in me, plucked from idleness.' The entire prologue to *Jacke Jugeler* (c1553–63), a play written for boys to perform, is another such plea in which Ovid, Plutarch, Cicero, and others are cited in support of Cato:

> For the mynd (saith he) in serious matters occupied
> Yf it haue not sum quiet mirthe, and recreacion
> Interchaungeable admixed, must niddes be weried.

The close relationship between Redford's *Wit and Science* and Westcott's presentation of *The Marriage of Wit and Science* appears to preclude the possibility of another source for the adaptation, unless, of course, an original could be found for Will, the only fresh character. The composition of such an interlude by John Heywood has recently come to light. Welcome as this is, it should be no surprise. Heywood's preoccupation with the wit-will conflict is shown in *The Firste Hundred of Epigrammes* (1556).

> Where will is good, and wit is yll,
> There wisdome can no maner skyll.
> Where wit is good, and will is yll,
> There wisdome sitteth all silent still.
> Where wit and will are both two yll,
> There wisdome no ware meddle will.
> Where wit and will well ordred bee,
> There wisdome makyth a trinitee.

Another poem, *Will and Wit*, the burden of which states the theme of *The Marriage* may also be by John Heywood.

> I wyll, said Wyll, folow my wyll:
> Not so, said Wytt, better be still.
> I wyll, said Wyll, if I list, spill;
> Therto, said Wytte, consent I wyll.
>   For he that by wyll dothe rule his witte,
>   Dothe oftymes loose, when he shulde knitte.
>
> I will, said Wyll, not leese my right;
> Sumtyme, said Witte, for all thy myght.
> I wyll, said Wyll, worke them dispite:
> Well than, said Witte, they will the quyte.
>   For he that by wyll doth rule his witte,
>   Must oftymes loose, when he shulde knytte.
>
> I will, said Wyll, avenged be:
> Not so, said Witte, be ruled by me.
> I wyll, said Wyll, their hurte ones see;
> Myght chaunce, said Witte, they myght hurte the.
>   For he that by wyll dothe rule his witte,
>   Doth oftymes loose, when he shulde knytte.

I wyll, said Wyll, talke wordes at large:
Well than, said Wytte, I take no charge.
I wyll, said Will, rowe in euerye barge:
Thyn oore, said Wytte, ys muche to large.
   For he that by wyll doth rule his wytte,
   Dothe oftymes lose, whan he shulde knytte.

I wyll, said Wyll, haue suerly bownde:
Thy knotte, said Wytte, is full onsownde.
I wyll, said Wyll, all things confownd:
Thy works, said Witte, haue slypper grownd.
   For he that by will dothe rule his witte,
   Dothe oftymes loose, when he shulde knytte.

I wyll, said Wyll, clyme hye alought:
Suche folke, said Wytte, fall much onsought.
I wyll, said Wyll, noowyse be towght:
Well than, said Witte, all will be nowght.
   For he that by wyll dothe rule his witte,
   Doth oftymes loose, whan he shuld knytte.

This wyllfull Wyll Wytte dothe leade,
Thorough folysshe fansyes in the headde.
But if Witte were ones in Wylles steade,
Than Wyll by Witte myght be leade.
   For wheras Witte dothe lead the wyll,
   The knot half knitte is fasten styll.

If wylfull Wyll wold ruled be
After Witts counsell, folye to flee;
Gods commaundements kepe shuld we,
And obey our kynge in eche degree.
   For wheras witte dothe rule the wyll,
   The knot half knytt is fasten styll;
   And wheras wyll dothe rule with witte,
   Oftymes dothe loose, when he shuld knytte.

FINIS[25]

---

25 The poem is one of six ballads contained in Corpus Christi College Manuscript No. 168,

The juggling reiteration, 'the trick of continuing the rhyme of a couplet over a quatrain,' and the incremental repetition are all poetic devices employed by Heywood; the first two of these are especially characteristic of his playful verse.[26]

The reference to John Heywood's play containing the character Will is made by Thomas Whythorne in his *Autobiography*.[27] Whythorne lived in Heywood's London household between 1545 and 1549, during which time he learned to play the virginals and the lute and to write verse. As 'servant and skoller' Whythorne was employed to make fair copy of his master's *A Dialogue of Proverbs* and also an interlude upon 'the parts of Man' commissioned by Thomas Cranmer, Archbishop of Canterbury. His statement 'all the which afforsaid befor they wer published I did wryt out for him, or had the yvs of them to read them' implies that the play was printed.[28] In a later passage of his autobiography Whythorne gives a tantalizingly brief excerpt which, slightly modernized, is as follows:

Bekawz I hav heer tofor towched sumwhat of the government of Reazon & will in mankynd, it seemeth vnto me that I shiuld not pas any furder in this diskowrs till I hav shewd you sumwhat mor plainly of their properties and governments, wherfor I will heer shew vnto yow the wurdz of my old master mr Haywood, the which hee did wryt in A komedy or play that hee mad of the parts of man, in the which after that he

edited for the Percy Society (vol. xiii) in 1884 by James Goodwin. On the first page of the ms Dr John Jegon, Master of Corpus Christi College (1590–1602), describes the contents as 'some fragments of that excellent man Rich. Cox, Bishoppe of Elie.' Cox lived from 1499 to 1581. In addition to the six anonymous ballads the ms 'contains a great number of specimens of his [Cox's] Latin verse,' some psalms versified and two poems by Sir Thomas Wyatt.

26 See Reed 121–8. Another ballad in the group entitled 'Say Well and Do Well' is similar in these respects and may also be the work of Heywood. Goodwin notes that 'it is doubtful … whether all the contents of the ms can rightly be attributed to Cox.' The relationship of wit and will appears as a minor theme in other poems of the period, see *The Paradise* (Rollins 96) for the subjection of wit to will, and *Tottel's Miscellany* (Rollins 1 146) for the co-operation between wit and will. In Jasper Heywood's sententious poem (*The Paradise*, Rollins 14–16) four lines of the fourth stanza neatly epitomize the moral of *Wit and Science* and of *The Marriage*:

> If thou to farre let out thy fancies slip,
> And witlesse wyll from reasons rule outstart;
> Then folly, shall at length be made they whippe,
> And sore, the stripes of shame, shal cause thee smart.

27 James M. Osborn, ed. (Oxford 1961)
28 See Osborn xix-xx and 13–14

hath mad Reazon to chalenge vnto him self the siuperiorite and government of all the parts of Man, and also to kommaund althings lyving vpon the earth, hee maketh reazon to say thus (in meeter) for him self.

And the diffrens between man the kommaunder, and beasts being by man kommaunded, iz only Reazon in man, the disserner of good and ill, the good in man elekted by me, and th'ill in man by mee rejekted. man obeing mee shynth in exsellensy, and disobeing mee, shewth mans insolensy. Now sins I reazon am th'only qualyte, that qualifiet man in such A temperans az setteth man in plas of prinsipalite abov all beasts to stand in governans who but I over man shiuld him self advans, to govern lykwyz, sins I bring man therto, and keep man therin doing az I bid him do.

when reazon hath thus said for him self, then kummeth in will, who dispiuteth with reazon for the siuprem government in man, whervpon in the end thei both ar dryven to graunt that man kan do nothing withowt will, and withowt reazon man kan do no good thing.

Whether or not Heywood's lost play was ever printed, all we know of the close relation between Redford, Heywood, and Westcott makes it very likely that whoever adapted *Wit and Science* was also acquainted with *The Parts of Man*. Did he transform Redford's messenger, Confidence, into the pert boy-servant, Will, in the light of John Heywood's creation?

THE WRITER AND THE DATE OF THE PLAY

The foregoing comparison of *The Marriage of Wit and Science* with its principal (perhaps its only) source illustrates, in a small way, changes of taste during the intervening three decades. The adaptor's indifference to, and impoverishment of, Redford's cunningly wrought allegory is perhaps the most noticeable of these. As we have seen, he chose to place his dramatic emphases elsewhere, upon the romantic courtship, for instance, and upon the saucy brilliance of his own invention, Will.

At first glance it would seem that the more extended treatment given to the wooing of Science by Wit was less successful. Judged realistically the romance appears lifeless, stifled by its own formality, luxuriously entombed beneath its own verbiage. When feelings are at their most intense, the communication of emotion appears to be at its most preposterous. To view the writer's achievement in this way, however, would be to misunderstand his intention as well as the very nature of his task. *The Marriage*, like its predecessor *Wit and Science*, was written to be performed by boys, and thus any attempt to portray convincingly an adult romantic situation would have been extremely difficult. What the writer has done is to provide the rhetorical lineaments of romantic passion for the boy actor's spontaneous grace and charm to transmute into an entertaining spectacle, at once tender and amusing, poignantly youthful yet highly sophisticated. For, concomitant with the spectacle, and making its appeal to the ears of the audience, is the verse, often elaborately rhetorical, and arranged in a variety of fashionable measures. The dramatist was quite familiar with the language, metres and conventions of the courtly poetry of the mid-century. Again and again, not only in the sententious passages connected with Wit's moral welfare and his lapse from grace, but especially in the wooing scenes, passages of verse expressing the feelings of the joyous or despondent lover are in the ardent vein of the popular Elizabethan verse anthologies, *Songs And Sonnets*, *The Paradise of Dainty Devices*, and *A Handfull of Pleasant Delights*. We are dealing with an author who, like so many of his contemporaries, has come by his Petrarch through an intimate knowledge of Wyatt and Surrey, and also one who is not often the inferior of the 'Uncertain Authors' of Tottel's *Miscellany*. A scrutiny of some representative passages in the play will best show this literary kinship. The three examined below reflect various phases of Wit's ardour for his lady, Science. Each is in poulter's measure, one of the characteristic measures in the anthologies, which, in the play, is always reserved for the writer's highest flights of gravity or passion.

> Nature, my soveraigne Quene and parent passyng dere,
> 30 Whose force I am inforst to know and knowledge every where,
> This care of myne, though it be bred within my breste,
> Yet it is not so rype as yet to brede me great unrest.
> So runne I to and fro with hap such as I fynde,
> Now fast, now loose, now hot, now cold, unconstant as the wind.
> 35 I feele my selfe in love, yet not inflamed so,
> But causes move me now and then to let suche fancies go,
> Whiche causes prevailyng settes eche thing els in doubte,
> Much like the nayle that last came in and dryves the former out.
> Wherfore my suite is thys; that it woulde please your grace
> 40 To settle this unsetled head in some assured place,
> To leade me through the thyck, to guyde me al the waye,
> To poynt me where I maye atcheve my most desyred praye.
> For nowe agayne of late I kyndle in desire,
> And pleasure pricketh fourth my youth to feele a greater fyre.

What though I be too young to shewe her sport in bed,   45
Yet are there many in thys lande that at my yeares doe wedde,
And though I wed not yet, yet am I olde inowe
To serve my Lady to my power and to begynne to woo.

In this passage Wit's feelings, though aroused, are not intense; after all, he has yet to see his lady. The long, sober alternate alexandrines and fourteeners are tolerably restrained. The rhymes are unforced, save for the last one, which, in the original, is matched with an eye-rhyme 'inowe/woe.' The rhetorical figures, *traductio* (doubled, 30) and (40), *asynedoton* (34), *anaphora* (40–2), and *epizeuxis* (47) are all skilfully functional, assisting the communication of Wit's incipient romantic desire. The proverb (38) is neatly integrated.

O pearle of passing price, sent downe from god on hye!   609
The swetest beauty to entise, that hath bene sene with eye:
The wel of wealth to all, that no man doth annoye:
The kaye of Kingedomes and the stall of everlasting joye:
The treasure and the store, whom al good things began:
The nurse of Lady Wisdom's lore: the lincke of man and man,
What wordes shal me suffice to utter my desyre?   615
What heate of talke shal I devise for to expresse my fyer?
I burne and yet I frese; I flame and coole as fast.
In hope to wyn and for to lese, my pensivenes doth last.
Why should my dulled spryte apal my courage so?
O salve my sore, or sley me quite by saying yea or no!   620
You are the marke at whome I shot to hit or misse.
My life it stayes on you alone; to you my sute it is.
A mate not much unmete, with you some griefe to fynde,
Dame Nature's sonne, my name it Wit, than fancieth you by kind;
And here I come this day to wayte and to attende,   625
In hope to have my hoped pray, or elles my life to ende.

As the verse well shows, Wit's first direct address to Science provides the writer with an ampler rehtorical scope. The main figures, *ecphonesis* (609, 620), *anaphora* (610–14, 615–16), *antitheton* (617–18), and *traductio* (626) are now more ostentatious, and these are combined with a further adornment, the internal rhyme throughout the passage. The Petrarchan conceit (617) and the phrase 'salve my sore' (620) are favourite poetic commonplaces of the contributors to the anthologies. The extravagance of the language, the elaboration of the devices, the clever and insistent rhymes all point to the writer's bent for conventional courtly verse.

> Eyther my glasse is wonderfully spotted,
> Or els my face is wonderfully blotted.
> This is not my Cote. Why, wher had I this weede?
> 1290 By the Masse, I loke like a very foole in deede.
> O heapes of happes! O rufull chaunce to me!
> O Idleness, woe worth the time that I was ruled by thee!
> Why did I lay my head within thy lappe to rest?
> Why was I not advised by her that wisht and will'd me best?
> 1295 O ten times troble! Blessed wights, whose corpes in grave do lye,
> That are not driven to behould these wretched cares which die!
> On me, your furies, all on me, have poured out your spite.
> Come nowe and slay me at the last, and ridde my sorowes quite.
> What coast shall me receyve? Wher shall I shew my head?
> 1300 The world wyll saye this same is he that, if he list, he sped:
> This same is he that toke an enterpryse in hand:
> This same is he that scarce one blow his ennemy did withstand:
> This same is he that fought and fell in open field:
> This same is he that in the songe of Idleness did yelde:
> 1305 This same is he that was in way to winne the game,
> To joyne himselfe wherby he should have won immortal fame;
> And now is wrapt in woe, and buried in dispayre.
> O happye case for thee, if death would rid thee quite of care!

In the final example, poulter's measure inevitably succeeds the irregular lines as soon as Wit is launched upon his lament. On the swelling tide of his self-pity, the rhetorical figures soon become prominent, formalising the outcries of grief and despair in accordance with the accepted conventional expression of the forsaken lover. A score of very similar lugubrious pieces may be seen in the anthologies.[29] Richard Edwards, himself a contributor to one of these anthologies, includes a lament of this type as a song sung by Pythias to the accompaniment of the regals in *Damon and Pythias*. It would

29 See explanatory notes. Cf. *Tottel's Miscellany* nos 10, 49, 66, 301; *The Paradise* nos 42, 83, 103; *The Gorgeous Gallery* 16 and 38 for a few in which the diction is particularly close to the example in the play. All references are to Rollins' editions. See also F.P. Wilson's discussion of the verse (*The English Drama* 73–4). He concludes: 'The rhetoric which Kyd and the early Shakespeare were to inherit is already to hand.'

be tedious to list the standardised devices. Of the many here employed, one notes that an identical use of *anaphora* (1301–5) occurs in Barclay's *Eclogues* (1805–8).

The evidence of these and other passages in the play points to the practised hand of the writer, his sense of craftsmanship, his keen concern with fashionable literary conventions, and suggests that the play was written not long before it was entered in the Stationers' *Register* in August 1569. *The Marriage of Wit and Science* is the work of a self-conscious dramatic poet who knows exactly what he wishes to do, and whose aim, above all, is to entertain. The highly adorned verse, with its stiffly formal rhetorical embroidery, has been composed as an appropriate vehicle for a courtly romance to be enacted by boys. Its very artificiality is its chief strength.

The writer's more purely literary talent may also be seen employed in the arrangement of his proverbial material.[30] The play is a fairly rich repository of proverbial sayings, comparisons, and phrases not found in Redford's original, which is noticeably bare of *paroemia*. Many of these fresh saws are subtly interwoven into contexts that are not overtly humorous or didactic. In addition to their conventional use throughout the play, witty adaptations of common sayings and cleverly apposite uses of others occur. In one passage (246–58) a cluster of proverbial phrases enriches the comic dialogue, and to another (579–88) proverbial *stychomythia* of a rare kind adds a racy colloquialism to the speech. Whiting has remarked that this latter proverb-capping dialogue between Wit and Will is the first example of its kind in the native drama.[31]

A few stylistic pecularities of the writer are worth drawing attention to, since they may be idiosyncratic and therefore may provide evidence of his hand at work elsewhere. These are: (i) a type of clausal construction, (ii) an addiction to eye-rhyme, and (iii) perhaps a distinctive trait of capitalisation.

The first of these is the use of an adverbial clause, beginning with the conjunction *or* followed by *else*, often employed in an admonitory sense as in 'Take tyme with all, or elles I dare assure thee of the foyle' (174). This construction occurs some dozen times throughout the text (174, 217, 218, 222, 272, 355, 598, 599, 626, 733, 1288, 1370). Neither the construction itself nor the regularity of its recurrence distinguishes it as a peculiarity of the writer, but its place within the context of its appearance, which is at the

---

30 B.J. Whiting's *Proverbs in The Earlier English Drama* (Cambridge, Mass. 1938) 138–42, contains a commentary upon this material. Additional uses of proverbial matter by the writer are also referred to in the explanatory notes.

31 Ibid. 63

conclusion of a sentence and often of a speech, perhaps does so. In two instances the construction is used in both lines of a concluding couplet (217–18, 598–9). In addition to forcing the rhymes occasionally, as in such examples as 'bestow/moe' (more), 'bloud' (blood),/'good' (goods), 'reache/ketche' (catch), the writer quite often adjusts final syllables of words in order to make the rhyme clear to the eye as well as to the ear. A few of the more obvious of such attempts are: 'woe' (woo)/'froe,' 'moe' (more)/'bloe' (blow), 'hye/eye,' 'ayde/denayde,' 'leave/geave' (give), 'hit/yit' (yet), 'furst' (first)/'curst,' 'fet' (feat)/'bet' (beaten), 'viewe/hiew' (hue), and 'eate/freete' (fret). Finally, there is the capitalisation. At first glance there appears to be an arbitrary use of capitals in the text. A closer scrutiny reveals that, in addition to the normal capitalisation of proper nouns, words of rank and status, the names of places and animals are almost invariably capitalised. Thus the following appear: 'Lord,' 'Lady,' 'Quene,' 'Dutches,' 'Knights,' 'Squiers,' 'Gentilman,' 'Ladyshipe,' 'Madam,' 'Mayster,' 'Childe,' 'Damsell,' 'Bachiler,' 'Giant,' 'Heaven,' 'Pernasus,' 'Kingedomes,' and 'Mare.' A few of these words, notably 'master,' 'chyld,' and 'madame,' also occur without capitals. Besides these that may be capitalised by rule, there are a number of unnecessarily capitalised words, almost all of which begin with 'C,' 'I,' or 'T': 'Creatures,' 'Curiouse,' 'Chuse,' 'Cote,' 'Closet,' 'Christal,' 'Counsell,' 'Idle,' 'Iot,' 'Ioynt,' 'Iurisdiction,' 'Iaveling,' 'Target,' and 'Thousāde.' These would appear to be either the compositor's or the writer's idiosyncracies.[32]

The author of *The Marriage* impresses one as a strongly individual and practised writer. He has not only a richly rhetorical poetic style, but also a marked gift for proverbial expression and a strong bent towards chivalric romance. In the creation of Will he has demonstrated a talent for comic characterisation of a high order. The nature of his adaptation of Redford's plot shows that his own creative instinct was very much alive, since he has adapted freely, and, while preserving the general outline of the original, has impressed upon it much of his own authority and transformed it into something entirely fresh. So marked are many of his characteristics, his comic dialogue, his turns of phrase, his handling of stock romantic situations – the formalised emotional displays of the lovers' joys and sorrows, for instance – that these and other traits prompt us to ask if they can be recognised elsewhere. As the notes appended to this text show, three other anonymous plays bear resemblances to *The Marriage of Wit and Science*.

---

32 A very similar form of capitalization is also to be found in *The Contention between Liberality and Prodigality*.

Two of these, *Common Conditions* (c1576) and *Clyomon and Clamydes*, printed in 1599, have already been suggested as being very likely the work of one author.[33] The third play, *Liberality and Prodigality*, not printed so far as is known until 1602, is in many respects even more closely connected with *The Marriage*.

THE STAGING

The action takes place before at least two specific locations providing entrances and exits for some of the characters: the dwelling-place of Science, Reason, and Experience, and the abode of the monster, Tediousness. These two 'houses' are in sharp scenic contrast to one another, befitting the allegory, and, to judge from the few allusions to them in the dialogue, visually arresting.

Lady Science invites Will to bring Wit 'within this house of myne' (l. 503). Earlier Wit had confessed to Dame Nature, 'I feele my selfe in love' and expressively indicates where his lady lives, 'Loe, where she dwelles! lo, where my harte is all possest!/Loe, where my bodie would abyde! lo, where my soule doth rest!' (ll. 62–3). From this house Science and her parents emerge to meet Will (l. 375), to meet Wit (l. 589), and again to meet Wit (l. 1204); at the close of these scenes the Science family withdraws into the house. Instruction, Study and Diligence are also resident there and at Reason's request enter 'the place' from the house to be introduced to Wit (l. 816). After Reason has ordered Shame to beat Wit, the penitent lover is invited to 'Come in and dwell with us' (l. 1384). Finally, Lady Science leads the victorious Wit and his helpmeets into her house at the close of the play. There is evidence to suggest that the house of Science was more solid and elaborate than the customary representational *domus* consisting of a lath and canvas façade framing a doorway. Wit vows to Nature 'before I slepe, I will to yonder forte repaire' (l. 181). Will informs the audience that he has 'come to the gate of this Ladye' (l. 374). When the second assault is to be made against the monster, Science tells Wit, 'Here in this Closet our selfe wil sitte and see/Your manly feates and your successe in fyght' (ll. 1428–9). Wit re-

33 See Tucker Brooke's edition of *Common Conditions*, Elizabethan Club Reprint (1915) App. 1 83–5; W.W. Greg's introduction to *Clyomon and Clamydes* MSR (1913); and B.J. Whiting, *Proverbs* 292–4. A critical edition of *Clyomon and Clamydes* has been edited by Betty J. Littleton (The Hague 1968), who thinks that the play and *Common Conditions* are not by the same author. *Common Conditions* and *Clyomon and Clamydes* have also been linked with Preston's *Cambises*. Some resemblances between them are obvious, but I find no trace in *Cambises* of the dramatic style discussed above.

sponds, 'Here in my sight, good Maddam, sitte and viewe/That, when I list, I may loke uppe on you' (ll. 1437–8). Farmer and Hazlitt have interpreted Wit's words 'to look upon you,' an emendation not subscribed to in this text. There is nothing irregular about the printing of 'upon' in the six appearances of the word in the text including 'and I wil loke upon' (l. 1120). We must therefore suppose that the closet or small inner room is situated in a raised place, perhaps an upper storey of her house, and that Science's viewpoint is a window large enough for her not only to see the combat below, but also large enough for her to be seen by the audience as she registers apprehension and joy while Wit engages her 'mortall foe.'

The other specific location is the 'deadly denne' of the 'monstrous Giant,' Tediousness, 'That lurketh in the woode hereby, as you come and goe' (l. 701). From this construction the monster emerges twice (ll. 951 and 1480) in response to the challenges of his adversaries. There is no detailed description of the appearance of Tediousness; because his head is cut off by Wit, placed upon a spear and uplifted as a 'joyfull sign,' one presumes that a false head was part of the costume and that this also served to increase his height as well as help present him either grotesquely or horribly. In both combats he wields a club. Unless Tediousness emerged and retired on all fours, his den required a sizeable opening. Perhaps it was in the relative obscurity of this entrance where Wit was able to sever the head.

The entrances and exits of all the other characters, Nature, Will, Honest Recreation, Shame, Idleness, and Ignorance are not made from or into 'houses.' Nor can it be said with any certainty that Wit had a representational *domus*. The two references to his domain are general and unlocated. 'Where shall I fynde you, when I come againe?' asks Will, and Wit's reply is 'At home' (ll. 359–60). Later Wit invites Instruction, Diligence, and Study to 'dwell in house wythe me' (l. 855) and they leave to the order of Wit's 'Come' and to the impertinence of Will's 'Goe.'

Professor Craik discusses the setting in relation to the movement of the play and in the light of other court presentations during the same festive season, namely *Orestes* and *Prodigality*, identified in surviving texts as *Horestes* and *Liberality and Prodigality*. The latter, as Hillebrand has shown and which this study has sought to confirm, was a Paul's play.[34] 'The castle gate and battlemented gallery above it' in *Horestes*, and the palace of Fortune in *Liberality and Prodigality* are said to be elaborate, central, two-level sets

34 *The Tudor Interlude* (Leicester 1958) 14–17. For further evidence that *The Contention between Liberality and Prodigality* is the play 'prodigallitie' performed at court in 1568, see pp 61 and 64.

which support the probability that Science's 'house' was similar in these respects. Professor Craik plausibly suggests that it, too, was a 'decorative and functional castle.' He concludes, 'Doubtless the castle stood centrally at the rear of the acting-space, flanked by the entrances used by Wit and Tediousness (both of which may have been representational *domus*) and another entrance used by Recreation, Idleness and their respective attendants.'

Was the house of Science, whether castle or something else, central, and, if Wit's house and the den of Tediousness flanked it, where was the opening for the entrances and exits of the other characters? The plot and movement of *Liberality and Prodigality* support the proposal that Fortune's palace was the principal piece of scenery and that it was centrally situated and dominant. In *The Marriage of Wit and Science*, however, the equality and apposition of two contrasted domains, the one associated with hope and fulfilment, the other with death and despair, would appear to offer a more valid visual reinforcement to the themes of the play, the educational morality, the chivalric pilgrimage, and the romantic courtship. Such an arrangement would be much more likely to give dramatic emphasis to the tensions and suspense upon which the play is craftily poised. For this reason we may suppose the setting to comprise two separate localities, on the one side the two-storey house of Science, on the other side the den of Tediousness associated with a forest. Between these scenic pieces would be a central opening by which Nature, Honest Recreation, Shame, Idleness, and Ignorance enter and leave 'the place' each in their turn, masked, as they soon would be, by the abutting façades of the opposing solid and high constructions. Thus Dame Nature begins the play, entering with Wit centrally between the 'houses' ('I come in place to treat with this my sonne') and retiring by the same way; she leaves Wit ready to commence his travail 'tyll tracte of time' has shown him the path 'whereby his Race in honour he may runne' through courtship, combat, dance, humiliation, and expiation to enter finally the house of his lady, Science. If the house of Science stood upon one side of the stage rather than centrally, Will's arrival there at the end of the first scene and his shift to stand 'amonge these fellowes' (the audience) 'to eye her' would surely be more fittingly accomplished.

Each of the stages of Wit's journey is appropriately supported by the simplest of properties: a picture of himself to be presented to Science by Will, a mirror given to him by Reason to remind him of his state, a fool's coat to dress his degenerate condition in the seductive lap of Idleness, a whip applied to his back by Shame under the rule of Reason, and lastly appropriate weapons – sword, buckler, dagger, and spear – to be used with proper tactics because Science herself has warned him that his monstrous match is to be won 'not by force but by slyght.' In all these scenes we may note the ordered variety of vocal and physical responses. The quieter passages of dialogue, whether leavened by the fashionable poetic cadences and rhetoric of the day, or by the sobrieties of Reason and Experience, are in contrast to the lively braggadacio of Wit and the bright improprieties of Will. Similarly, the action alternates between stasis, even prostration as Wit is felled by Tediousness or sinks exhausted an easy prey to Idleness, and the heightened activity of dances and combats. That the play is able to amuse and interest a modern audience with the universality of its appeal, its immediacy of speech and action, has been attested at the University of Calgary where it was performed before public audiences in 1968.

THE HEIRS OF WIT AND SCIENCE

In concluding this introduction we may take brief notice of the fruits of the popular union of Wit and Science. In the quarter century following *The Marriage* several plays derive from it. There are Francis Merbury's *The Contract of a Marriage between Wit and Wisdom*, the anonymous *Play of Plays and Pastimes*, perhaps also called *Delight* after one of the main characters, bespoken by Stephen Gosson, and Anthony Munday's clever parody, *The Marriage of Wit and Wisdom*, a play within the play of *Sir Thomas More*.

Merbury's *Wit and Wisdom* survives in a single manuscript dated 1579. There are, however, indications that it may have been printed.[35] Although there is evidence that Merbury knew both the earlier 'Wit' plays (his interlude incorporates some elements of each), the extant version is a very different composition from either Redford's original or the adaptation presented by Westcott. It impresses one, at first, as the product of a writer unskilled in dramatic composition who quickly loses interest in the pedagogical allegory of his chief sources, and who becomes wholly concerned with the presentation of a series of farcical episodes dominated by the vice, Idleness, and largely culled from other plays such as *Gammer Gurton's Needle*, *Cambyses*, and *Misogonus*. It has been suggested that the play exemplifies the degeneration of allegoric morality and that it marks the trend toward 'purely comic entertainment.' It has also been inferred that *Wit and Wisdom* was written for the popular stage and intended for performance by an adult troupe. Examination of the text and enquiry into the career of its author suggest that the manuscript should be interpreted with greater caution.[36]

35 See introduction to the Malone Society Reprint, 1966 (1971).
36 See 'Francis Merbury, 1555–1611,' *SP* LXV (April 1968) 207–22.

The extant version may not be a complete transcription of the original. The structural imbalance may have resulted from cutting, particularly of the morality element; certainly in its present form the play is unusually short.

Perhaps a safer estimate of *Wit and Wisdom* may follow the recognition that, despite Merbury's use of incidents and characters from the earlier 'Wit' plays, his play is essentially a 'prodigal son' morality and not an educational allegory. Hence the introduction of Wit's parents, Severity and Indulgence, whose contrasted temperaments in the opening scene prepare us for the misadventures of their errant son. Hence also the greater comic licence, and the rejection of many of the allegoric characters. My suggestions that *Misogonus* was one of Merbury's sources and that he wrote the play at Cambridge strengthen this proposal. At any rate, it is doubtful that he wrote it for the popular stage. On the other hand, the supposed printed version, insofar as it is reflected by the existing manuscript, may well have been arranged to make its appeal to a small professional troupe and to the audiences that such a company would entertain.

While the copy we have may not do full justice to Merbury's talent as a dramatist, the play provides sufficient evidence for us to draw some tentative conclusions about him. Except for the promising opening scene, the play is largely imitative. The use Merbury makes of his chief and secondary sources is, furthermore, hackneyed, and betrays his incapacity for inventive transformation. When allowances are made for the possible structural imperfection of the copy, it must still be admitted that the Vice was more mischievous than perhaps even Merbury intended. Idleness has attracted too much of his creator's imaginative energy, impoverished the dramatic existence of the other characters, and run away with the show. This weakness points to Merbury's lack, not so much of re-creative skill but to his rudimentary grasp of form. His chief asset – a vein of droll and vital speech steeped in proverbial wisdom and salted with a coarse wit – cannot mask his ineptitude as a playwright.

Stephen Gosson in *Playes Confuted in Five Actions* (1582) summarizes the plot of the lost *Play of Plays and Pastimes* written, in all probability, to defend the presentation of stage plays against puritan complaint.

He [Tediousness?] tyeth Life and Delight so fast together, that if Delight be restrained, Life presently perisheth; there, zeale perceyuing Delight to be embraced of Life, puttes a snafle in his mouth, to keepe him under. Delight beinge bridled, Zeale leadeth life through a wildernesse of lothsomenesse, where Glutte scarreth them all, chafing both Zeale and Delight from Life, and with the clubbe of amasednesse strikes such a pegge into the heade of Life, that he falles downe for dead vpon the Stage. Life beinge thus fainte, and ouertrauailed, destitute of his guyde, robbed of Delight, is readie to giue vp the Ghost, in the same place; then entereth Recreation, which with music and singing rockes Life a sleepe to recouer his strength. By this meanes Tediousnesse is driuen from Life, and teinte is drawne out of his heade, which the club of amasednes left behinde. At last Recreation setteth vp the Gentleman vpon his feete, Delight is restored to him againe, and such kinde of sportes for cullices are brought in to nourishe him as none but Delighte must applye to his stomache. Then time being made for the benefite of Life, and Life being allowed to followe his appetite, amongst all manner of pastimes, Life chooseth Commedies, for his Delight, partly because Commedies are neither chargable to yᵉ beholders purse, nor painful to his body; partly, because he may sit out of the raine to viewe the same, when many other pastimes are hindred by wether.[37]

The correspondences with the 'Wit' plays are obvious and, one might add, ingenious. It is reasonable to conjecture that this was the play called *Delight* performed by Leicester's Men at court on the 26 December 1580, and, according to Gosson, at The Theatre thereafter.

The 'Wit' play selected by Sir Thomas More from the 'diuers' repertory of 'The Lord Cardinal's Men' for the entertainment of his guests appears in that section of the manuscript of *Sir Thomas More* (c1590–1600) in the hand of Anthony Munday. It was an apt choice of Munday to make for More – 'The mariage of witt and wisdom? that my lads/ Ile none but that.'[38] Saving the presence of the characters Wit and Wisdom however, what is eventually performed has nothing to do with Merbury's play; rather it is a clever mélange which more accurately deserves the title 'The Marriage of Disobedient Juventus' because the presentation is a compound of three fragments, one from *The Disobedient Child* and two from *Lusty Juventus* together with Inclination, the vice, and a hint of a situation from *The Trial of Treasure* – all of these, mid-century moralities. The play within the play has been taken quite seriously as valid evidence of the size, repertory, and *modus operandi* of an early professional troupe.[39] In fact Munday is having fun and the delightful entertainers he presents are as far removed from historical authenticity as a great deal of fancy and a little knowledge have brilliantly combined to place them.

The contribution made by the 'Wit' interludes to the dramatized romances such as *Common Conditions* and *Clyomon and Clamydes* and through them to the form of the pre-Shakespearean 'romantic comedy' has been pointed out by Werner Habicht.[40]

37 See Chambers IV 217–18.   38 See pp 95–6.
39 See F.S. Boas, 'The Play Within The Play,' *Shakespeare and the Stage* (London 1927) and David Bevington, *From 'Mankind' to Marlowe* (Cambridge, Mass. 1962) 18–20.
40 See p 91.

Finally, T.W. Baldwin has suggested that Shakespeare intended *Love's Labour's Lost* to be 'a school morality in reverse' or, as he put it in another way, that 'love won by study is love's labour lost.'[41] The young lords vow to pursue wisdom for three years and are provided with recreation. They forswear study, behave foolishly, are chastized, shamed, and duly repent. If they do not win their ladies, at least they learn through love's labours that 'the ground of study's excellence' far from being a bookish acquisition lies in 'the beauty of a woman's face' and, as Berowne sweetly argues, that women 'are the ground, the books, the academes,/From which doth spring the true Promethean fire.' Such, I take it, is the nature of the reversal to which Baldwin refers. He does not appear to have generated any interest in his view whatsoever, perhaps because his remarks about the educational moralities are general and he did not attempt to show that Shakespeare's play might have been shaped to some extent by anyone in particular. It may be worthwhile to take a closer look at the goings-on at the court of Navarre.

Navarre and his companions are wits who would be scholars seeking 'the light of truth' – wisdom. Their respective qualities of wit are acutely noted by the ladies. Longaville 'is a sharp wit match'd with too blunt a will' (II.i.49).[42] Dumaine has 'wit to make an ill shape good,/And shape to win grace though he had no wit' (II.i.59–60). As for Berowne, according to Rosaline 'His eye begets occasion for his wit' (II.i.69). Their individual and collective wittiness is, of course, exercised and, alas, rudely mocked, throughout the play. One disastrous display of it prompts the Princess to ask, 'Are these the breed of wits so wondered at?' (v.ii.267), and upon another occasion acidly to comment, 'Such short-liv'd wits do wither as they grow' (II.i.54). These observations and aspersions by no means exhaust their delineation of the lords as wits.

The bookmen-wits are not to be without some diversion during the term of their proposed labour. Berowne asks, 'But is there no quick recreation granted?' (I.i.159). Recreation there is in the person of Armado, another 'negligent student' according to Moth, quick perhaps, but not very honest, since Navarre loves 'to hear him lie' and whom the king will use 'for my minstrelsy' (I.i.174–5).

The Princess and her fair ladies are witty too, but they are also 'wise girls' as befits their divinities, at least in the view of the wooers, who hail their exalted state in song and sonnets. The Princess is a 'queen of queens': Katherine is 'most divine Kate' for whom Jove would deny himself and turn mortal; Maria will be proved 'a goddess' and possesses eyes capable of

---

41 *William Shakespeare's Five Act Structure* (Urbana 1947; reprinted 1963) 579ff.
42 Line references are to the New Kittredge Shakespeare (1968).

'heavenly rhetoric,' and Rosaline ('the fairest goddess on the ground') has dark eyes which have a regenerative power. Collectively these beautiful, celestial creatures are the teachers and the light-givers and so represent 'that angel knowledge' (I.i.113), Science/Wisdom, for which the wits are to lose their oaths and find themselves (IV.iii.258–361). Berowne's sonnet offers further testimony to this:

> Study his bias leaves and makes his book thine eyes,
>> Where all those pleasures live that art would comprehend.
> If knowledge be the mark, to know thee shall suffice;
>> Well learned is that tongue that well can thee commend,
> All ignorant that soul that sees thee without wonder;
> …
> Celestial as thou art, O, pardon love this wrong,
> That singës heaven's praise with such an earthly tongue.
>
> (IV.ii.102–11)

The wits break their vows and embrace folly, as the wise girls mockingly observe. 'The blood of youth burns not with such excess/As gravity's revolt to wantonness,' remarks Rosaline (V.ii.73–4) and Maria responds:

> Folly in fools bears not so strong a note
> As fool'ry in the wise when wit doth dote;
> Since all the power thereof it doth apply
> To prove, by wit, worth in simplicity.　　　　(V.ii.75–8)

The Princess is another clear-eyed witness: 'None are so surely caught, when they are catch'd,/As wit turned fool' (V.ii.69–70). It is fitting that spokesman Berowne is the first of the wits to recognize the metamorphosis: 'Well, "set thee down sorrow!" for so they say the fool said, and so say I, and I the fool. Well proved, wit' (IV.iii.3–5). He is in no solitary state; his fellow-scholars are similarly transmuted and the guilt-stricken Berowne must soon confess, 'That you three fools lack'd me fool to make up the mess' (IV.iii.203). Indeed they all don the equivalent of motley, as Rosaline points out when she advises her companions, 'Let us complain to them what fools were here,/Disguiz'd like Muscovites in shapeless gear' (V.ii.303–4), and as Berowne confirms later, ruefully admitting to Rosaline that he has been wearing 'the parti-coloured presence of loose-love/Put on by us' (V.ii.752–3). The ultimate ignominy, however, is reserved for Berowne alone. In the 'Wit' plays Wit is not only dressed as a fool; his face is blackened. Berowne recognizes himself to be in a similar condition of degradation as a result of falling in love with a black-haired beauty – 'The King he is hunting the deer: I am coursing myself. They have pitch'd a toil; I am toiling in a pitch – pitch that defiles. Defile! a foul word' (iv.iii.1–3). He is hard put to vindicate Rosaline from the ridicule of his fellow-fools, who wittily connect her dark attributes with those of the devil. As Navarre says, 'Black is the badge of hell....' The besmirched face of Wit in *The Marriage of Wit and Science* shocks Lady Science who cries, 'Thy loke is like to one that came out of hell.'

Shame and punishment follow degradation. In the two earlier 'Wit' plays it is Shame who whips Wit. Navarre and the lords suffer likewise from the pitiless 'tongues of mocking wenches' and also from Boyet, whose 'eye wounds like a leaden sword' (v.ii.480). The wits are twice scourged. After the muscovite foolery they 'depart away with shame' as the Princess had intended (v.ii.156) and, as the humiliated Berowne admits, 'By heaven, all dry-beaten with pure scoff!' (v.ii.264). Rosaline has observed their discomfiture. 'O, they were all in lamentable cases./The king was weeping-ripe for a good word' (v.ii.274–5). Unmasked, the transgressors return to receive further chastisement, for, as Boyet has correctly judged, 'it can never be/That they will digest this harsh indignity ... though they are lame with blows' (v.ii.289–292). Rosaline had promised 'That same Berowne, I'll torture ere I go' (v.ii.60) and he, her fool (v.ii.384), who had once been 'love's whip' (iii.i.161) and who later confesses, 'For your fair sakes, we neglected time,/Play'd foul-play with our oaths' (v.ii.741–2) is now prepared to face the cutting edge of her tongue:

> Here stand I, lady. Dart thy skill at me,
>   Bruise me with scorn, confound me with a flout,
> Thrust thy sharp wit through my ignorance,
>   Cut me to pieces with thy keen conceit. (v.ii.397–400)

Unlike the 'Wit' plays there is no 'world-without-end bargain' between the lovers in *Love's Labour's Lost*; after all, as Berowne declares, 'Our wooing doth not end like an old play' (v.ii.860). Nonetheless, the wits do at least kiss the hands of wisdom.

We may now turn to consider which of the 'Wit' plays perhaps gave Shakespeare the idea of reversing the precepts of the educational morality and offered him matter and incident he was to diffuse throughout *Love's Labour's Lost*.

The Marriage of Wit and Science is the only surviving printed version of the 'Wit' plays and it includes all the plot elements summarised above. Moreover, it is a thoroughly romantic piece in which the courtship of Wit and Science is given a far greater prominence than in either the earlier or the later version. There are additional resemblances to note between *The Marriage of Wit and Science* and *Love's Labour's Lost*. Young Wit sends Science a picture of himself as a token of his esteem and seriousness. Later, Reason, Science's father, presents Wit with a token, a 'glasse of Christal cleare' to

> Marke what defectes it wil discover and discrye;
> And so syth judgement rype, and curiouse eye,
> What is a mysse indevor to supplye. (III.iii.842–4)

These tokens are made much of when Wit confronts Reason and Science after his transmutation into a fool. 'The fairings' and 'tokens' of the lords are put to teasing use by the Princess and her ladies. Reason's mirror eventually reflects Wit's blackened face and fool's garb – the truth of his degraded condition. The Princess charmingly embarrasses the Forester by deliberately misunderstanding the meaning of his words 'thou speak'st the fairest shoot' (IV.i.10). She concludes the brief contretemps with,

> Nay, never paint me now!
> Where fair is not, praise cannot mend the brow.
> Here (good my glass) take this for telling true.

As the Arden editor has noted, 'The forester is the mirror that shows the Princess her face at its true value.' In drawing attention to this parallel I hope that I am not seeing through a glass too darkly! Perhaps more convincing is the similarity beteween the pages, Moth and Will. They are impertinently brilliant boys and both are in nicely ambivalent relationships with their respective masters, Armado and Wit. Both are employed as ambassadors of love. Will's embassy to Science wins commendation from Experience: 'I have not harde a meyssage more trymlee done,' and Reason concludes, rightly, 'He hath bene instructed this errand....' Moth the 'herald is a pretty knavish page/That well by heart hath conn'd his embassage' (v.ii.97–8), and, in rehearsal at any rate, satisfies the wits that 'A better speech was never spoke before' (v.ii.110). Will is instrumental in persuading Wit to forswear his promises to Nature and Reason. Word-play between Navarre and the Princess reflects this situation in the Paul's Play.

PRIN. Our Lady help my lord! He'll be forsworn.

FERD. Not for the world, fair madam, by my will.

PRIN. Why, will shall break it; will and nothing else.

FERD. Your ladyship is ignorant of what it is.

PRIN. Were my lord so, his ignorance were wise,
Where now his knowledge must prove ignorance.

(II.i.197–202)

A few years ago Alfred Harbage challenged the prevailing orthodoxy about *Love's Labour's Lost*.[43] His remarkable lecture raised some exceedingly awkward, if not unanswerable, questions for those who would support the claim that the play in its first form belonged to the period 1593–5, and, among other things, drew attention once more to the structural and tonal affinities the play has with those of the Chapel and Paul's boys of the eighties and with the work of John Lyly and others who wrote for them. He found 'it more congenial to imagine *Love's Labour's Lost* originally in the repertory of the boy actors, rather than that of grown men' and he proposed that Shakespeare's play 'in its original form was written for Paul's in 1588–9.'[44] My attempt to show that when Shakespeare conceived the romantic imbroglio between the lords and ladies, he had in mind the moral pattern of the 'Wit' interludes and in particular *The Marriage of Wit and Science*, may perhaps lend substance to his view. From the knowledge and remembrance of that 'Wit' play Shakespeare appears to have begot the root idea which, 'nourished in the womb of pia mater' as Holofernes has it, was eventually 'delivered upon the mellowing of occasion.'

A NOTE ON THE TEXT

In this edition it has been my aim to preserve as much as possible of the original text. Clarification of the meaning, however, has made alteration unavoidable. The text has been repunctuated throughout. A few words, the spellings of which were likely to cause uncertainty, have been changed, and the originals placed in the notes at the foot of the page. Unusual spellings, the result of an attempt to force the rhyme, have been left unaltered. The ligatures ee and oo have been replaced by single vowels in words where

43 '*Love's Labour's Lost* and the Early Shakespeare,' *Stratford Papers on Shakespeare* (Toronto 1962) 107–34, and PQ XLI no. 1 (1962)

44 Harbage 123 and 125

modern usage requires single vowels. Doubled vowels and consonants have been retained. Misprints and turned letters have been silently corrected. Throughout the text the initial use of i for j, v for u, and the medial use of u for v have been silently transposed; but no change has been made to the use of y for i, or the use of 'then' for 'than' and vice versa. Abbreviations have been silently expanded. Emendations are either noted below the text or discussed more fully in the notes. Additions have been inserted within square brackets. The names of all characters have been normalised. In the notes below the text only significant or unusual emendations, readings and suggestions by previous editors have been referred to. More extensive references are offered in the explanatory notes. The following abbreviations are used in the footnotes.

H – W. Carew Hazlitt, 'The Marriage of Wit and Science,' in *Dodsley's Old English Plays*, 2 (London 1874)

F – John S. Farmer, 'The Marriage of Wit and Science,' in *Five Anonymous Plays*, Fourth Series (London 1908)

B – Arthur Brown, *The Marriage of Wit and Science*, Malone Society Reprint, 1960 (1961)

A new and
Pleasaunt enterlude in-
tituled the marriage of Witte
and Science

[Ornament]

Imprinted at London in
Fletestrete, neare unto Sainct
Dunstones churche by
Thomas Marshe
[n.d.]

[CHARACTERS OF THE PLAY]

DAME NATURE
WIT, her son
WILL, his page
REASON
EXPERIENCE, his wife
SCIENCE, daughter of Reason
INSTRUCTION
STUDY
DILIGENCE
SHAME
IDLENESS
IGNORANCE, her son
TEDIOUSNESS, a monster
RECREATION
Companions to Recreation

[ACT I SCENE 1]

[*Enter*] NATURE, WIT AND WILL

[NATURE]

Graunde Lady, mother of every mortall thynge:
Nurse of the worlde, conservatyve of kynd: 5
Cause of encrease, of lyfe and soule the spring,
At whose instincte the noble Heaven doth winde,
To whose award all Creatures are assynde,
I come in place to treate with this my sonne,
For his avayle, howe he the path may fynde   10
Wherby his Race in honour he may runne.
Come tender Childe, unrype and greene for age,
In whom the parent settes her chiefe delite.
Wit is thy name, but farre from wisdome sage,
Tyll tracte of tyme shall worke and frame aryght   15
This perelesse brayne, not yet in perfect plyght
But when it shalbe wrought, me thinkes I see,
As in a glasse before hand with my syghte,
A certaine perfect peece of worke in thee.
And now, so farre as I gesse by signes,   20
Some great attempte is fyxed in thy brest.
Speake on, my sonne, wherto thy harte inclynes,
And let me deale to set thy hart at rest.
He salves the sore that knowes the pacient best,
As I doe thee, my sonne, my chiefest care,   25
In whom my speciall prayse and joye doth rest;
To me therfore these thoughtes of thyne declare.

WIT

Nature, my soveraigne Quene and parent passyng dere,
Whose force I am inforst to know and knowledge every where,   30
This care of myne, though it be bred within my breste,
Yet it is not so rype as yet to brede me great unrest.

---

1 Act and scene heading omitted
2 *Enter ... Will*| Nature, *witte and will*
13 *parent*| paret

19 *thee*| the
29 *parent*| paret
31 *bred*| bread

So runne I to and fro with hap suche as I fynde,
Now fast, now loose, now hot, now cold, unconstant as the wind.
35 I feele my selfe in love, yet not inflamed so,
But causes move me now and then to let suche fancies go,
Whiche causes prevailyng settes eche thing els in doubte,
Much like the nayle that last came in and dryves the former out.
Wherfore my suite is thys; that it woulde please your grace   [A.ii.ᵛ]
40 To settle this unsetled head in some assured place,
To leade me through the thyck, to guyde me al the waye,
To poynt me where I maye atcheve my most desyred praye.
For nowe agayne of late I kyndle in desire,
And pleasure pricketh fourth my youth to feele a greater fyre.
45 What though I be too young to shewe her sport in bed,
Yet are there many in thys lande that at my yeares doe wedde,
And though I wed not yet, yet am I olde inowe
To serve my Lady to my power and to begynne to woo.

NATURE

50 What is that Ladye, sonne, which thus thy hart doth move?

WIT

A Ladye whom it myght be seeme hygh Jove hym self to love.

NATURE

Who taught thee her to love, or hast thou seene her face?

55   WIT
Nor this nor that, but I hard menne talke of her apace.

NATURE

What is her name?

WIT

60 Reason is her sire, Experience her dame;
The Ladye nowe is in her flower and Science is her name.

---

34 *loose*] lose   *the*] that: B. suggests 'ẙ' (= that) has been mistaken for 'ẙ'
45 *too*] to   54 *thee*] the
48 *woo*] woe   61 *flower*] flowers
50 *Ladye*] Ladyes

Loe, where she dwelles! lo, where my harte is all possest!
Loe, where my bodie would abyde! lo, where my soule doth rest!
Her have I borne good wyll these manye yeares tofore,
But nowe she lodgeth in my thought a hundred partes the more;   65
And since I doe perswade my self that thys is she
Which ought above all earthly wyghtes to be most deare to me;
And since I wote not howe to compasse my desyre;
And since for shame I can not now, nor mynd not to retyre,
Helpe on, I you besech, and bring thys thyng about   70
Wythout youre hurte to my great ease, and set all out of doubte.

NATURE

Thou askest more than is in me to gyve;
More than thy cause, more then thy state will beare.
They are two things to able thee to live,   75
And to live so that none should be thy peer.
The first from me proceedeth everye where;
But this by toyle and practise of the mind   [A.iii]
Is set full farre, god wot, and bought full deare
By those that seeke the fruite therof to finde.   80
To match thee then with Science in degree;
To knit that knot that few may reach unto,
I tel thee playne, it lyethe not in me.
Why should I challenge that I cannot do?
But thou must take another way to woo,   85
And beate thy brayne and bende thy Curiouse head,
Both ryde and runne and travayle to and froe,
If thou entend that famous Dame to wed.

WIT

You name your selfe the Lady of this world.   90

NATURE

It is true.

WIT

And can there be within this world a thing too hard for you?

76 *peer*] peare   85 *woo*] woe
83 *thee*] the   94 *too*] to
84 *do*] doe

NATURE

95   My power, it is not absolute in jurisdiction,
For I cognise an other Lord above,
That hath receaved unto his disposition
The soule of man, which he of speciall love
100   To gyfts of grace and learning eke doth move.
A worke so farre beyonde my reach and call,
That in to part of prayse with him my selfe to show
Myght sone procure my well deserved falle.
He makes the frame and [I] receive it soe;
105   No jotte therin altered for my head.
And, as I it recive, I let it goe,
Causyng therin suche sparkles to be bredde,
As he commyttes to me by whom I must be ledde,
Who guides me first and in me guides the rest,
110   All which in their due course and kind are spedde
Of giftes from me such as may serve them best.
To thee, sonne Wit, he will'd me to inspire
The love of knowledge and certayne seedes devine,
Which, ground, might be a meane to bring thee hiere,
115   Yf therunto thy self thou wilt encline.
The massy golde the connyng hand makes fyne:
Good groundes are tilde, as well as are the worste: [A.iii.ᵛ]
The rankest flower will aske a springyng tyme;
So is man's wit unperfit at the first.

120   WIT

If connyng be the key and well of worldly blysse,
My thinketh god might at the first as well endue al with this.

NATURE

As connyng is the kay of blysse, so it is woorthy prayse;
125   The worthiest things are wonne with pain in tract of time alwaies.

104 *I receive*| so H. and F.
112 *will'd*| wild
114 *ground*| so F. ; B. suggests *grown*, see note   *hiere*| ie 'higher' ; H. *here*

119 *man's*| mans   122 *the*| yᵉ
121 *worldly*| wordly   125 *are*| ar *with*| wᵗ

WIT

And yet right worthy things ther are, you wil confesse, I trow,
Which notwithstanding at our birth god doth on us bestow.

NATURE

There are; but such as unto you that have the great to name,   130
I rather that bestow then wynne therby ymmortal fame.

WIT

Fayne would I learne what harme or detriment ensued,
If any man were at his byrth with these good gyftes endued.

NATURE   135

There should be nothing lefte wherin men might excell,
No blame for sinne, no praise to them that had defyned wel.
Vertue should lose her price, and learning would abounde;
And, as man wold admire the thing that echewher might be found,
The great estate, that have of me and fortune what they wil,   140
Shold have no nede to loke to those whose heads are fraght with skil.
The meaner sorte that nowe excells in vertues of the minde
Should not be once accepted there, wher now they succor find;
For gret men should be spedde of al and wold have nede of none;
And he that were not borne to land should lacke to live upon.   145
These and five thousand causes moe which I forbeare to tel,
The noble vertue of the mind have caused there to dwell,
Where none may have accesse but such as can get in
Through many doble dores, through heat, through cold, through thick
                                             and thinne.

WIT   150

Suppose I would addresse my selfe to seeke her out,
And to refuse no paine that lieth there about,
Should I be sure to spede?

NATURE

                              Trust me and have no doubte.   155
Thou canst not Chuse but spede with travell and with tyme;   [A.iv]
These two are they that must dyrect thee how to clime.

139 *as man*| see note
141 *with*| w^t

153 *sure*| suer
156 *travell*| H. travail

[WIT]
With travel and with time, must they needs joyne in one?

160   NATURE
Nor that nor this can do thee good, if they be toke alone.

WIT
Time worketh all with ease, and gyves the greatest dynt:
In tyme softe water dropes can hollowe hardest flynt.
165   Agayne, with labor by it selfe, great matters compaste be.
Even at a gyrde, in very lyttel time or none wee see.
Wherfore in my conceyte good reason it is,
Eyther this with out that to looke, or that with out this.

NATURE
170   Set case thou dyddest attempte to clyme Pernasus hill.
Take tyme, five hundreth thousand yers and longer if thou will.
Trowest thou to touch the top there of by standyng still?
Againe, worke out thy harte, and spend thy selfe with toyle.
Take tyme with all, or elles I dare assure thee of the foyle.

175   WIT
Madame, I trust I have your licence and your leave –
With your good will and so much helpe as you to me can gyve,
With further ayde also, when you shal spye your tyme –
To make a proof to give attempt this famouse hil to clime.
180   And now I here request your blessyng and your prayer,
For sure, before I slepe, I will to yonder forte repaire.

NATURE
I blesse thee here with al such gifts as nature can bestow,
And for thy sake I would they were as many hundred moe.
185   Take therwith all this childe to wayte upon thee stil,
A byrde of myne, some kinne to thee, his name is Will.

158 Wit] Will, see note   177 good will] good wil
159 needs] neds   travel] H. travail   179 proof] proffe
161 thee] the   185 thee] the
174 thee] the   186 Will] Wyll

WIT

Wellcome to me my Will! What service canst thou doe?

WILL

All thinges forsooth, sir, when me liste, and more too.   190

WIT

But when wilt thou list? When I shall list, I trowe!

WILL

Trust not to that, paradventure yea, paradventure noe.

WIT   [A.iv.^{v}]

When I have neede of thee, thou wilt not serve me soe.

WILL

If ye byd me runne, perhappes I will goe.

WIT

Cock soule, this is a boye for the nonse amongest twentie moe!   200

WILL

I am plaine, I tell you, at a worde and a bloe.

WIT

Then must I pricke you, childe, if you be drowned in slouth.

NATURE   205

Agree, you twayne, for I must leave you both.
Farewel, my sonne. Farewel myne owne good Will;
Be ruled by Wit, and be obedient still;
Force thee I cannot, but as farre as lies in me,
I wil helpe thy master to make a good servant of thee.   210
Farrewell.   *Exit* [NATURE]

WIT

Adue, Lady mother, with thankes for al your paine!
And now let me bethincke my self againe and eke again.

190 *too*] to   213 *paine*] peine
209 thee] the

215 To matche with Science is the thinge that I have toke in hande,
A matter of more weight, I see, then I did understande.
Will must be wonne to this, or els it wil be hard;
Will must goe breake the matter first, or els my gaine is marde.
Sir boye! are you content to take such parte for me
220 As god shall sende, and helpe it forth as much as lyes in thee?

WILL

Yea, Mayster, by his wounds, or els cut off this head.

WIT

Come then and let us two devise what trace were best to tredde.
225 Nature is on my syde and Will, my boye, is fast.
There is no doubt I shall obtayne my joyes at last.
                    Exe[u]nt

ACT II SCENE 1

[*Enter*] WIT AND WILL

230   WIT
What, Will! I say, Will boye, come againe, folishe elfe!

                         WILL   [B.i]
I crye you mercy, sir, you are a tall man your selfe.

                          WIT
235 Such a cokbraine as thou art, I never saw the like to it.

                         WILL
Truth, in respect of you that are nothing els but Wit.

                          WIT
Canst thou tel me thy errand, because thou art gone so sone?

222 *off*] of   *this*] his; H. retains *his*   231 *Will boye*] Wilboye
228 Act 2 sena 1   235 *the*] y̅ᵉ
229 *Enter ... Will*] *Witte and Will*   237 *Wit*] Wtt

WILL   240
Can I remember a longe tale of a man in the moone,
With such a circumstance and such flym flam?
I wyll tell at a worde whose servante I am,
Wherfore I come, and what I have to saye,
And cal for her aunswere, before I come awaye.   245
What, should I make a brode tree of every litell shrubbe,
And kepe her a great whyle with a tale of a tubbe?

WIT
Yet thou must commend me to be rich, lusty, pleasaunt and wyse.

WILL   250
I can not commend you but I must make twentie lies.
Rich, quoth you – that appeareth by the port that you kepe –
Even as rich as a newe shorne sheepe;
Of pleasaunt conceiptes, ten busshells to the pecke;
Lusty like a herringe with a bell about his necke;   255
Wyse as a woodcocke; as brage as a bodylouse;
A man of your handes, to matche wyth a mouse.
How say you, are not these proper qualities to prayse you with?

WIT
Leave these mad toyes of thyne and come to the pythe.   260
One part of the errande should have bene
To give her this picture of mine to be seene,
And to request her the same to accepte
Safely, untill my comminge to be kepte,
Which I suspende till thy returne and then,   265
If it like her Ladyshippe to appoint me where and when,
I will waite upon her gladly out of hande.

WILL
Sir, let me alone; your mynde I understand.
I will handle the matter so that you shall owe me thankes.   270
But what if she finde fault with these spindle shankes,   [B.iᵛ]
Or els with these blacke spottes on your nose?

WIT
In fayth, sir boy, this talke deserveth blowes.

275
WILL

You will not misuse your best servant, I suppose?
For, by his nayles and by his fingers too,
I will marre your mariage if you do.

WIT

280   I praye thee goe thy wayes and leave this clatter.

WILL

First shal I be so bold to breake to you a matter.

WIT

Tushe! Thou art disposed to spende wordes in wast,
285   And yet thou knowest this busines asketh hast.

WILL

But even two wordes, and then I am gon.

WIT

If it be worth the hearing, say on.

290
WILL

I would not have you thinke that I, for my part,
From my promise or from your service wil depart;
But yet now and then it goeth to my hart,
When I thinke how this mariage maye be to my smart.

295
WIT

Why so?

WILL

I would tell you the cause, if I durst for shame.

WIT

300   Speke hardely what thou wilt without any blame.

277 *too*] toe
278 *do*] 'clitter' appears immediately after this word; see note
280 *thee*] the

WILL

I am not disposed as yet to be tame,
And therfore I am loth to be under a Dame.
Now you are a Bachiler, a man may sone win you.
Me thinks there is some good felowshippe in you.   305
We may laugh and be mery at bord and at bedde.
You are not so testy as those that be wedde.
Myld in behavior and loth to fall out,
You may runne, you may ryde and rove round about,
With wealth at your will and all thinge at ease,   [B.ii]
Free, franke and lusty, esye to please.
But when you be clogged and tyed by the toe
So faste that you shal not have power to let goe,
You will tell me another lesson sone after,
And cry *peccavi* too, except your lucke be the better.   315
Then farewel goodfellowshyp, then come at a call,
Then waite at an inche, you idle knaves all.
Then sparyng and pynchinge and nothing of gift,
No talke with our maister, but al for his thrift.
Solemne and sower and angry as a waspe,   320
Althinges must be kept under locke and haspe.
At that which will make me to fare ful ill,
All your care shalbe to hamper poore Will.

WIT

I warrant thee, for that, take thou no thought.   325
Thou shalt be made of, whosoever be set at nought;
As dere to me as myne owne dere brother,
Whosoever be one, thou shalt be an other.

WILL

Yea, but your wyfe wyl play the shrew; perdy, it is she that I feare.

WIT

Thy message wyll cause her some favor to beare   332
For my sake and thy sake, and for her owne likewyse,
If thou use thy selfe discretly in this enterpryse.

323 *Will*] wyll   325 *thee*] the

WILL

335   She hath a father, a testy sower old man;
I doubt lest he and I shall fall out nowe and than.

WIT

Give hym fayre words, forbeare him for his age.
340   Thou must consider hym to be auncient and sage.
Shew thy selfe officious and servisable stil,
And then shall Reason make very muche of Will.

WILL

If your wyfe be ever complayning, how then?

345   WIT

My wyfe wyll have nothing to doe wyth my men.

WILL

If she doe, beleve her not in any wyse.
And when you once perceyve her stomacke to aryse,   [B.ii^v]
350   Then cut her short at the first, and you shall see
A mervaylouse vertue in that medisen to be.
Give her not the bridle for a yeare or twayne,
And you shal see her bridle it without a reine.
Breake her betymes and bring her under by force,
355   Or elles the graye Mare wil be the better horse.

WIT

If thou have done, begone, and spende no time in vayne.

WILL

Where shal I fynde you, when I come againe?

360   WIT

At home.   [*Exit* WIT]

WILL

Good enough! Take your ease, let me alone with this.
Surely a treasure of all treasures it is
365   To serve such a mayster as I hope him to bee,
And to have such a servant as he hath of mee;

For I am quicke, nimbell, proper and nise.
He is ful good, gentle, sober and wyse.
He is full loth to chide or to checke,
And I am as willinge to serve at a becke.   370
He orders me well and speakes me so fayre,
That, for his sake, no travayle I must spare.
But now am I come to the gate of this Ladye,
I wyll pause awhyle to frame myne errande fynelye.
And loe, wher she commeth; yet will I not come nye her.   375
But amonge these fellowes wyl I stande to eye her.

ACT II SCENE 2

[Enter] REASON, EXPERIENCE [and] SCIENCE

SCIENCE

My Parentes, ye knowe howe many fall in lappes   380
That do ascribe to me the cause of their mishappes;
Howe many seeke that come too short of their desyre;
Howe many do attempt that dayly do retire;
How many rove about the marke on every syde;
How many thinke to hit, when they are much too wyde;   385
Howe many runne too farre; how many light too lowe;
Howe fewe to good effecte their travayle do bestowe,
And howe all these impute their losses unto mee –   [B.iii]
Should I have joye to thinke of mariage, nowe trowe ye?
What doth the worlde? My love alone, say they,   390
Is bought so dere that life and goodes for it must paye.
Stronge youth must spende it selfe; and yet, when al is done,
We hear of fewe or none that have this Lady wonne.
On me they make outcryes, and charge me with the bloud
Of those that for my sake adventure life and good.   395

374 *errande*] errante; H. errant
377 Act 2 sena 2
378 *Enter ... Science*] *Reason, Experience, Science and Will*
380 *lappes*] H. and F. *lapse*, see note
382 *too*] to   386 ¹ & ²*too*] to
385 *too*] to   393 *hear*] here

This griefe doth wound my hart so, that suters more as yet
I se no cause nor reason why I shold admyt.

REASON

Ah, daughter, say not so. There is great cause and skill
400   For which you shold mislike to live unmaried thus alone.
What comfort can you have remayning thus unknowne?
How shal the common wealth by you advaunced be,
If you abide enclosed here, where no man may you see?
It is not for your state, your selfe to take the payne
405   All straungers that resort to you to entertayne:
To suffer free accesse of all that come and goe:
To be at eche man's call: to travayle too and fro:
What then! Synce god hath plast such treasure in your brest,
Wherwith so many thousand thinke by you to be refresht,
410   Needes must you have some one of hyd and secret trust
By whom these things may be well ordered and discuste.
To him you must disclose the depth of all your thought;
By him, as time shall serve, all matters must be wrought;
To hym above you must content your selfe to be at call;
415   Ye must be his, he must be yours, he must be al in all.

EXPERIENCE

My Lord your father telles you truth, perdie!
And that in time your selfe shall fynde and trye.

SCIENCE

420   I could aledge more then as yet I have sayde,
But I must yelde, and you muste be obayed.
Fall oute as it will, there is no helpe, I see,
Some one or other in time must mary me.

WILL   [*Advances*]

425   In time? Nay, out of hand, Madame, if it please you.
In fayth, I knowe a yonker that will ease you,
A lyvelye younge gentilman, as freshe as any flower,   [B.iiiᵛ]
That wyll not sticke to marye you within this hower.

396 *that*] yͭ
407 *man's call*] mannes cal
408 *then*] the
410 *hyd*] see note

SCIENCE

Such haste myght hapelye turne to wast to some;   430
But I pray thee, my pretye boye, whence art thou come?

WILL

If it pleace youre good Ladyshype to accepte me so,
I have a solemne message to tel ere I goe;
Not anye thynge in secrete your honour to stayne,   435
But in the presence and hearinge of you twayne.

REASON

Speake.

WILL

The Lady of this world, which Lady Nature hyght,   440
Hath one, a peereles sonne, in whom she taketh delyght.
On hym she chargeth me to be an tendant styll;
Both kynde to her, hys name is Wit, my name is Will.
The noble chyld doth feele the force of cupyde's flame
And sendeth now for ease by counsel of hys dame.   445
Hys mother taught hym fyrst to love, whyle he was younge,
Which love with age encreaseth sore and waxeth wondrous stronge.
For verye fame displayes youre bountye more and more,
And at thys pyntch he burneth so as never heretofore.
Not fantasy's force, not vayne and Idle toyes of love,   450
Not hope of that whych commenlye doth other suiters move,
But fixed fast good wyll that never shall relent,
And vertue's force that shines in you, bade him geve this attempte.
He hath no neade of wealth; he wooes not for youre good.
His kynred is such, he nede not to seke to match with noble bloud. 455
Such store of fryndes that, where he list, he may commaunde,
And none so hardy to presume hys pleasure to withstand.
Youre self it is, your vertue and youre grace,
Youre noble giftes, youre endles praise in every place;

430 *some*| sum
433 *so*| soo
434 *ere*| or
442 *me*| men   *an tendant*| antendant; see note

450 *fantasy's*| fanteses
453 *that*| y^t
456 *list*| lest
459 *praise*| prayes

460 You alone, I saye, the marke that he would hit,
    The hoped joye, the dearest pray, that can befale to wit.

EXPERIENCE

I have not harde a meyssage more trymlee done.

SCIENCE

465 Nor I. What age art thou of, my good sonne?

WILL

[B.iv]

Betwene eleven and twelve, Madame, more or lesse.

REASON

He hath bene instructed this errand, as I gesse.

SCIENCE

470 How old is the gentilman thy maister, canst thou tell?

WILL

Seventene or there aboute, I wote not verye well.

SCIENCE

475 What stature, of what makyng, what kynde of port beares he?

WILL

Such as youre Ladyshipe can not myslike, trust me;
Well growen, wel made, a stripling clean and taule,
Wel favored, somwhat black and manlye therewithal.
480 And that you may conceave hys personage the better,
Lo, here of hym the verye shape and lively picture!
Thys hath he sente to you to viewe and to behoulde.
I dare advouch no Joynt therin, no Jote, to be controulde.

SCIENCE

485 In good fayth, I thancke thy mayster with my hart.
    I perceyve that Nature in him hath done her part.

---

461 *to wit*| to witte; H. and F. *to Wit*   481 *here*| heare *verye*| vearye
467 *twelve*| xii   486 *Nature*| nature

WILL

Farther, if it please your honour to knowe,
My master would be glad to runne, ryde or goe
At your commaundment to any place farre or neere,   490
To have but a sight of your Ladyshippe there.
I beseech you appoint him the place and the hower.
You shal se how redyly to you he will scoure.

REASON

Do soe.   495

EXPERIENCE

Yea, in any wise, daughter, for heare you mee,
He semeth a right worthy and trymme younge man to bee.

SCIENCE

Command me then to Wit, and let him understande   500
That I accept with all my hart this present at his hande;
And that I would be glad, when he doth see his tyme,
To heare and se him face to face within this house of myne.
Then maye he breake his mind and talke with me his fyll.
Tyll then, adew, both hee and thou myne owne swete little Will.   505

Exe[u]nt SCIENCE, REASON [*and*] EXPERIENCE   [B.iv^v]

ACT II SCENE 3

WILL

Ah, flattering Queene, how neatly she can talke!   510
How minionly she tryps; how sadlye she can walke!
Well, wanton, yet beware that ye be sound and sure,
Fayre wordes are wont oft times fayre women to allure.
Nowe must I get me home and make report of this
To him that thinkes it longe till my returne, I wys.   [*Exit*]

497 *Yea*| Ye   *daughter*| daugher   *heare*| heere
507 Act 2 sena 3

515 ACT III SCENE 1

[Enter] WIT *and* WILL

WIT
Sayst thou me so, boye, will she have me in deede?

WILL
520 Be of good cheere, sir, I warrant you to spede.

WIT
Did both her parentes speake wel to her of mee?

WILL
As hart can thinke: go on, and you shall see.

525 WIT
How toke she the picture; how lyketh she my person?

WILL
She never had done toting and loking theron.

WIT
530 And must I come to talke with her my fyll?

WILL
When soever you please, and as oft as you will.

WIT
O my sweet boy, how shall I recompence
535 Thy faythfull hart and painfull diligence?
My hope, my stay, my wealth, the kaye of al my joye!

WILL
I praye you, sir, call me your man and not your boy.

515 Act 3 sena 1   534 *sweet* | sweat
516 *Enter … Will.* | *Witte and Will*

WIT

Thou shalt be what thou wilt, all in all. 540

WILL

Promise me faythfully that, if your wyfe brall,
Or set her father to checke me out of measure,
You will not see me abused to their pleasure. [c.i]

WIT 545

Give me thy hande; take here my fayth and troth.
I wil maintayne thee, how soever the world goeth.

ACT III SCENE [2]

WIT

What shall we doe? Shall we stande lingring here? 550

WILL

If you be a man, preasse in and go neare.

WIT

What if there be some other suter there?

WILL 555

And if there be, yet nede you not to feare. ·

WIT [c.iii^v, l.14]

Perhappes we may fynd them at this time in bedde.

WILL

So much the rather loke you to be sped. 560
Care for no more, but once to come within her,
And when you have done, then let another win her.

544 *see*| se
548 Act 3 sena 1
556 After this line the text is dislocated, see introduction.

WIT

To come within her, child? What meanst thou by that?

565   WILL

One masse for a penye, you know what is what!

WIT

Heard you ever such a counsell of such a Jacke Sprot?

WILL

570   Why, sir, do ye thinke to doe any good,
       If ye stande in a corner like Roben Hood?
       Nay, you must stoute it, and face it out with the best.
       Set on a good countenaunce; make the most of the lest.
       Who soever skippe in, loke to your part,
575   Any whyle you live, beware of a false hart.

WIT

Both blame and shame rashe boldnes doth breede.

WILL

You must adventure both; spare to speake, spare to speede.
580   What, tell you me of shame! It is shame to steale a horse.

WIT

More hast then good speede makes many fare the worse.

WILL   [c.iv]

But he that takes not such time, while he maye,
585   Shal leape at a whyting, when time is a waye.

WIT

But he that leapes before he loke, good sonne,
Maye leape in the myre, and mysse when he hath done.

[Enter SCIENCE, REASON and EXPERIENCE]

568 Heard] Hard   Jacke Sprot] Iacke sprot
571 Roben Hood] Roben hood

SCIENCE   590

Me thinke I heare the voyce of Will, Wit's boye.

WIT

I see her come, my sorow and my Joye,
My salve and yet my sore, my comfort and my care,
The causer of my wound, and yet the well of my welfare.   595
O happye wight, that have the saynte of your request!
O hoples hope, that holdeth me from that which likes me best!
Twixte hope and feare I stande, to marre or els to make;
This day to be relieved quite, or else my death wound to take.

REASON   600

Here let us rest a whyle and pause all three.

EXPERIENCE

Daughter, sit downe. Belike this same is he.

WILL

Be of good chere, sir; be ruled by me.   605
Women are best pleased, tyll they be used homely.
Loke her in the face and tell your tale stoutely.

WIT

O pearle of passing price, sent downe from god on hye!
The swetest beauty to entise, that hath bene sene with eye: 610
The wel of wealth to all, that no man doth annoye:
The kaye of Kingedomes and the stall of everlasting joye:
The treasure and the store, whom al good things began:
The nurse of Lady Wisdom's lore; the lincke of man and man,
What wordes shal me suffice to utter my desyre?   615
What heate of talke shal I devise for to expresse my fyer?
I burne and yet I frese; I flame and coole as fast.
In hope to wyn and for to lese, my pensivenes doth last.

591 *Wit's*] Wittes   609 *price*] pryse
593 ¹*my*] her   612 *stall*] steale, see note
595 *well*] wil   614 *Wisdom's*] wysedoms
599 *relieved quite*] reliued quit   618 *lese*] ie, 'lose,' see note

Why should my dulled spryte apal my courage so?
620 O salve my sore, or sley me quite by saying yea or no!
You are the marke at whome I shot to hit or misse.
My life it stayes on you alone; to you my sute it is.
A mate not much unmete, with you some griefe to fynde,   [c.iv^v]
Dame Nature's sonne, my name is Wit, that fancieth you by kind;
625 And here I come this day to wayte and to attende,
In hope to have my hoped pray, or elles my life to ende.

SCIENCE

Good cause there is wherfore I should embrase
This loving hart whyche you have borne to me;
630 And glad I am that we both in place,
Ech one of us eche other's lookes to see.
Your picture and your person doth agree.
Your princelike port and ecke your noble face,
Wherin so many sygnes of vertue be,
635 That I must needes be moved in your case.

REASON

Friend Wit, are you the man in dede whych you intend?
Can you be well content untill your life doth ende
To joyne and knit most sure with this my daughter here,
640 And unto her alone your fixed fayth to beare?

WIT

As I am bente to this, so let my suite be sped.
If I do fayle, ten Thousande plagues and more lighte on my head.

EXPERIENCE

645 There are that promise fayre, and meane as well,
As any here can thinke, or tongue can tell,
Which at the first are hot, and kindle in desyre,
But in one month or twayne, quite quenched is the fyre.
Such is the trade of youth whome fancy's force doth lede,
650 Whose love is only at the plonge and cannot longe procede.

---

620 *sley*| slee
623 *A mate*| Amitie, see note
624 *Nature's*| Natures   *that*| y^t

646 *here*| heare, see note
648 *quite*| quit
649 *fancy's*| famies

WIT

Credit my wordes, and ye shall find me true.

EXPERIENCE

Suppose you kepe not touch, who shuld this bargaine rue?

WIT   655

I will be sworne here solemnly before you both.

EXPERIENCE

Who breaketh promise wil not sticke likewyse to breake his othe.

WIT

I wyll be bound in all that ever I can make.   660

EXPERIENCE   [D.i]

What good were that to us, if we th'advantage take?

WIT

Wyll neyther promyse serve, nor othe, nor bandes?
What other assuraunce wyll ye aske at my handes?   665

WILL

My maister is a gentilman, I tell you, and his word,
I would you knewe it, shall with his deedes accord.

REASON

We know not whom to trust, the world is so ill.   670

WILL

In dede, sir, as you say, you may mend when ye wyll.
But in good earnest, Madam, speake – off or on?
Shal we speede at your hand, or shall we begone?
I love not these delayes. Say so, if we shall have you;   675
If not, say no, and let another crave you.

WIT [Aside]

Soft and fayre, sir boye. You talke you wot not what.

662 *th'advantage* | thaduantage   675 *these* | this
673 *off* | of

WILL   [*Aside*]

680   Can you abyde to be driven off wyth this and that?
Can they aske any more then good assuraunce at your hands?

EXPERIENCE

All is now too litle, sonne, as the matter standes.

WILL

685   If al be too little, both goodes and landes,
I know not what will please you, except Darbye's bandes.

[SCIENCE]

I have an enemy, my frend Wit, a mortal foe to me,
And therwithall the greatest plague that can befall to thee.

690   WIT

Must I fyght wyth him?

REASON

Can you fyght, if neede be?

WILL

695   If any such thing fall, count the charge to me.
Trouble not your selfe.

WIT

Hould thy peace, elfe!

SCIENCE

700   Hear out my tale. I have a mortall foe
That lurketh in the woode hereby, as you come and goe.   [D.iᵛ]
This monstrous Giant beares a grudge to me and mine,
And wyll attempt to kepe thee backe from this desier of thine.
The bane of youth, the roote of ruine and destres,
705   Devouring those that sue to me, his name is Tediousness.
No soner he espyes the noble Wit beginne
To styr and payne him selfe the love of me to winne,

680 *off*] of
683, 685 *too*] to
688–9 These lines are erroneously given to Will.
688 *foe*] fo

689 *thee*] the
700 *Hear*] Here
701 *hereby*] hearby
707 *him selfe*] it selfe

But forth he steppes and with strong hands, by might and maine,
He beates and buffettes downe the force and livelynes of braine.
That done, in deepe dispayre he drownes him villanously.   710
Ten thousand suters in a yere are cast away therby.
Now, if your mind be surelye fixed soe,
That for no toyle nor cost my love you will forgoe,
Bethinke you well, and of this monster take good heede;
Then may you have with me the greater hope to speede.   715
Herein use good advise to make you strong and stout
To fend and kepe him off a whyle, untill his rage be out.
Then, when you feele your selfe well able to prevayle,
Byd you the battell, and that so coragiously assayle.
If you can wyn the field, present me wyth his head.   720
I aske no more, and I forthwith shall be your owne to bedde.

WIT

Il might I thrive, and lacke that likes me best,
If I be not a scourge to him that bredes your unrest.
Madam, assure your selfe, he lives not in the land   725
Wyth whom I would not in your cause encounter hand to hand.
And, as for Tediousness that wretch, your common foe,
Let me alone; we twayne shall cope before I sleape, I troe.
Untill I bringe his head to you upon a speare,   [c.i, l.14]
I will not loke you in the face, nor in your syght appeare.   730

REASON

Nay, Wit, advise your selfe and pause a while,
Or els this hast of yours will you beguile.

SCIENCE

No hast but good; take tyme and learne to fyghte;   735
Learne to assault; learne to defende a ryght.
Your matche is monstrous to beholde and full of might
Whom you must vanquish, not by force but by slyght.

WIT

Madame, stande to your promyse. If I wynne, I am sped,   740
Am I not?

717 *fend*] send *off*] of

SCIENCE

Yea, trulye.

[WIT]

745 Good enough, if we fyght not, I would we weare dead.
No man shal stay us that beres a head.

EXPERIENCE

Young man, a word or twayne, and then adue.
Your yeares are fewe, your practise grene and newe;
750 Marke what I saye, and ye shal fynde it true.
You are the fyrst that shall this rashnes rue.
Be ruled here; our counsell do therafter.
Lay good ground, your worke shal be the faster;
This hedlong hast may soner misse then hit;
755 Take hede both of Wit's wyll and wilfull wit.   [c.iⱽ]
We have within a gentilman, our retayner and our friend,
With servauntes twayne that do on him attende.
Instruction, Study, Diligence – these three
At your commaundement in this attempt shalbe.
760 Hear them in stede of us, and as they shall devyse,
So hardely cast our cardes in this enterpryse.
I will send them to you, and leave you for now.

WIT

The more company the merier! Boy, what saist thou?

765   WILL

It is a good faulte to have more than enowe.
I care not, so as we may pul the knave downe.
I would we were at it, I passe not how sone.

WIT

770 If it shal please you to send those three hyther,
We wyll follow your counsell and go together.
                    [Exeunt EXPERIENCE and SCIENCE]

744 Wit| Will, see note   760 Hear| Here
755 Wit's| Wittes   767 knave| knaues

WILL

I warrant her a shrewe, whosoever be an other.
God make the daughter good, I like not the mother.   775

REASON

Yet would not I for no good to have forgone her.

WILL

Mary, sir, in deede she talkes and takes on her
Lyke a Dame, nay, like a Dutches or a queene,   780
Wyth such a solemnitie as I have not seene.

REASON

She is a queene, I tell thee, in her degree.

WILL

Let her be what she list, with a vengaunce for me.   785
I will keepe me out of her reach, if I can.

REASON

If this mariage goe forward, thou must be her man.

WILL

Mariage or mariage not, be shrewe me than!   790
I have but one maister, and I will serve no moe,
And if he anger me, I wil forsake him too.

REASON

She shal not hurt thee, unless her cause be juster.

WILL   [c.ii]

By the fayth of my bodye, sir, I intend not to trust her.

REASON

Whye?

WILL

Take me this woman that talkes so roundly,   800
That be so wyse, that reason so soundly,

792 *too*| to   794 *thee*| the

That loke so narrow, that speake so shryll,
Their words are not so curst, but their deedes are as ill.

REASON

805   It is but thy fansy. I see no such thing in her.

WILL

Perhappes you had never occasion to try her.

REASON

That were great marvayle in so many yeares.

810   <center>WILL</center>

She hath wonne the mastery of you, it appeares.

WIT

Will, quiet your selfe, thou shalt take no wronge.
Me thinke oure three companions tary very longe.

815   <center>ACT III SCENE 3</center>

[Enter] INSTRUCTION, STUDY [and] DILIGENCE

INSTRUCTION

Sir, we are come to know your pleasure.

REASON

820   You are come in good tyme, Instruction, our treasure.
This Gentilman craveth your acquaintaunce and ayde.
What you may do for him, let him not be denayde.

WIT

Welcome, good fellowes! Wyll ye dwell wyth me?

825   <center>DILIGENCE</center>

If all partes be pleased, content are we.

813 *Will*] Well, see note   815 *Act 3 sena 3*
816 *Enter ... Diligence*]*Instruction, Studie, Diligence, Reason, Witte, Will*

WIT

Wellcome, Instruction, wyth al my hart.

WILL   [*Aside*]

What, three newe servaunts! Then farewell my part.   830

INSTRUCTION

I hartely thanke you, and loke what I can doe;
It shalbe always redye to pleasure you.

REASON   [c.ii^v]

Consider and talke together with these,   835
And you shall fynd in your travayle great ease.
Take here of me, before I take my leave,
This glasse of Christal cleare, which I you geave.
Accept it, and reserve it for my sake most sure;
Much good to you in time it may procure.   840
Behold your selfe therin, and view and prye;
Marke what defectes it wil discover and discrye;
And so wyth judgement rype, and curiouse eye,
What is a mysse indevor to supplye.
Farewell!   845

WIT

Farewell to you, right honourable sir,
And commend me to my love, my harte's desyre.
Let her thinke on me, when she sees me not, and wyshe me wel.

WILL   850

Fare wel mayster Reason, thincke upon us, when you see us not,
And in any wyse, let not Will be forgot.   [*Exit* REASON]

WIT

Synce I must take advise and counsell of you three,
I must entreat you all to dwell in house wyth me,   855
And loke what order you shall prescribe as needefull;
To kepe the same you shall fynd me as heedefull.
Come.

836 *ease*] e <a, see note   841 *Behold*] Bedold

INSTRUCTION

860 Come.

WILL

Goe.   [*Exeunt omnes*]

ACT IV SCENE 1

[*Enter*] WIT, WILL, INSTRUCTION, STUDY [*and*] DILIGENCE

865   WILL
[*To Instruction*] Tushe, tushe, Instruction, your talke is of no force.
You tell us a tale of a rosted horse.
[*To Wit*] Wit, by hys woundes, except we set to it,
As fast as we make, these fellowes wyll undo it.
870 Their talke is nothing but 'soft,' and 'fayre,' and 'tary.'
If you folow their counsell, you shall never mary.

INSTRUCTION   [c.iii]
To followe our counsayle youre charge and promys was.

WIT

875 I would I had never knowen you, by the masse!
Muste I looke so longe and spend my lyfe wyth toyle?
Naye, sure, I will eyther wynne it, or take the foyle.

STUDY
The surer is your grounde, the better you shall beare it.

880   WILL
Ground us no ground, let him winne it and weare it.

INSTRUCTION
Good sir, be ruled, and leave this pevish elfe.

863 Act 4 sena 1
864 *Enter ... Diligence*] *Witte, Will, Instruction, Studie, Diligence*
868 *Wit*] Whych, see note
869 *these*] this

WIT

I had even as lief ye bad me hange my selfe.   885
Leave him? No, no, I would you all knewe,
You be but loyterers to him; my Will telles me true.
I could be content with a weke, yea, a month or twaine,
But three or four yeares! Mary, that were a payne
So longe to kepe me, and lyve like a hogge.   890

WILL

A life, wythall my hart, I would not wyshe a dogge.

WIT

Wyll a weke serve?

STUDY   895

Noo.

WIT

A monthe?

STUDY

Neyther.   900

WIT

Two?

STUDY

Not so.

INSTRUCTION   905

No, nor so many moe.

WIT

Then farewell all, for as I hope to thrive,
I wyll prove him, ere I sleape, if I be alive.
And if ye be mine, and good fellowes all three,   910
Goe thyther out of hand, and take your chaunce wyth mee.

885 *lief*] leafe   902 *Two?*] Noo, see note
889 *three or four*] 3 or 4   909 *ere*] or
890 *lyve*] lye

INSTRUCTION [c.iiiᵛ]

For my part, I know I can do you no good.

WILL

915 You are a proper man of your handes, by the Roode!
Yet welfare hym that never his maister forsaketh.

WIT

What sayst thou, Study?

STUDY

920 My head aketh.

WIT

Out upon thee, coward! Speak, Diligence.

[DILIGENCE]

Agaynst Instruction's mynd, I am lothe to go hence;
925 Yet I will make one, rather than you should lacke.

WILL [D.iᵛ, l.29]

Lustely spoken! Let me claw thee by the backe.
Howe say you now, sir! Here are three agaynst twayne.

STUDY

930 Go, that go list, I wil at home remayne.
I have more neede to take a nappe in my bedde.

WILL

Do soe, and here you couche a codde's head.

INSTRUCTION

935 Well, since it wyl none otherwyse frame,
Let us twayne, Study, and retourn from whens we came.

STUDY [D.ii]

Agreed!   [Exeunt STUDY and INSTRUCTION]

922 thee] the   936 see note
923 [Diligence]] see note   938 sd Exeunt ... Instruction] Exit

WIT

And let us three bestyre our selves like men. 940
Unlikely thinges are brought to passe by courage now and then.
My Will be alwayes prest, and ready at an ynche.
To save thy selfe, to succour me, to helpe at every pinche.
Both twayne on eyther syde, assaulte him if ye can,
And you shal see me in the middes, howe I wil play the man. 945
Thys is the deadly denne, as farre as I perceave.
Approche we neere and valiantly let us the onset geve.
Come forth thou monster fell, in drowsy darkenes hydde,
For here is Wit, Dame Nature's sonne, that doth thee battaile bid.

ACT IV SCENE 2 950

[Enter] TEDIOUSNESS

TEDIOUSNESS

What pryncox have we heere that dares me to assayle?
Alas, poore boy, and weenest thou against me to prevaile?
Full smal was he thy frend, whoever sent thee hyther, 955
For I must drive thee backe with shame, or slay thee altogether.

WIT

Great bost, small rost! I warrant thee, do thy best!
Thy head must serve my tourne this day, to set my hart at rest.

WILL 960

And I must have a legge of thee, if I can catche it.

TEDIOUSNESS   *Fight; strike at* WILL
First, I must quise this brayne of thine, if I can reach it.

942 *Will*] wyll	954 *weenest*] winest
947 *onset*] vnset	956 ¹ & ² *thee*] the
949 *that*] y̌	961 *thee*] the
950 Act 4 sena 2	962 *Will*] will
951 *Enter Tediousness*] *Tediousness,*	963 *quise*] see note
Witte, Will, Diligence	

WIT

965   Well shifted Will; now have at thee, sir knave.

TEDIOUSNESS

These friscoles shal not serve your tourne for al your vauntes so brave.
Hoh, hoh! Did I not tell thee, thou camst to thy payne.   [*He fells* WIT]

DILIGENCE

970   Helpe, helpe, helpe, our maister is slaine!   [*Exit*]

WILL

Helpe, helpe, helpe! etc.   [*Exit*]

TEDIOUSNESS

Where are these lustye blouds that make their matche with mee?
975   Here lyes a pattorne for them all to loke at and to see,
To teach them to conspire against my force and might,   [D.ii^v]
To promise for their woman's love to vanquishe me in fight.
Nowe let them goe and crake howe wiselye they have sped;
Such is the end of those that seke this curious Dame to wed.
980   Hoh, hoh, hoh!   [*Exit*]

ACT IV SCENE 3

[*Enter*] WILL, RECREATION [*and her companion(s)*]

WILL   *Rub and chafe him*
For godde's love, hast! See, loe, where he doth lye!

985   RECREATION
He is not cold, I warrant him, aye.   *Singe* [*both*]

Give a legge, geve an arme, aryse, aryse!
Hould up thy head, lift us thy eyes!

981 Act 4 sena 3   986 *aye*] I
982 *Enter ... companion(s)*] *Will, Recreation, Witte*   987 *Singe*] see note
983 sd *Rub and chafe him* printed in BL

1 A legge to stand up right,
2 An arme to fyght amayne,   990
1 The head to hould thy braynes in plight,
2 The eyes to loke agayne.
[1] Awake ye drowned powers!
    Ye sprites, for-dull with toyle,
    Resyne to me this care of yours,   995
    And from dead sleape recoyle.
    Thinke not upon your lothsome lucke,
    But arise and daunce with us a plucke.
      Both sing 'Give a legge' as is before.
 2 What thoughe thou hast not hit   1000
    The toppe of thy desyre,
    Tyme is not soo farre spent as yit
    To cause thee to retyre.
    Arise and ease thy self of payne,
    And make thee stronge to fight agayne.   1005
      Singe bothe ['Give a legge,' etc.]
[1] Let not thy foes rejoyse,
    Let not thy frendes lament,
    Let not thy Lady's ruful voice
    In sobbes and sighes be spent.   1010
    Thy fayth is plight, forget it not,
    Twixt her and thee to knit the knot.
      Singe [both,] 'Give a legge,' etc.
[2] This is no deadly wounde;   [D.iii]
    It may be cured well.   1015
    Se here what Phisicke we have found.
    Thy sorowes to expell.   WIT *lyfting himselfe up, sitting on*
                                        the grounde

    The way is plaine, the marcke is fayre,
    Lodge not thy selfe in deepe despaire.

            [WIT]   1020
What noise is this that ringeth in my eares?
Her noyse that greveth my myshap with teares.

1003 *thee*] the   1013 *Singe ... etc.*] Singe/Gyue a legge &c. in BL
1009 *Lady's*] Ladies   1020 *Wit*] Will, see note
1012 *thee*] the

Ah, my mishap, my desperate mishap!
On whom ill fortune poureth downe all mishap at a clappe,
1025 What shall become of me, where shal I hyde my head?
Oh, what a death is it to live for him that would be dead!
But since it chanceth so, what ever wyght thou be
That fyndeth me here in heavy plight, goe, tel her this from me.
Causles I perishe here and cause to curse I have
1030 The time that erst I lyved to love; and now must die her slave.
The matche was over much for me, she understoode.
Alas, why hath she this delite to lap in giltles blode?
How did I give her cause to shewe me this despyght,
To matche me wher she wist full wel I should be slaine in fight?
1035 But go, and tell her playne, although too late for me,
Accursed be the time and hower, which first I did her see.
Accursed be the wyght that will'd me first thereto,
And cursed be they all at once that had therwith to doe.
Nowe get thee hence in hast, and suffer me to die,
1040 Whom scornful chaunce and lawles love have slaine most
trayterouslye.

RECREATION

O noble Wit, the miracle of God and eke of Nature,
Why cursest thou thy selfe and every other creature?
What causeth thee thine innocent deare Lady to accuse?
1045 Who would lament it more then she to heare this wofull newes?
Why wylt thou dye, wheras thou mayst be sure of health,
Wheras thou seeth a playne path waye to worship and to wealth?
Not every foyle doth make a fal, nor every foyle doth slaye.
Comfort thy selfe! be sure thy lucke wyll mend from day to daye.

1050   WILL
These gentil newes of good Will are come to make you sound.
They know which way to salve your sore, and how to cure your
wound. [D.iii]
Good sir, be ruled by her then, and pluck your spirite to you.
There is no doubt but you shall find your loving lady true.

1024 *On*| In
1035 *too*| to
1037 *will'd*| wilde
1039 *thee*| the

1044 *thee*| the
1045 *heare*| here
1051 *These*| This, see note

WIT

Ah, Will, art thou alive? That doth my hart some ease.
The sight of thee, swete boy, my sorowes doth appeace.
How hast thou scapte? What fortune thee befell?

WILL

It was no trusting to my handes, my heeles did serve me wel.   1060
I ran wyth open mouth to cry for helpe amayne,
And, as good fortune would, I hit upon these twayne.

WIT

I thanke both thee and them. What wyll ye have me do?

RECREATION   1065

To ryse and daunce a litle space with us two.

WIT

What then?

RECREATION

That done, rapayre agayne to Study and Instruction.   1070
Take better hould by their advise your foe to set upon.

WIT

Can any recompence recover this my fall?

RECREATION   1075

My life to yours, it may be mended all.

WIT

Speake, Will.

WILL

I have no doubt, sir, it shalbe as you would wishe.

WIT   1080

But yet this repulse of myne they wyll lay in my dishe.

1057, 1058 *thee*| the

RECREATION

No man shall let them know therof, unlesse your selfe do it.

WIT

1085 On that condicion, a god's name, fall we to it.

WILL

Naye, stande we to it, and let us fall no more.

WIT

Will daunsing serve, and I will daunce until my bones be sore.

1090 Pype us up a Galiard, mynstrel, to begynne.   [WIT *and* RECREATION

dance]

WILL [*To* RECREATION'*s companion*]   [D.iv]

Come Damsell, in good fayth, and let me have you in.

Let WILL *call for daunces, one after an other*

RECREATION

1095 Enough at once, now leve, and let us part.

WIT

This exercise hath done me good, even to the very hart.

Let us be bould with you, more acquaintance to take,

And daunce a round yet once more for my sake.

1100   [RECREATION]

Enoughe is enoughe, farewel, and at your neede

Use my acquaintaunce, if it may stande you in steede.

WIT

Right worthy Damsels both, I knowe you seke no gaynes

1105 In recompence of this desert your undeserved paynes:

But loke what other thinge my service maye devise,

To shewe my thankefull harte in any enterprise.

Be ye as bolde therwyth as I am bold on you,

And thus wyth hartye thankes I take my leave as nowe.

1090 The text appears to be disordered after this line, see notes.

1093 sd *Will*] Will

1100 *Recreation*] lines 1101–2 are given to *Wit*, see note

1101 *Enoughe*] Enouge

RECREATION   1110

Farewell, frend Wit, and since you are relieved,
Thynke not upon your foyle whereat you were so grieved,
But take your hart to you, and give attempte once more.
I warrant you to speede much better then before.

[*Exeunt* RECREATION *and her companion(s)*]   1115

ACT IV SCENE 4

WIT

One daunce for thee and mee, my boye, come on.

WILL

Daunce you, sir, if you please, and I wil loke upon.   1120
Let him practise in daunsing al things to make
himselfe brethles. [*Enter* IDLENESS *and* IGNORANCE]

WIT

This geare doth make me sweate and breath a pace.

IDLENESS   1125

Sir, ease your selfe a whyle; here is a restinge place.

WIT

Home, Will, and make my bedde, for I will take a nappe.   [*Exit* WILL]

IGNORANCE

Sure, and it please youre mastership, here in my Dame's lap.   1130

IDLENESS   *Syngeth*   [D.iv^v]

Come, come lye doune, and thou shalte see
Non lyke to mee to entertayne
Thye bones and thee opprest wyth payne.
Come, come and ease thee in my lappe,   1135
And yf it pleace thee, take a nappe,

1116 Act 4 sena 4. Immediately below: *Witte, Will, Idlenes, Ignoraunce*
1118 *thee*] the
1121–2 sd printed in BL and given to *Will* in preceding scene; see note
1126 *here*] heare

A nappe that shall delight thee so
That fancies all wyll thee forgoe.
Bye musinge styll, what canst thou fynde
1140 But wantes of wyll and restles mynde,
A mynde that marres and mangles all
And breadeth jarres to worke thy falle?
Come, gentle Wit, I thee requyre,
And thou shalt hytt thy chiefe desyre,
1145 Thy chiefe desire, thy hoped praye;
Fyrste ease thee here and then away.

WIT   *Falle doune in to her lapp*
My bones are styff, and I am wearyed sore,
And still me thynck I faynte and feble moore and moore.
1150 Wake mee agayne in tyme, for I have thinges to doe,
And, as you wyll mee for myne ease, I doe assent thereto.

IDLENESS   *Lul hym*
Welcome, wyth all my harte! Syr boye, houlde here thys fan,
And softly coole his face. Slepe sowndly, gentleman.
1155 Thys chayer is chaired well now, Ignorance, my sonne.
Thou seest all this, how fittlye it is done,
But wotste thou whye?

IGNORANCE
Nay, bumfaye, mother, not I.
1160 Well I wotte tis a gaye whorchit tricke and tryme:
Choulde rejounce my harte to chaunce cootes with hym.

IDLENESS
Doste thou remember how many I have served in the like sorte?

IGNORANCE
1165 It doth my hart good to thyncke on this sporte.

IDLENESS
Wylte thou see thys proper fellowe served soe?

1137 *so*] soo
1145 *hoped*] hooped   1155 *chaired*] chared

IGNORANCE

Choulde geve twaye pence to see it and tway pence moore.

IDLENESS   [E.i]

Come off, then, let me see thee in thy doublet and thy hose.

IGNORANCE

You shall see a taule felow, mother, I suppose.

IDLENESS   [*Puts the Fool's coat on* WIT]

Helpe off with this sleve, softly, for feare of waking.   1175
Wee shal leave the gentilman in a pretie takinge.
Give me thy Cote; hold this in thy hand.
This fellowe would be maried to Science, I understand;
But ere we leave him, tell me an other tale.
Now let us make him loke some what stale.   [*Daubs* WIT's *face*] 1180
There laye and there be; the proverbe is verified –
I am neither idle, nor yet wel occupied.

IGNORANCE

Mother, must I have his Cote, now mother, must [I]?
Chal be a lively lad with hey tistye tosty.   1185

IDLENESS

Sleape sound and have no care to occupie thy head,
As neare unto thy body now, as if thou hadst ben dead.
For Idleness hath wonne, and wholly thee possest,
And utterly dishabled thee from having thy request.   1190
Come on with me, my sonne, let us goe coutche againe,
And let this lusty, ruffling Wit here like a foole remayne.
        [*Exeunt* IDLENESS *and* IGNORANCE]

ACT V SCENE 1

WIT   1195

Up and to goe! Why sleape I here so sound?
How fals it out that I am left upon the naked ground?

1171, 1175 *off*] of   1184–5 see note
1179 *ere*] or   1189 *thee*] the
1194 Act 5 sena 1. Immediately below: *Witte, Science, Reason*

God graunt that all be well, whylest I lye dreaming here.
Me thinckes all is not as it was, nor as I would it were.
1200 And yet I wot not why; but so my fancies give mee
That some one thinge or other is my tyer that greves me.
That are but fancies, let them goe. To Science now wyll I,
My sute and busines yet once againe to labor and aplye.

[*Enter* SCIENCE *and* REASON]

SCIENCE
1205 What is become, trow yee, of Wit, our spouse that would be?

REASON
Daughter, I feare all is not as it should be.

WIT
1210 Yes, yes, have ye no doubt, all is and shalbe well.   [E.1ᵛ]

REASON
What one art thou? Therof, howe canst thou tell?

WIT
Reason, most noble sir, and you, my Lady deare,
1215 How have you done in all this time, since first I sawe you here?

SCIENCE
The foole is mad, I wene. Stand backe and touch me not!

WIT
You speake not as you thinke, or have you me forgot?

SCIENCE
1220 I never saw thee in my life until this time, I wotte.
Thou art some mad braine, or some foole, or some disguised Scot.

WIT
God's fishe, hostess, and knowe you not mee?

1200 *give*] giues   1224 *hostess*] hostes
1201 *tyer*] tryer

SCIENCE   1225
I had bene well at ease, in deede, to be acquainted wyth thee!

WIT
Hope haliday, mary, this is pretty cheere!
I have lost my selfe, I can not tell where.
An olde sayd sawe it is, and too true, I finde –   1230
Soone hot, sone cold: out of sight, out of mind.
What, maddam, what meaneth this sodaine change?
What meanes this scornefull looke, this countenance so straunge?
Is it your fashion so to use your lovers at the furst,
Or have all women this delite to scould and to be curst?   1235

REASON
Good felow, whence art thou? What is thy name?

WIT
I wene ye are disposed to make at me some game.
I am the sonne of Lady Nature; my name is Wit.   1240

REASON
Thou shalt say soe longe enough ere we beleve it.

SCIENCE
Thou, Wit! Nay, thou art some madde braine out of thy wit.

WIT   1245
Unto your selves this triall I remit.
Loke on me better and marke my personne well.

SCIENCE   [E.ii]
Thy loke is like to one that came out of hell.

REASON   1250
If thou be Wit, let see what tokens thou canst tell.
How comst thou first acquainted here? What sayd we?
How did we like thy sute? What intertaynment made we?

1230 *too*| to   1242 *ere*| or
1234 *Is it*| It is

WIT

1255 What tokens?

SCIENCE

Yea, what tokens? Speake, and let us know.

WIT

Tokens good store, I can reherse a rowe.
1260 First, as I was advised by my mother, Nature,
My lackey, Will, presented you with my picture.

SCIENCE

Stay there! Now loke how these two faces agree.

WIT

1265 This is the very same that you receyved from me.

SCIENCE

From thee! Why loke, they are no more like
Then chalke to cheese, then blacke to white!

REASON

1270 To put thee out of doubt, if thou thinke we saye not true,
It weare good for thee in a glasse thy face to viewe.

WIT

Well remembred, and a glasse I have in deede,
Whych glasse you gave me to use at neede.

1275   REASON
Hast thou the glasse, which I to Wit did gyve?

WIT

I have it in my purse, and will kepe it while I lyve.

REASON

1280 These markes me muse. How should he come therby?

WIT

Sir, muse no more, for it is even I
To whome you gave the glasse, and here it is.

REASON

Wee are content thou trye thy case by this. 1285

WIT [*Looks in the glass*]

Eyther my glasse is wonderfully spotted,

Or els my face is wonderfully blotted. [E.ii^v]

This is not my Cote. Why, wher had I this weede?

By the Masse, I loke like a very foole in deede. 1290

O heapes of happes! O rufull chaunce to me!

O Idleness, woe worth the time that I was ruled by thee!

Why did I lay my head within thy lappe to rest?

Why was I not advised by her that wisht and will'd me best?

O ten times troble! Blessed wights, whose corpes in grave do lye, 1295

That are not driven to behould these wretched cares which die!

On me, your furies, all on me, have poured out your spite.

Come nowe and slay me at the last, and ridde my sorowes quite.

What coast shall me receyve? Wher shall I shew my head?

The world wyll saye this same is he that, if he list, had sped: 1300

This same is he that toke an enterpryse in hand:

This same is hee that scarce one blow his ennemy did withstand:

This same is he that fought and fell in open field:

This same is he that in the songe of Idleness did yelde:

This same is he that was in way to winne the game, 1305

To joyne himselfe wherby he should have won immortal fame;

And now is wrapt in woe, and buried in dispayre.

O happye case for thee, if death would rid thee quite of care!

ACT V SCENE 2

REASON 1310

Shame!

[*Enter* SHAME]

SHAME

Who calls for Shame?

1292 *woe*] woo   1295–8 see note
1294 *will'd*] wil   1308 ^{1 & 2} *thee*] the
1309 Act 5 sena 2. Immediately below: *Shame, Reason, Science, Witte*

1315
REASON

Here is a marchant, Shame, for thee to tame.

SHAME

A shame come to you all, for I am almost lame
Wyth trudging up and downe to them that lose their game.

1320
REASON

And here is one, whom thou must rightly blame,
That hath preferde his folly to his fame.

SHAME

Who, this good fellowe? What call you his name?

1325
REASON

Wit, that on wooing to Lady Science came.

SHAME   [E.iii]

Come aloft, child! Let me see what friscoles you can fet.

REASON

1330 He hath deserved it; let him be well bet.

WIT

O spare mee wyth the whippe, and sley me with the knife.
Ten thousand times more deare to me were present death then lyfe.

SHAME

1335 Naye, naye, my frend, thou shalt not die as yet.

REASON

Remember in what case Dame Nature left thee, Wit,
And how thou hast abused the same.

SHAME

1340 A shame come to it!

1338 and 1345 see note

REASON

Remember what fayre words and promises thou diddest make,
That for my daughter's love no paynes thou wouldest forsake.
Remember in what sorte we had a care of thee:
Thou hast deceyved all our hope, as all the world may see.   1345

SHAME

A shame come to it!

REASON

Remember how Instruction should have bene followed styll;
And howe thou wouldest be ruled by none but by Will   1350
How Idleness hath crept, and raigneth in thy breast;
How Ignorance, her sonne, hath wholly thee possest.

SHAME

A shame come to it!

WIT   1355
O wofull wretch! To whom shall I complaine?
What salve may serve to salve my sore, or to redresse my payne?

[REASON]

Naye, I can tell thee more. Remember howe
Thou was subdued of Tediousness right nowe.   1360
Remember with what crakes thou went unto hys denne
Against the good advise and Counsell of thy men;
What Recreation did for thee in these thy rufull happes,
And howe the second tyme thou fell into the lappe[s].

SHAME   [E.iii^v]

A shame come to thee!

WIT
O let me breath a whyle, and hold thy heavy hand!
My grevouse faultes with shame enoughe I understande.

1344 *thee*| the
1358 *Reason*| lines 1359–64 are given to Wit
1359 *thee*| the

1363 *thee*| the
1364 *lappe*[s]| lappe, see note

1370 Take ruthe and pittie on my playnt, or els I am forlorne.
Let not the world continue thus in laughing mee to scorne.
Madame, if I be hee to whom you once were bente,
With whom to spend your time, sometime you were content.
If any hope be left, if any recompence,
1375 Be able to recover this for-passed negligence.
O helpe mee now, poore wretche, in this most heavy plight,
And furnishe me yet once agayne wyth Tediousness to fyght.

SCIENCE

Father, be good to these yonge tender yeares.
1380 See howe he doth bewayle his folly past with teares.

REASON

[To Shame] Hould, slave, take thou his Cote for thy labor.
[To Wit] We are content, at her request, to take you to our favor.
Come in and dwell with us, til time shall serve,
1385 And from Instruction's rule loke that thou never swerve.
Wythin we shall provide to set you up once more:
This scourge hath taught you what defaulte was in you heretofore.
[Exeunt omnes]

ACT V SCENE 3

1390 [Enter WILL]

WILL

Once in my life I have an odd haulfe hower to spare
To ease my selfe of all my travaile and my care.
I stoode not still so longe these twenty dayes, I weene,
1395 But ever more sent forth on messages I have bene.
Such trudging and such toyle, by the masse, was never seene!
My body is worne out, and spent with labor cleane.
And this it is that makes me loke so leane,
That lettes my growth, and makes me seene a squall.
1400 What then, althoughe my stature be not tall,

1389 Act 5 sena 3   1394 these twenty | this xx
1392 odd | od   1399 growth | groth

Yet I am as proper as you: so neate and clenlye,
And have my joyntes at commaundement full of actevitie.
What should a servaunt do with all this fleshe and bones
That makes them runne with leaden heeles, and stur them selves like
                                                        stones?

Give me a proper squier much after my pitche,   1405
And marke howe he from place to place will squitche.   [E.iv]
Fayre or foule, thicke or thinne, mire or dusty,
Clouds or rayne, light or darke, cleare or mystie,
Ride or runne, to or froe, badde or good,
A neate litle fellowe on his busynes wyll scud.   1410
These great laborers are neyther active nor wyse
That feede till they slepe, and sleape out their eyes.
So heavy, so dul, so untoward in their doinge,
That it is a good sight to see them leave working.
But all this while, while I stand prating here,   1415
I see not my mayster. I left hym snorting here.

ACT V SCENE 4

[*Enter*] SCIENCE, WIT, INSTRUCTION, STUDY [*and*] DILIGENCE

SCIENCE

Myne owne deare Wit, the hope of mine availe,   1420
My care, my comfort, my treasure and my trust,
Take hart of grace our ennemye to assaile.
Lay up these thynges whych you have heard discust:
So doinge, undoubtingly you can not fayle
To winne the fyeld, to scape all these unhappy shewers,   1425
To glad your frendes, to cause your foes to wayle,
To matche wyth us, and then the gayne is youres.

1404 *selves*| self
1411 *laborers*| labores
1417 Act 5 sena 4
1418 *Enter ... Diligence*| Science, Witte, Will, Instruction Studie Diligence Tediousnes
1420 *owne*| one

Here in this Closet our selfe wil sitte and see
Your manly feates and your successe in fyght.
1430 Strike home couragiously for you and me.
Learne wher and howe to fende, and howe to smite.
In any wyse, be ruled by these three.
They shall direct both you and Will aryght.
Farewell, and let our loving counsell bee
1435 At every hande before you in your fyght.

WIT

Here in my sight, good Maddam, sitte and viewe,
That, when I list, I may loke uppe on you.
This face, this noble face, this lively hiew
1440 Shal harden mee, shall make our enemye rue.   [SCIENCE *goes to her*
closet]

O faythful mates, that have this care of mee,
How shal I ever recompence your paynes wyth gold or fee?
Come now, and as you please, enjoyne me how to doe it,
And you shall see me prest and servisable to it.

1445   WILL   [*Advances*]   [E.iv^v]
Why mayster, whyther away? What hast, am I no body?

INSTRUCTION

What, Will, we maye not mysse thee, for no money.

WIT

1450 Welcome, good Will, and do as thou art bydde.
This daye or never must Tediousness be ridde.

WILL

God spede us well! I will make one at all assayes.

INSTRUCTION

1455 [*To* WILL] Thou shalt watche to take him at certayne bayes.
Come not in the thronge, but save thy selfe alwayes.

1428 *sitte*] sette   1444 *prest*] preest
1438 *uppe on*] vppe on   1446 *away*] way

[*To* STUDY *and* DILIGENCE]
You twayne on eyther syde, first wyth your sword and buckler;
After the first conflict, fight wyth your sworde and daggers.
[*To* WIT] You, sir, with a Javeling, and your Targett in your hand,
See how ye can his deadly strokes wythstand.   1461
Kepe at the foyne, come not wythin his reache,
Untyll you see what good advauntage you may ketche.
Then hardly leave him not, tyll time you strike him dead;
And of all other partes, especially save your head.   1465

WIT

Is this all, for I would fayne have done?

WILL

I would we weare at it, I care not how sone.

INSTRUCTION   1470

Now, when ye please, I have no more to tell,
But hartely to praye for you, and wyshe you well.

WIT

I thancke you. Goe thou and bidde the battayle, Will.

WILL   [*Advances to den of* TEDIOUSNESS]   1475
Come out thou monster fell, that hast desire to spill
The knot and linked love of Science and of Wit.
Come, trie the quarel in the fyeld, and fyght with us a fitte.

ACT V SCENE 5

[*Enter*] TEDIOUSNESS   1480

TEDIOUSNESS
A doughtie durte these four boyes will doe.
I will eate them by morsels two and two.

1479 Act 5 sena 5
1480 *Enter Tediousness*| Tediousnes, Witte, Will, Instruction, Studie, Diligence
1482 *four*| iiii

[*To* WIT] Thou fyghteste for a wyfe – a rod, a rodde!   [F.i]
1485   Had I wist this, I would have layed on loade,
       And beate thy brayne and thys my cloobe together,
       And made thee safe inoughe for retourninge hyther.

WILL

A foule horesone, what a sturdie thife it is!
1490   But we wyll pelt thee, knave, untill for woe thou pisse.

TEDIOUSNESS

Let me come to that elfe.

WIT

Nay, nay, thou shalt have worke inoughe to save thy selfe.   [*They*]
                                                              fight

1495   INSTRUCTION
       Take breath and chaunge your weapones: playe the men.

[TEDIOUSNESS]

Some what it was that made thee come agaen.
Thou stickest some what better to thy takling, I see;
1500   But what, no force, ye are but Jack Sprot to mee.

WIT

Have houlde! Here is a morsell for thee to eate.

STUDY [*and*] INSTRUCTION

Here is a pelt to make youre knave's hart freete.

1505   DILIGENCE
       There is a blowe able to fell a hogge.

[WILL]

And here is a foyne behynde for a madde dogge.
                       [*Trips* TEDIOUSNESS]

1497 [*Tediousness*]] lines 1498–1500 are given to Instruction
1500 *Jack Sprot*] Iack sprot   1507 Will] *Wit*, see note
1502 *here*] heare   1508 sd] *Let will trippe you downe*

WIT

Houlde, houlde, houlde, the lubber is downe!   1510

TEDIOUSNESS

Oh!

WILL

Stryke off his hed whyle I houlde hym by the crowne.

WIT   1515

Thou monstrous wretch, thou mortall foe to me and myne,
Which evermore at my good lucke and fortune didest repyne,
Take here thy juste desert and payment for thy hire.
Thy hed this day shall mee prefer unto my harte's desyre.
              [*Beheads* TEDIOUSNESS]   1520

INSTRUCTION

O noble Wit, thee prayse! The game is thine.

STUDY   [F.iᵛ]

Hove up his head upon your speare; loe, here a joyfull signe.

DILIGENCE   1525

O valiant Knighte, O conquest full of prayes!

WILL

O blest of god, to see these happie dayes!

WIT

You, you, my faithfull Squiers, deserve no lesse,   1530
Whose tried trust, well knowen to mee in my distres,
And certain hope of your fixt fayth and faste good will,
Made me attempt this famouse fact most nedefull to fulfill.
To you I yeald great thancks; to me redownds the gaine.
Now home a pace and ringe it out that Tediousness is slayne.   1535
[*Say all at once*] Tediousness is slaine!

1522 *thee*| the   1530 *deserve*| deserues
1524 *loe*| soe   1536 sd see note

ACT V SCENE 6

[Enter] SCIENCE

SCIENCE

1540 I heare and see the joyfull newes, wherin I take delight,
That Tediousness, our mortall foe, is overcome in fight.
I see the signe of victorye, the signe of manlines,
The heape of happy happes, the joy that tongue cannot expresse.
O welcome fame from day to day for ever shal arise!

1545   WIT
Avaunt ye griping cares, and lodge no more in mee!
For you have lost, and I have wonne continuall joyes and fee.
Nowe let me freely touche and freely you embrace,
And let my frendes with open mouth proclame my blisful case.

1550   SCIENCE
The world shall know, doubt not, and shal blow out your fame;
Then true report shall send abrode your everlasting name.
Nowe let our parentes dere be certifyed of this,
So that our mariage may forthwith procede, as meete it is.
1555 Come after me, all five, and I will lead you in.

                                        WIT
My payne is paste, my gladnes to beginne;
My taske is done, my hart is set at rest;
My foe subdued; my Ladye's love possest.   [F.ii]
1560 I thancke my frends, whose helpe I have at neede,
And thus you see how Wit and Science are agreed.
We twaine, hence forth, one soule in bodyes twayne must dwel.
Rejoyse, I praye you all with mee, my frendes, and fare ye well.

1564   FINIS

1537 Act 5 sena 6   1543 that| ẙᵗ
1538 *Enter Science|Science, Witte*

Explanatory Notes

Definitions of words and explanations of meanings are derived from the *Oxford English Dictionary, A Tudor and Stuart Glossary* by W.W. Skeat and A.L. Mayhew (Clarendon Press 1914), *A Shakespeare Glossary* by C.T. Onions (Clarendon Press 1949), and *A Dictionary of Slang And Unconventional English* by Eric Partridge (Routledge & Kegan Paul, Fifth Edition 1961). All line references to the plays *Wit and Science, Liberality and Prodigality*, and *Clyomon and Clamydes* are to the respective reprints of the Malone Society. Line references to *Common Conditions* are to the Elizabethan Club edition by Tucker Brooke (Yale University Press 1915). The proverbial material is noted with reference to *The Proverbs in England* by Morris P. Tilley (University of Michigan Press 1950), and to *Proverbs in the Earlier English Drama* by B.J. Whiting (Harvard University Press 1938).

ACT AND SCENE DIVISION

The division of the play into five acts appears to be marked by a cleared stage. Between Acts I and II, II and III, III and IV, the stage is empty. In the printed version, however, the division between IV and V breaks the consistency. At the end of IV.4 Wit is left asleep on the stage and at the beginning of V.1, the next scene, he awakens to continue the action. There is some reason for thinking that the Act division at this point in the printed text may not accurately reflect the original. It has already been suggested that IV.3 and IV.4 show evidence of hasty revision, and one naturally wonders if this has also affected the numbering of the scenes immediately following. It will be noticed that scenes 3 to 6 of Act v compose the final structural unit of the action. Therein, Wit, now purged of his wilfulness under the correction of Shame and Reason, overcomes his enemy with the aid of Instruction, Diligence, and Study and wins his Lady. Scenes 1 and 2 of Act v would seem to belong to the preceding structural unit, which portrays Wit's downfall and disgrace. It is, therefore, not surprising to find that the stage is clear after v.2. A tabulation of the division of the action as it stands in the text, together with a hypothesis of how it may have appeared in the original, helps to clarify the statement of this problem.

ACT AND SCENE DIVISION		ACTION
Printed Text	Hypothetical Original	
I.1	I.1	Nature counsels Wit and gives him Will.
Stage clear		
II.1	II.1	Wit instructs Will.
2	2	Will, on behalf of Wit, makes formal
3	3	overture to Science and to her parents.
Stage clear		
III.1	III.1	Wit courts Science. He is advised to
2	2	be patient and to prepare himself for
3	3	his ordeal with Tediousness.
Stage clear		
IV.1	IV.1	Wit rejects the advice of Reason.
2	2	He is beaten by Tediousness.
3	3	He is revived by Recreation.
4	4	He is seduced by Idleness.
V.1	5	He is rejected by Science.
2	6	He is corrected by Shame and Reason.
Stage clear		
3	V.1	Will reappears.
4	2	Wit, aided by his helpers, re-engages
5	3	and overcomes Tediousness.
6	4	Wit is united with Science.

For other discussions of the act and scene divisions see T.W. Baldwin, *Shakespeare's Five-Act Structure* (Urbana: University of Illinois Press 1947) and R.S. Varma, 'Act and Scene Divisions in "The Marriage of Wit and Science,"' NQ (March 1963). Professor Baldwin's observations are based upon an examination of the faulty original text and are consequently erroneous in a number of ways. Professor Varma thinks that the act and scene divisions were an afterthought and not authorial. He may well be right.

Title-Page. Original, 'A new and/Pleasaunt enterlude in-/tituled the mariage of Witte/and Science./lace ornament/Imprinted at London in/Fletestrete, neare vnto Sainct/Dunstones churche by/Thomas Mars he./

Title-Page. *The Players' Names*. In original, 'The players names' appears on the verso of title-page (sig. A.i^v). Below the list is an ornament which also appears upside down at end of text (sig. F.2^r). The list is in three columns. At the foot of the middle column of names appears 'Recreation,/with thre o-/ther women/singers.'

Line 1, *Act I Scene 1* Before Wit's house.

2, sd In this and subsequent scenes of the original (except II.3 and III.2.), a list of characters in the scene appears below the act and scene heading. I give Will an entrance here, although he is not introduced by Nature until ll. 185–6. Since there is no signal or any other indication explaining his sudden appearance there, it seems probable that he was present attending Nature from the start. H. and F. apparently assume that Will is present throughout the scene.

4–11. In these opening lines Nature introduces herself in a manner more usually appropriate to a prologue. For similar self-explanation of Nature cf. Medwall's *Nature* and Rastell's *Four Elements*.

5, *conservatyve of kinde*. Nature is the conserver of species.

7, *At whose instincte ... winde*. Nature receives her motion and power from Heaven.

11, *Race ... runne*. Cf. *Misogonus*, 'he is but yonge he must nedees runne his race' (II.iii.38).

15, *Tyll tracte of tyme shall worke and frame aryght*. An often iterated and important theme of the play (see ll. 125, 159–65, 172–4, 735, 753–4 and 865–910). Wit is constantly exhorted that travail (toil), travel (his pilgrimage), and the passage of time are the necessary elements of a successful attainment of wisdom. The proverbs *'Tempus omnia revelat'* (Tilley, T333), and 'Time tries all things' (Tilley T336) are probably alluded to in this and other related statements. Cf. *Liberality and Prodigality* (ll. 701–7) for similar expression of this concept. Heywood's *Dialogue*, l. 130, 'And than tract of tyme trayne her me to forsake.'

16, *perfect plyght*, in a good state or condition

20, *I gesse*. H. and F. emend to *I can guess*.

24, *He salves the sore that knowes the pacient best*. This is one of the recurring variations in the play of several related proverbs: 'He has but one salve for all sores,' 'Seek your salve where you got your sore,' and 'There is a salve to every sore' (Tilley, S82–4). For further examples see ll. 594, 1052, and 1357. One of the characteristics of the author is his facility for combining proverbs. Perhaps here he is also alluding to the proverb, 'He is a good Physician who cures himself' (Tilley, P262). Similar usage of a like expression may be found in *Common Conditions* (ll. 78 and 312). The use of the expression 'to salve the sore' is a poetic commonplace in the Elizabethan verse anthologies.

30, *knowledge*, acknowledge

33, *hap*, luck. H. prints *hap luck* for *hap such*.

38, *Much like the nayle ... out.* Proverb, 'One nail drives out another' (Tilley, N17).

42, *praye* ie, *prey*, booty, spoil, winnings. Perhaps also used in the scriptural sense – that which one saves from a contest. See also ll. 461, 626, and 1145. 'Pray' used in this sense also occurs in *Common Conditions* (l. 1479).

47, *inowe*, enough

62–3, *Loe, lo.* Cf. *Clyomon and Clamydes* (ll. 639–40).

75–80, *They are two things ... finde*, ie, the 'cause,' Wit's natural endowment from Nature, and the 'state,' the effort by 'toyle and practise' needed by him for the fulfillment of his desire.

78–79, *But this ... deare.* Whiting (p 140), 'We have here a somewhat curious application of the proverb, "Far fet and deare bought is good for ladies!"'

86, *Curiouse*, anxious; see also l. 979.

87, *ryde and runne.* A frequently recurring expression in the play (see ll. 198, 309, 489, and 1409). Cf. *Common Conditions* (l. 70), *Clyomon and Clamydes* (ll. 1246 and 1251), *Liberality and Prodigality* (l. 596), *Enough Is as Good as a Feast* (l. 176).

travayle. H. and F. alter to *travel*, but originally 'travail' and 'travel' were identical, and the modern word does not do justice to the concepts of bodily and mental toil and hardship implicit in 'travayle' and these are relevant to the meaning of the allegory of Wit's pilgrimage. The original spellings of the word are therefore left unaltered at ll. 156, 159, 372, 387, 407, and 1393.

90, 440, *the Lady of this world.* Cf. *Liberality and Prodigality*. (l. 229) where Dame Fortune is described as 'The god of this world.'

102, *That in to part ... show.* Nature declines to compete for praise with her 'other Lord above,' Jove, from whom she receives her authority and power.

104, *and I receive it so.* Hazlitt's interpolation of 'I' clarifies the sense and balances the measure.

107, *sparkles.* Used either in the rare sense of 'a vital or animating principle,' or perhaps figuratively 'with the allusion to the kindling of fire or conflagration.'

110, *spedde.* H. and F. wrongly emend to *spread.* 'Speed' in its many forms is a word often used in the play. Here it signifies 'provided' or 'furnished.' For various other senses, see below passim. A frequent use of 'speed' in its various senses may also be seen in *Liberality and Prodigality*, *Common Conditions*, and *Clyomon and Clamydes*.

113, 114, *The love of knowledge and certayne seedes devine,/Which, ground, might be a meane to bring thee hiere.* B. would resolve the ambiguity by suggesting that *groune* (ie, 'grown') should be read in place of *ground*. This is persuasive, but elsewhere in the text 'grown' is spelled *growen* (l. 478), and so I interpret *ground* to mean 'grounded.' Thus the divine seed, given by Nature under the authority of Jove, is planted in Wit, enabling him to fulfill himself, if he should have the inclination. Allegorically, it enables him to ascend Mt Parnassus, if he undertakes the travail of a pilgrimage to wisdom.

122, *My thinketh.* See OED. 'Methinks': 'In the 16–17c there occur the forms *my think*, *my thought(s)*, which are attempts to obtain a normal syntax by taking *think*, *thought* as sbs.' Cf. *Common Conditions* (l. 1299).

124, *connyng*, knowledge, expertise

137, *defyned*, determined, decided. H. and F. *designed.*

139, *as man wold admire.* B. suggests reading *no man*. This is tempting in view of the series of negatives that precede this clause; but no emendation seems necessary. Nature is cautioning Wit of the evil results that would proceed from a superabundance of her gifts. Those in 'great estate' would become self-sufficient, and thus upset the natural balance of mankind.

141, *fraght*, fraught

144, *be spedde*, equipped, or skilled

153, *to spede*, to prove successful

156, 159, *travell*, *travel*, see n. l. 87.

158, *Wit*. Original has *Will*, but the Page is not introduced until l. 185.

163, *dynt*, impression

164, *In tyme … flynt*. Proverb, 'Time wears out all things' (Tilley, T326). 'The Marble stone, is pearst at length,/With little droppes, of drislyng rayne' in M.T.'s poem, *The Paradise of Dainty Devices* (Rollins, p 23). Rollins gives classical sources of the proverb and a list of Elizabethan usages.

166, *gyrde*, a sudden movement or a spurt of action

174, *foyle*, a repulse or defeat; see also ll. 877, 1048, and 1112.

185–186, Will appears to have been present from the beginning of the scene (see n. on l. 2).

194, *paradventure yea … noe*. Cf. *Liberality and Prodigality* (l. 796).

200, *Cock soule*, a euphemism for *God's Soul*, ie, *cock* for *God* in oaths

202, *I am plaine*, ie, 'I am one who complains.'
at a worde and a bloe. Proverb, 'He is but a word and a blow' (Tilley, w763). Cf. *The Longer Thou Livest* (l. 819).

208, *Be ruled*, a common expression. A slightly varied and often repeated request in the play (see ll. 605, 752, 883, 1292, 1350, and 1432). Cf. *Liberality and Prodigality* (ll. 894 and 1090), and *Common Conditions* (l. 129).

218, *gaine*. H. silently alters to *game* ; F. prints *gaine*, but incorrectly notes 'original *game*, probably a printer's error.' Both 'gain' and 'game' are used as distinct concepts in the play ; for 'gain' see ll. 1427 and 1534, and for 'game' see ll. 1319 and 1522.

222, *this head*. Original, *his head*. F.'s emendation thus preserves Will's amusing impudence throughout the play from this single tincture of gratuitous blasphemy. I follow F., but cf. l. 277.

224, *what trace were best to tredde*. Cf. *The Marriage between Wit and Wisdom*, 'trading (ie, 'treading') vertues trace' (l. 44) ; *Misogonus* (I.i.96). 'To tread the trace' is a fairly common expression in the Elizabethan verse anthologies ; see, for instance, *The Paradise of Dainty Devices* (Rollins 96).

225, *Nature is on my syde*. Wit here demonstrates that he has not fully understood his mother's cautionary advice.

228, *Act II Scene 1* Wit and Will enter from Wit's home.

233, *a tall man*, an ironical expression signifying 'valiant'

235, *cokbraine*, a silly light-headed person (DOS)

237, *Truth, in respect … Wit*. Perhaps an echo of the proverb, 'You have little Wit and it does you good' (Tilley, w571).

241, *Can I remember*. H. alters to *I can remember* ; but Will is continuing to be ironical.

242, *flym flam*, nonsense, idle talk. Heywood's *Dialogue* (l. 572), 'She maketh ernest matters of euery flymflan.'

247, *a tale of a tubbe*, a nonsensical story. A proverb (Tilley, T45) with similar meaning as 'A tale of a roasted horse' (see l. 867) ; Heywood, *Dialogue* (l. 2517), 'A tale of a tub, your tale no truthe auowth' ; *Misogonus*, III.ii.50.

253, *a newe shorne sheep*. Cf. *Liberality and Prodigality* (l. 740) ; Heywood, *Dialogue* (l. 1098), 'Tyll tyme ye be as riche as a newe shorne shepe.'

256, *Wyse as a woodcocke*. Proverb, 'As wise as a woodcock' (Tilley, w746) ; *Apius and Virginia*, l. 125
as brage as a bodylouse. Proverb, 'As brisk (busy, brag) as a body louse' (Tilley, B504). *Misogonus*, 'as busy as a body louse' (II.iv.225) ; also *Gammer Gurton's Needle*, II.iv.32.

269, *let me alone*. This expression is also used at ll. 363 and 728. Cf. *Common Conditions*, ll. 574, 1705, and 1779.

278, *if you do*. H. has noticed that the word *clitter*, which appears after *do*, is superfluous to both the rhyme and sense ; accordingly he substitutes *so*. He explains that 'the compositor's eye must have caught *clitter* (for clatter) from the next line. *So* is agreeable to the metre and the sense.' F. prints original, *if you do clitter*. I follow H., omitting *clitter* for the reason he gives, but I do not think that his addition of *so* improves the line and therefore reject it. *Clitter* is a parallel form of *clatter* and together they made a commonly used expression for 'chatter' as in *Gentleness and Nobility* (ll. 179–80): 'Now here is a bybbyll babbyll clytter clatter/I hard neuer of so folysh a matter.' Cf. also *Nice Wanton* (ll. 1457–9), *Wealth and Health* (ll. 261–2), *The Longer Thou Livest* (ll. 826–8), *The Tide Tarrieth No Man* (sig. B.ii), *New Custom* (I.i.) and *All for Money* (sig. D.iiij^v).

284, *Tushe!* an extremely common exclamation. Also at l. 866 *Tushe, tushe!* Both forms of the exclamation occur frequently in *Liberality and Prodigality* (ll. 52, 365, and 567), *Common Conditions* (ll. 207, 262, 377, 396, 609, 824, and 968) and *Clyomon and Clamydes* (ll. 529, 598, 603, 667, 676, 956, 1899, and 2032).

300, *hardely*, boldly, courageously

315, *And cry peccavi*. Original, peccaui. Proverb, 'To cry peccavi' (Tilley, P170).

317, *waite at an inche*, be ready instantly; see also l. 942.

322, *At that*. H. emends to *All that*; but this does not clarify the sense. B. suggests *At*, ie, 'But.' This may be so; however, if the suggested punctuation of the preceding sentence is correct, no alternative seems necessary.

325, *I warrant thee*. See also ll. 520, 774, 958, and 1114. Cf. *Liberality and Prodigality* (ll. 365, 547, 800, 1035, and 1196).

330, *perdy*, By God! Here merely an asseveration; see also l. 417.

332, *Thy*. H. Silently emends to *The*.

349, *her stomacke to aryse*. 'Stomach' here perhaps used in the proverbial sense for anger, bad temper, but Will may also be mocking Wit's claim (l. 346) 'My wyfe wyll have nothing to doe wyth my men.'

355, *graye Mare*. Proverb, 'The grey mare is the better horse' (Tilley, M647), ie, the wife rules the husband; Heywood, *Dialogue* (1659–60), 'She is (quoth he) bent to fors you per fors/To know, that the grey mare is the better hors.'

363–76, During this speech Will traverses the 'place' and advances to Science's house.

373, *the gate of this Ladye*, the door of Science's house; see also l. 503.

377, *Act II Scene 2*. Continuing action. Reason, Experience, and Science enter from Science's house.

380, *lappes*. H. and F. print *lapse*; F. notes '*lappes* (="error").' Perhaps it is an intentional pun; on the allegorical level one of Wit's later errors is to fall in the lap of Idleness (see ll. 1147, 1293, and 1363–4).

390, *What doth the worlde?* ie, 'What does the world think or say?' H. alters *doth* to *saith*.

395, *good*, ie, 'goods,' perhaps the singular enforced for the sake of the rhyme; see also l. 454.

399, an unrhymed line. There does not appear to be anything missing.

410, *hyd*. H. alters to *high*. Note that 'high' is spelled 'hye' (l. 609), and that 'hid' is 'hydde' (l. 948).

414, *above*. H. changes to *alone*, unnecessarily. Reason is suggesting that his daughter's future husband is not only to be her helpmeet, but also to be her superior.

417, *perdie*, By God! See n. on l. 330.

426, *yonker*, a young fellow, especially a gay or fashionable one. Cf. *Patient Grissell* (ll. 915 and 1155).

430, *Such haste ... some*. Proverb, 'Haste makes waste' (Tilley, H189).

431, *my pretye boy*. Similar endearments occur at ll. 207, 327, 505, 534, 1057, and 1420, see note. Cf. *Liberality and Prodigality* (ll. 549 and 835–6); *Tom Tyler and his Wife* 'I mean a play set out by prettie boyss' (l. 6).

440, *The Lady of this world*, see note l. 90.

442, *On hym ... styll*. Original, 'On hym she chargeth men to be antendant styll.' H. and F. emend 'antendant' to 'attendant'; F. also emends 'men' to 'me.' The succeeding line makes it clear that *me* is correct, and thus the only alteration necessary is to separate *an* from *tendant*.

443, *kynde*, an abbreviated form of kindred; see also l. 186. H. and F. print *kin*.

445, *sendeth*. H. unnecessarily alters to *seeketh*.

449, *pyntch*, strait, exigency

454, *good*, goods, see n. l. 395.

458, *Youre self it is*. H. interpolates 'madam' after this.

460, *marke*, target

461, *hoped joye, the dearest pray*. Cf. ll. 42 and 626. *Common Conditions* (l. 1479) has 'my wished pray....'
  to wit. Original, 'to witte.' H. and F. print *to Wit*, thus weakening the possibly intended ambiguity, ie, 'to wit' to be sure, truly.

480–1, *better,/picture*. The writer seems to have had difficulty in rhyming 'better,' see also ll. 314–15.

483, *I dare ... controulde*, ie, 'I vouch that not even the smallest element of it can be censured.'

507, *Act* II *Scene 3* Continuing action. Will remains to deliver his mocking soliloquy.

509, *Queene*, ie, 'quean,' an ill-behaved woman. H. and F. alter *Queene* to *quean*; Will is clearly disparaging Science in this and successive lines.

510, *sadlye*, gravely

515, *Act* III *Scene 1* Stage clear. Wit and Will enter from Wit's home and during the course of the dialogue move towards Science's house.

520, *to spede*, to prosper

528, *toting*, looking or gazing. In proverbial use in north of England down to

Warwickshire, in the sense of peeping and prying. Cf. *Respublica*, 'Theare was suche tooting suche looking and suche priing....' (I.iii.159).

536, *the kaye of al my joye*. Cf. *Wit and Science* (l. 1052), '... a key of my most Ioye.'

542, *brall*, scold, chide, brawl

548, *Act* III. *Scene* 2 Original, Act 3 sena 1. H.'s stage-direction is *'The house of* SCIENCE. WILL, WIT; *also* REASON *and* SCIENCE *behind'*; F. follows H. exactly. This is misleading. Wit and Will have approached the house of Science (indicated earlier by her as the proposed rendezvous, l. 503) and Will now encourages his master, a hesitating lover, to press his suit. Their amusing but inconclusive debate is interrupted by the entrance (from her house, presumably) of Science and both her parents. H. and F., one supposes, have been misled by their failure to observe a major dislocation of the text after l. 556.

557, The text is dislocated here; see introduction. From this place in the original (l. 13, sig. c.i.), the dialogue continues at l. 14 on sig. c.iii.ᵛ.

566, *One masse for a penye*, enough said? Noted as proverbial phrase by Whiting (p. 140), but not explained by him. I can find no reference in Tilley.

568, *Jacke Sprot*. Original, *Iacke sprot* to rhyme with *what* (l. 566). Probably, but not certainly, Jack Sprat is a scornful allusion to one who would teach his elders, as in the proverb, 'Jack Sprat would teach his grandame' (Tilley, J26). Perhaps it is also a term of contempt for a diminutive person, ie, 'sprot,' a chip, splinter. See also l. 1500.

577–88, Whiting notes these lines as 'the first example of proverbial stichomythia in the English drama' (see pp. 63 and 139).

579 and 582, *spare ... speede*. Proverb, 'Spare to speak, spare to speed' Tilley, S709): Heywood, *Three Hundred Epigrammes*, no. 188, 'spare to speake, spare to speede. If speech bring speede,/Then wilt thou speede, for thou speakst more then neede.'

580, *It is a shame to steale a horse*. Proverb, '... but a worse to bring him home' (Tilley, s269).

582, *more hast then good speede....* Proverb (Tilley, H197).

585, *leape at a whyting*, to let slip an opportunity, as in proverb, 'You have leaped a whiting' (Tilley, w 318). Heywood, *Dialogue* 'There lepte a whitying ...' (l.2071).

587–8, *But he that leapes before he loke, good sonne,/Maye leape in the myre, and mysse when he hath done*. This expression appears to combine two proverbs: 'Look ere you leap' (Tilley, L429), and 'He that leapeth before he looke, may hap to leap into the brook!' cited by Tilley from Pettie, *Pet. Pal.*, II, 61.

593, ¹*my*. Original, *her*. My is needed for the consistency of Wit's antipodal statements.

595, *the well of my welfare*. Original, *wil*. I accept H.'s emendation and this is supported by parallel references: (i) 'well of worldly blysse' (l. 121), and (ii) 'The wel of wealth' (l. 611).

598, *to marre or els to muke*. Cf. *Liberality and Prodigality* (1.268). Heywood, *Three Hundred Epigrammes*, no. 39:

> 'Make or mar I wyll, so saist thou euer:
> But thou doost euer marre, thou makst neuer.'

606, *tyll*, ie, 'when'
homely, familiarly

609, *passing*, surpassing; see also l. 29.

612, *The kaye of Kingedomes and the stall of everlasting joye*: Original, *the steale of euerlasting ioye*. B., who suggests reading *stall* for *steale*, notes the need for interior rhyme with *al* (l. 611). H. and F. print *seal*.

614, *lore*. H. unnecessarily alters to *love*. Note interior rhyme *store* (l. 613).

618, *lese*, lose. H. and F. *lose*, but *lese* needed for interior rhyme with *frese* (l. 617). In original, the medial vowels of both words are ligatures. Cf. *Wit and Science*, 'leese her' (l. 24), and *Common Conditions*, 'Ile leese my life' (l. 417).

619, *spryte*. H. and F. *spirit*, but *spryte* needed for interior rhyme with *quite* (l. 620), as well as for the metre.

623, *A mate ... fynde*. H. has *A suit not much unmeet with you some grace to find*. He was no doubt puzzled by the Amitie (for *A mate*) in the original and felt compelled to alter two words. F. preserved the original, even though the sense is not clear. This line is the first on sig. c.iv[v] and the catchword on the preceding signature is 'Amate.' Wit claims to be a suitor to Science, as the next line makes quite clear. H.'s second alteration from *griefe* to *grace* is also wrong, although a superficial understanding of the speech may mislead one to think it has merit. Wit has attempted to express the torment of his feeling for Science in a series of opposing concepts (ll. 617–18), and all these suggest the grief latent in his longing. Further, Science has made it clear that her suitors grieve and complain when they fail to bring their wooing of her to fulfillment (ll. 394–5); this is exactly what Wit does after Tediousness overcomes him (ll. 1023–40).

626, *hoped pray*, ie, 'hoped for prey'; see also n. on l. 461.

642, *be sped*, be promoted

646, *here*. Original, *heare*. H. and F. print *heart*. Line 524 'As hart can thinke ...' would appear to support the change. But 'heart' is always either 'hart' or 'harte' in the text (see ll. 22, 23, 50, 62, 173, 501, 524, 535, 575, 629, 848, 959, 1097, 1107, 1113, 1153, 1161, 1165, 1422, 1504, 1519, and 1558. 'Heare' or 'hear' for 'here,' on the other hand, occurs a number of times (see ll. 481, 1126, and 1502). In view of this, one is reluctant to accept heart here, especially as an interpretation of lines 645–8 can be made without it. Experience is sceptical of Wit's extravagant promise.

She says, 'There are those that make fine promises, with the best intentions, as any of us can imagine, or anybody can tell.'

647, *Which at the first are hot, and kindle in desyre,/But in one month or twayne, quite quenched is the fyre.* In *Wit and Science*, Experience cautions her daughter against Wit's ardour with 'thys proverbe old/hastye love is soone hot & soone cold' (ll. 708–9).

649, *trade*, way, course, manner. H. *train*

662, *if we th'advantage take*, ie, 'if we avail ourselves of your offer'

664, *bandes*, bonds

674, *speede*, prosper

675, *these delayes*. Original, *this delayes*. This for *these*, see notes at ll. 800 and 1051.

678, *wot not what*. Cf. *Nice Wanton*, 'You talk, sir, me think, you wot not what' (l. 1459) and *Common Conditions* 'Wot you what?' (l. 249).

686, *Darbye's bandes*. H. notes, 'A proverbial expression not found in the collections. It may signify the hangman's cord'; but rather as in *TSG*, 'supposed to have orig. meant a very strict bond exacted by some usurer of that name. ... Later it meant fetters,' citing Gascoigne, *Steel Glass* (l. 787, ed. 1576), 'To binde such babes in father Derbies bands.' Tilley gives the expression 'To bind in Derby's bands' and cites R. Carew, *Surv. Cornwall* 149, 'For which poor wretch is bound in Darby's bonds to deliver him two hundred weight of tin at the next coinage.'

688–689, These two lines belong to Science. Both editors correctly emend, H. silently.

698, 883, 1492, *elfe*. In each instance it is Will who is so called. Similarly the Vice in *Common Conditions* (ll. 406 and 1006) is so described.

700–721, Science's account of her subjection to the monster, Tediousness, is paralleled in *Clyomon and Clamydes* (ll. 46–58) by Juliana's description of her subjection to the flying serpent.

709, Tediousness' attack upon the brain is appropriate to the allegory.

715, *to speede*, to succeed

717, *fend*. Original, *send*. Both editors correctly emend.

721, *I aske no more* etc. Science betrays a full measure of feminine insouciance.

724, *bredes*. F. *breedeth*

727, *common*, familiar, well-known. F. alters *your common foe* to *our common foe*.

728, *Let me alone*. Cf. ll. 269 and 363; see n. on l. 269.

729, At this point in the original (l. 27, sig. D.i^v) the dialogue continues at l. 14, sig. c.i.

735, *No hast but good*. Proverb, see Heywood's *Dialogue* (l. 2601), 'No hast but good....'

738, *slyght*, a cunning trick

740, *sped*. Original, *If I wynne, I am sped,/Am I not?* ie, 'If I conquer Tediousness, shall my suit with you succeed?'

744, *Wit*. B., whom I follow, suggests this speech (ll. 745–6) belongs to Wit. H. and F. retain for Will. It might be argued that Will is impertinently interrupting the conversation of his elders with a characteristic piece of swagger. On the other hand, in the next speech Experience addresses herself to Wit, as if he had done the boasting.

755, *Wit's wyll and wilfull wit*. This quibble has caused confusion. H. prints *witless Will and wilfull Wit*, and F., *Wit's will and wilful Wit*. The original has been retained to do full justice to the play upon words and names.

761, *hardely*, boldly; see l. 300.

764, *The more company the merier*. Proverb, 'The more the merrier, the fewer the better cheer' (Tilley, M1153).

766, *more than enowe*. Proverb, 'More than enough is too much' (Tilley, M1152). Will impertinently opposes proverbial wisdom.

767, *knave*. Original, *knaues*; H. and F. print original, presumably suggesting that Will is directing his animus against Instruction, Study, and Diligence. However, this speech indicates Will's impatience to fight the monster. His first line is a grudging welcome to the three helpers, and therefore it is hardly likely that he would wish their downfall so precipitately.

776, H. and F. misattribute Reason's line to Wit. After the departure of Experience and Science (l. 772), the dialogue is entirely between Will and Reason, until it is concluded by Wit's check of his impudent page (l. 812).

800–3, *Take me this woman ... ill.* As noted (l. 675) *this* is often supplied for *these* and therefore F.'s observation that the 'context would suggest *these women*' may be correct; however, both F. and H. retain original as I do. Whether this is an error or not, as a result of it, Will's speech gains in psychological depth. He begins by sharply abusing Experience, and suddenly, aware that he is speaking to her husband, modifies his condemnation of her in particular, by making his remarks inclusive of all shrews.

813, *Will*. Original, *Well*. Will's cheek appears to warrant the sharper rebuke by his master.

815, *Act* III *Scene 3*. Continuing action. Instruction, Study, and Diligence enter from Science's house.

826, *partes*, ie, 'parties'

833, *It*. H. emends to *I*. I interpret, 'It (=what I can doe) shalbe alwayes redye to pleasure you.'

836, *ease*. Original, *e< a; a* is partially visible. As there is no trace of ink, it would seem likely that the frisket was out of register, and so prevented the letters from catching ink.

838–44, *This glasse … supplye*. Cf. *Wit and Science* (ll. 1–9) wherein Reason gives Wit 'a glas of reson.'

860 and 862 H. and F. unnecessarily interpolate *I* before the respective requests of Instruction and Will.

863, *Act* IV *Scene 1*. Stage clear. This scene takes place outside Wit's house. Wit and his helpers presumably make their entrance from Wit's house which is mentioned a little earlier (l. 855). They are continuing their argument outside, having failed to agree within, about the length of time necessary for Wit to perfect himself for combat with the monster.

867, *a tale of a rosted horse*, a nonsensical story; see also l. 247.

868, *Wit*. Original, *Whych*. I follow B. After disparaging Instruction, Will turns to Wit to complain of the dilatoriness of Instruction and his companions.

869, *these*. Original, *this*; see also n. on l. 675.

877, *foyle*, a repulse, a defeat; see also ll. 174 and 1111.

881, *Ground us no ground*. Cf. *Common Conditions* (l. 430), 'tinke mee no tinks,' said by the Vice about the tinkers.

let him winne it and weare it. Proverb, 'Win it and wear it' (Tilley, W408).

890, *lyve*. Original, *lye*. The following line by Wit confirms F.'s emendation.

890 and 892 *hogge/dogge*. See also ll. 1506–8. Cf. *Liberality and Prodigality* (ll. 982–3).

902, *Two?* Original, *Noo*; H. and F. *No*. B. suggests reading *Twoo*. I follow B., despite the fact that a doubled vowel in words such as 'no,' 'to,' and 'so' occurs elsewhere in the text. Instruction's response to this question (l. 906) suggests that Wit has extended his request for a further period of time and not merely made a negative enquiry. Wit, himself, furthermore, has stated the limit of his patience, 'yea, a month or twaine' (l. 888). The compositor's slip may be the result of his use of an unusual number of upper case *n*'s between ll. 896 and 906, or perhaps it resulted from foul case.

920, *My head aketh*. Cf. *Wit and Science* (ll. 127 and 210), 'my hed akth sore.'

924–5, In the original these two lines are given to Wit. This misattribution is very probably connected with the textual dislocation already noted. At this place (l. 13, sig. C.iii^v) the dialogue continues at l. 29 on sig. D.i^v.

933, *couche a codde's head*. Cod's head, a fool (*OOS*). The proverb, 'To couch a Hogshead' (Tilley, H504), ie, 'to go to sleep,' is here neatly adapted by Will to show his contempt for Study. Both editors give this as an 'Aside,' Will's impudence in this and other places, one feels, is better left overt. For 'Cod's head' see *Damon and Pithias* (ll. 1247–9), *Apius and Virginia* (ll. 254 and 572), *Susanna* (ll. 465–7) and

Misogonus iv.14–16. Heywood, *Dialogue* (ll. 1509–10), 'And in meane tyme, my akyng hed to ease/I wyll couch a hogs hed.'

936, *Let us twayne, Study, and retourn from whens we came.* H. deletes 'and'; F. prints *Let us twain study, and return* etc., but no emendation appears necessary. Instruction is merely responding to Study's declaration (l. 930).

940–949. During Wit's speech, Wit, Will, and Diligence advance to the den of Tediousness.

942, *ready at an ynch*, see n. on l. 317.

946, *Thys is the deadly denne*. Cf. *The Marriage between Wit and Wisdom* (ll. 815–16).

947, *onset*, assault. Original, *vnset*

950, *Act* IV *Scene* 2. Continuing action. Tediousness enters from his den (see l. 946).

953–954, *What pryncox have we heere that dares me to assayle?/Alas, poore boy, and weenest thou against me to prevaile?* Cf. *Clyomon and Clamydes* (ll. 1374–5):
Cly. Yet therefore do defend thy selfe, for her I thee assaile.
Thras. Alas, poore boy, thinkest thou against me to preuaile?
pryncox, a conceited young fellow. This common epithet occurs in *Common Conditions* (ll. 1312 and 1321) and in *Clyomon and Clamydes* (ll. 441 and 1779) in the same context as it appears here. It is used by one of two opponents in the exchange of taunts before combat. In *Liberality and Prodigality* (l. 931), Vanity applies it to Prodigality.

954, *weenest*, thinkest. Original, *winest*

955, *Ful smal ... frend.* It is not clear exactly to whom Tediousness is alluding, but probably it is to Will.

958, *Great bost, small rost!* Proverb, 'Great boast (and) small roast' (Tilley, B488); Heywood, *Dialogue* (ll. 921–2), 'but great boste & small roste/Maketh vnsauery mouthes....'

963, *quise*. H. and F. emend to *quite*; I follow B., who interprets 'quise' ie, 'quease' (to press or to squeeze).

967, *friscoles*, capers; see also l. 1328.

970, 972, Neither H. nor F. gives exits to Diligence and Will.

978, 1361, *crake*, boast. Cf *Nice Wanton*, 'a craking braggar' (l. 1619), *Gentleness and Nobility*, 'But I wold thou knewist it for all thy krakkys' (l. 24).

979, *curious*, fine, delicate, exquisite

981, *Act* IV *Scene* 3. Continuing action. Wit after being felled by Tediousness lies unconscious. Will brings Recreation and her companions to him.

982, sd *Enter ... companion(s)*. The determination of the exact number of characters in this scene is a problem. Those listed beneath the Act and Scene heading are: Will, Recreation and Wit. As F. has pointed out, 'the song is marked for two voices,' but it should be noted also that this arrangement is rather tentative. In the text there are explicit references to two women (ll. 1062, 1066, and 1104), Recreation and her companion singer, presumably. Another character, a 'mynstrel,' is called upon to 'Pype us up a Galiard' (l. 1090). Yet on the verso of the title-page, under 'The players names,' Recreation is listed 'with thre other women singers.' F. suggests, 'it would seem that *Idleness* is present, or standing aside, in this scene,' but this is clearly wrong.

983, sd *Rubs ... Wit*. In original, 'Rub and chafe him' is printed in BL and placed after *Will*. This is a stage-direction for Will; H. and F. assume that it is a part of his speech and print accordingly.

987, sd *Singe both*. The incomplete and somewhat confusing arrangement of the song is misleading. It is basically arranged here for two voices, and it would appear likely that Recreation is one of the singers, though there is no direct evidence to indicate this. The song consists of four six-line verses sung alternately by each voice. The first three verses have a six-line refrain, the first two lines of which are sung in unison, the remaining four, alternately by each voice. The refrain in full appears above the first verse, and the brief directions referring to its repetition are placed centrally between the verses. It does not appear after the last verse. The appearance of the song in the text thus suggests that the compositor may have thought the refrain should be sung before each of the four verses. However, it was the custom to place the refrain in full at the head of the song in dramatic texts, because very often the song took its title from the opening line of the refrain (see *Common Conditions*, l. 213 and l. 1125, also *Wit and Science*, l. 1033). H. prints the song as it stands in the text; F. has made some attempt to arrange it for two voices.

The printed version of this song could conceivably be a rearrangement for two voices of an original designed for four – hence the 'Recreation, with three other women singers' (see intro., p 89). In *Wit and Science*, Honest Recreation has three companions. Comfort, Quickness and Strength, who sing a six-verse song 'Gyue place, gyue place,' as they revive Wit (l. 240). Individual lines of these verses are sung by each character, though most of the lines are sung in unison. Certain parallel words and phrases are to be found in both Redford's song and this one; no doubt the author of this play has used Redford's song as a model.

988, *lift us*. Original, *vs*; H. *us*. F. alters to *up*, and B. concurs. I do not think any change is required; note 'Pype us up a Galiard' (l. 1090).

991, *plight*, in a good state

998, *plucke*, a snatch; here, figuratively, 'an attempt,' 'a go'

1018, *marcke*, token, sign

1020, *Wit*. In the original, ll. 1021–40 are erroneously given to Will. In these lines Wit is clearly the victim of the 'deep despayre' foretold by Science (l. 710). Science has also anticipated (ll. 394–5) the kind of accusations which Wit here makes against her.

1021–40, Wit's self-pitying lament upon adversity has its close parallels in *Common Conditions* (Clarissa, ll. 371–6, Galiarbus, ll. 478–83) and in *Clyomon and Clamydes* (Clyomon, ll. 760–7, Clamydes, ll. 921–31). Cf. also *Liberality and Prodigality* (ll. 462–7). This kind of lament is a poetic commonplace in the Elizabethan verse anthologies (cf. nos. 168 and 301 in Tottel's *Miscellany*, and no. 83 in *The Paradise of Dainty Devices*, Rollins' editions).

1024, *On whom*. Original, *In whom*; H. prints *On whom*, which makes better sense of ll. 1024–5.

at a clappe, suddenly

1047, *seeth*. H. silently alters to *seest*.

1051, *These gentil newes of good Will*. Original, *This gentil newes.* ... H. prints *These gentlewomen of good skill*; and F., *These gentle news of good Will*. B. suggests 'This (= these) gentil women of good will (ie, "of their charity").' 'These gentil newes' of Wit's good servant, Will, is the delivery of the heartening message by Recreation, who, together with her companion(s), have been brought by Will to the place of Wit's defeat, and is a direct contrast to 'this wofull newes' (l. 1045) which Science will hear when she learns of Wit's repulse and suffering. Perhaps 'these gentil newes' was intended to refer to both the message and the messengers. In the sixteenth century 'news' was still used plurally.

1090, From this point – the last line of sig. D.iii^v – until the sudden appearance of Idleness thirty-two lines later on sig. D.iv., the text presents a number of problems: (i) Wit calls for a Galliard, yet an immediately following stage-direction designates the 'call for daunces' to Will (MSR, ll. 1084–5); (ii) the catchword on sig. D.iii.^{v}. is 'Will' printed in BL, yet the stage-direction at the top of the next signature begins with the word 'Let' printed in italic; (iii) a stage-direction 'Let him practise in daunsing al things to make himself brethles' is printed in BL and given as speech to Will (MSR, l. 1088), although it would be quite appropriate as a direction after l. 1113; (iv) two lines obviously belonging to Recreation are given to Wit (MSR, ll. 1095–6); (v) no exeunt is given for Recreation and her companion(s); (vi) no entrance is given to Idleness and Ignorance; (vii) no exit is given for Will. All these errors and omissions occur within the limit of thirty-four lines and so it may be inferred that this page of the copy from which the play was printed contained some loosely arranged revisions which confused the compositor (see nn. on ll. 1128 and 1416).

H. and F. reproduce the original without comment, except to notice that the stage-direction printed as speech has no companion line, and, therefore, to conclude that a line or lines 'may have been dropped here.'

1090, *mynstrel*, perhaps one of Recreation's companions

1092, *Come Damsell* etc. Wit is partnered by Recreation, and I assume that Will now invites her companion to dance with him.

1093, sd *Let Will call for daunces, one after an other.* It is odd that Wit does not continue to direct the dancing. In *Wit and Science* Honest Recreation and Wit also dance a Galliard.

1101–2, In original, these lines are given to Wit, but they clearly belong to Recreation. H. and F. retain for Wit.

Enoughe is enoughe. Proverb (Tilley, E159)

1114, *to speede,* to fare

1116, *Act* iv *Scene* 4. Continuing action. Wit, watched by Will, continues to dance until Idleness and Ignorance enter.

1121–2, sd *Let him practise* ... [*Enter* ... *Ignorance.*] See n. on l. 1090. It seems appropriate that, while Wit is dancing himself breathless, Idleness and Ignorance should unobtrusively enter here; the allegory calls for Idleness to creep up on Wit (l. 1351). Cf. sd in *Wit and Science* (ll. 324–8), 'here they dawnce & ⟨ ⟩ in the mene whyle Idellnes cūth in & sytth downe & when the galyard is doone wyt sayth as folowyth & so falyth downe [on evrysyde] in Idellnes lap.'

1128, *Home, Will,* etc. This peremptory order by Wit to his servant is complied with immediately, at a moment when Will's candour must have been hard to restrain. Will's silent departure here is quite uncharacteristic, and is, perhaps, another reason for thinking this scene was very likely revised. See also n. on l. 1416.

1142, *jarres,* quarrels, discords.

1152, sd *Lul[l]hym.* Cf. *Wit and Science* (l. 366), 'Idelnes. I must now lull hym. ...'

1155, *chaired.* Original, *Thys chayer is chared well now.* H. prints *This char is char'd well now,* and interprets 'That business is despatched. See Hazlitt's ''Proverbs,'' 1869, p. 352.' F. has *This char is charr'd well now.* In addition to the proverb cited by H., it seems likely that another proverb is also aptly alluded to here: 'For want of a wise man a fool is set in the chair' (Tilley, W30). Idleness' 'chair' (her lap) is well chaired by the sleeping fool, Wit.

1156, *fittlye,* aptly, skilfully

1159, *Nay, bumfaye,* ie, 'No, by my faith.' Ignorance's rustic speech is taken over from *Wit and Science.* Redford's Ignorance, however, speaks much less broadly than the character here.

1160–1, *Well I wotte* ... *hym,* ie, 'I know that it is a gay and neatly worked trick. It would rejoice my heart to change coats with him.'

1169, *Choulde geve twaye pence.* Cf. *Common Conditions* (l. 1775), 'I would giue my life for two pence.'

1171, *Come off, then, let me see thee in thy doublet and thy hose.* H. unnecessarily alters to *his doublet and his hose.* F. prints original and remarks, 'the meaning is quite clear. Idleness is speaking to Ignorance after he has changed (or is changing)

clothes with Wit.' This explanation is not precise. Idleness is about to remove Wit's
coat with the help of Ignorance, and she refers to it as though it already belonged to
her son. This situation has its parallels in *Wit and Science* (ll. 562–614), *The
Marriage between Wit and Wisdom* (ll. 417–19), and in *The Longer Thou Livest*
(ll. 1819–20).

1180, sd *Daubs Wit's face*. The blackening of Wit's face (see his recognition of this ll.
1287–8) closely parallels the incidents in *Wit and Science* (fol. m^r, 806–7) and in
The Marriage between Wit and Wisdom (fol. 10^v, sd).

1181–2, *the proverbe ... occupied* (Tilley, 18). Cf. *Wit and Science* (l. 441), 'nother
Idle not yet well occupyde.'

1184, *must I?* Original, *must?* B. suggests this interpolation. H. prints *I must*, and
tust for *tostye* (l. 1188). F. has *must?* and *tust*.

1185, *hey tistye tosty*, an ejaculation of triumph. Cf. *Common Conditions* (l. 213),
'Hay tisty tosty.'

1194, *Act v Scene 1*. Continuing action. Wit awakens from sleep to be confronted by
Reason and Science.

1198, *lye*. H. alters to *lay*.

1201, *That some one thing or other is my tyer that greves me*. Original, *is my tryer*.
H. alters to *in my tire*, and F. follows with *in my 'tire.'* Obviously *tryer* is an error
for tyer ('attire'); but there is no need to change *is* to *in*. I interpret ll. 1200–1: 'And
yet I do not know why, but my instinct tells me that the thing which grieves me is
my attire.' The strain for rhyme and the weak result probably caused the odd
syntax.

1202, *That*. H. alters to *They*.

1204, sd *Enter Science and Reason*. They enter from Science's house.

1222, *Scot*. H. alters to *sot*.

1224, *God's fishe, hostess*. Original, *Gods fishe hostes*. God's fish, an oath. I adopt
B.'s suggested reading. H. and F. print *God's fish-hooks*. Cf. *Misogonus* 'Gods-
fishe lettes be gone' (ii.ii.45) and *Tom Tyler and his Wife* 'Gods fish you knave'
(l. 625).

1228, *Hope haliday*. H. prints *Hop haliday* and notes, 'A colloquialism, of which the
exact import must be a matter of guess. ... Perhaps a corruption of "upon my
haliday".' F. follows H. It could be a corruption of the ancient formula for the
taking of oaths: 'as helpe me God and halidome'; halidom, originally, were the
holy relics upon which oaths were sworn. (TSG 183).

1231, *Soone hot ... out of mind*. Two proverbs (Tilley, H732 and S438).

1249, *Thy loke ... hell*. She is referring to the blackened face of Wit.

1263, *Now loke how these two faces agree*. Cf. *Wit and Science* (ll. 784–6), 'yf that
be youre pycture then shal we/soone se how you & your pycture agree.'

1267–8, *they are ... to white*. Two proverbs (Tilley, C218 and B438).

1280, *These markes me muse*. 'Muse' = bemuse; H. and F. emend to *This makes me muse*; but perhaps Reason is directly referring to Wit's daubed face.

1287–8, *Eyther my glasse is wonderfully spotted,/Or else my face is wonderfully blotted*. Cf. *Wit and Science* (ll. 830–1). 'other this glas is shamefully spotted/or els am I to shamefully blotted.'

1289, *weede*, garment

1291, *O heapes of happes!* An exclamation denoting catastrophic misfortune. H. prints *O haps of haps*. Cf. *Common Conditions* (l. 373), 'heapes of woes' and (l. 376), 'heapes of greif'; *Clyomon and Clamydes* (l. 1180), 'the hugie heapes of care.'

1292, *woe worth the time*, a common expression. Cf. *Common Conditions* (l. 140), 'Woe worth the time,' and *Clyomon and Clamydes* (l. 773), 'Woe worth the wind.' The expression is a poetic commonplace; Stephen Hawes (*The Pastime of Pleasure*), Wyatt in several poems in Tottel's *Miscellany*, and Richard Edwards (*A Paradise of Dainty Devices*) are particularly fond of using it. In *Damon and Pythias* the Muses sing: 'Alas what happe hast thou poore Pithias now to die,/Wo worth the which man for his death hath geven vs cause to crie' (ll. 1895–6).

1295–6, *O ten times troble ... die!* Original, *O ten times troble blessed wights, whose corpes in graue do lye:/That are not driuen to behould, these wretched cares which die*. H. alters *troble* to *treble* and *die* to *I*, explaining the latter change thus: 'The same appears to be "That are not driven to behold those wretched cares, which I *am driven &c.*"' F. prints *treble*, but retains *die*. There appears to be no need for either emendation. The awkward construction here, as elsewhere in the text, is the result of the author compromising his syntax for the sake of the rhyme. Wit's exclamation 'O ten times trouble!' figuratively sums up the calamities listed in the preceding lines. Next, in contrast to his own misfortune, he apostrophises the dead, who are 'blessed' because their earthly cares have ceased ('which die'). The final line of Wit's lament reinforces this interpretation. He, too, longs for death's acquittance.

   Wit's jeremiad has its close parallels of tone, phrase and allusion with passages in *Common Conditions* (Sedmond, ll. 450–77, and Lamphedon, ll. 950–62, 1871–9), in *Clyomon and Clamydes* (Clyomon, ll. 760–80, Clamydes, ll. 872–95), and in *Damon and Pythias* (Song, ll. 691–723).

1297–8, *On me, your furies, all on me, have poured out your spite,/Come nowe and slay me at the last, and ridde my sorrows quite*. Original, *On me your furies all on me. ...* H. and F. alter to *you furies*. Cf. the lament sung by Pythias (*Damon and Pythias*, ll. 710–15):

'Let sorow sinke in to my brest
and ransacke euery vayne:/
You Furies all at once,
on me your tormentes trie:/
Why should I liue, since that I heare/
Damon my friend should die?'

I retain *your furies*, uncertain whether the allusion is to the Eumenides or to the
mental torments described by J.L. Vives in *De Tradendis Disciplinis* (1531), 'The
vices of the mind of the first kind should be explained and disclosed fully ... as, in
pride, anger, hate, envy, which torment and torture men's minds ... so that not
unjustly they are called "furies".' For similar invocations to the Furies, see
Misfortunes of Arthur (1587), I.ii. 39–44 and *Macbeth*, I.v. 39–44.

1300, *sped*, prospered

1309, *Act* v *Scene 2*. Continuing action. Shame enters to chastise Wit.

1316, *marchant*, merchant. H. notes, 'Fellow. The word is frequently used, as we
now use the word *chap*, which is in fact the same [similar meaning?] being an
abbreviation of *chapman*.'

1328, *fet*, fetch (Dial.), or possibly as H. notes, 'Fet (or feat) seems to be here
employed in the sense of *play* or *perform*.'

1330, *He hath deserued it; let him be well bet*. Cf. *Wit and Science* (ll. 882–3),
'wherfore spare him not shame bete him well there/he hath deservyd more then he
can beare.' H. interpolates 'If' before 'He.'
bet, beaten

1338, *And how thou hast abused the same*. B. has suggested that this short unrhymed line may be defective. Immediately after, in the original, appears 'Thou
hast deceyued all our hope, as all the world may see,' which, in a proper context and
with an appropriate rhyme, is placed also at the conclusion of a speech by Reason (l.
1345). I delete it; H. and F. retain. It would seem that 'A shame come to it!' (l.
1340) completes the rhyme of l. 1338, and, if so, nothing would appear to be
missing here.

1361, *crakes*, brags; see also n. on l. 978.

1364, *lappes*. Original, *lappe*. Preserving the rhyme with 'happes,' l. 1364, preserves the pun on 'lapse' and the consistency of the usage at ll. 380–1.

1371, *Let not the world continue thus in laughing mee to scorne*. Cf. *Wit and
Science* (ll. 848–9), 'evrye man I se lawhe me to scorne/alas alas that ever I was
borne.'

1375, *for-passed*, surpassing

1382, *Hould, slave ... labour*. Similarly, Reason gives Wit's fool's coat to Shame in
Wit and Science.

1389, *Act* v *Scene 3.* Stage clear. Will enters from Wit's house.

1399, *lettes,* hinders

    seene, seen. H. and F. silently alter to *seem.*

    squall, a small or insignificant person. The term appears to have been in usage either as a term of contempt or a term of endearment (see TSG). This slang diminutive occurs in *Common Conditions* (l. 1006).

1404, *leaden heeles.* This allusion to servants with leaden heels perhaps finds an echo in *The Marriage between Wit and Wisdom* (ll. 1358–9), 'some leden heeled lubber'; lubber, ie, 'drudge, scullion.'

    them selves. Original, *them self*; see n. on l. 675.

1405, *pitche,* stature.

1406, *squitche,* move quickly. H. notes: 'A word of most uncommon occurrence and of dubious meaning. From the immediate context we should infer that it signified *skip, move lightly and quickly.*' TSG, 'Probably identical with prov. E. *switch,* to move quickly.'

1407–8, *Fayre or foule ... mystie.* Cf. *Liberality and Prodigality* (l. 52), 'fairc or foule, farre or nccre.'

1411, *laborers.* Original, *labores.* H. and F. print *lubbers.*

1416, *snorting,* sleeping heavily. Will's statement is at variance with the facts. He was sent home by Wit (l. 1128) before Wit fell asleep. Perhaps this is yet more evidence for suggesting that IV.3 and IV.4 were revised; see n. on l. 1090.

    All editors give Will an exit here. However, his last lines do not indicate that he departs from the scene. I take it that he remains in the background throughout Science's farewell to Wit and, resentful of being overlooked, advances (l. 1445) with his exclamation, 'What haste, am I nobody!'

1417, *Act* v *Scene 4.* Continuing action. Science, Wit, Instruction, Study, and Diligence enter from Science's house.

1420–1, *Myne owne deare Wit, the hope of mine availe,/My care, my comfort, my treasure and my trust.* Cf. *Liberality and Prodigality* (ll. 835–6): 'Oh, my sweeting, my darling, my chewel, my ioy,/My pleasure, my treasure, mine owne prettie boy.'

1425, *shewers,* showers; figuratively, 'copious misfortunes'

1438, *list,* please

    uppe on you. Original *vppe on you.* H. and F. print *upon*; but it would be incautious to emend, because it may very well be that the 'Closet' from which Science is to view the fight (l. 1428) is a raised place. Craik (*The Tudor Interlude* 16), suggests 'perhaps an upper window of her house.'

1445, sd *Advances.* See n. on l. 1416.

1453, *spede,* prosper

1455, *Thou shalt watche to take him at certayne bayes.* Probably Instruction intends Will to engage Tediousness only at those times when the giant is at bay, or engaged by the others.

1455–65 Instruction's order of battle includes tasks for all but himself, and does not much differ from Wit's earlier deployment of forces (ll. 940–5). Wit is to be flanked by Study and Diligence, and is rightly honoured with the most dangerous position. Will is given a mobile and relatively safe role.

1460, *Javeling*, javelin. It is interesting to notice that an element of Redford's allegory has been dropped here. Wit does not fight with Science's 'sword of comfort.'

1462, *foyne*, thrust; see also l. 1508.

1463, *ketche*, catch

1478, *fitte*, bout

1479, *Act* v *Scene 5*. Continuing action. Tediousness enters from his den.

1482, *durte*, dirt. H. prints *dust*, fray, disturbance. Cf. *Misogonus*, 'but you nede no more men I am sure for this dust' (I.iv.47).

1486, *cloobe*, club

1489, *what a sturdie thife it is!* Cf. *Wit and Science* (l. 86), Wit calls Tediousness 'a fowle theafe.'

1490, *pelt*, strike

1499, *Thou stickest … takling*. Proverb, 'To stand to one's tackling' (Tilley, T7). Cf. *Common Conditions* (l. 993) and *The Marriage between Wit and Wisdom* (l. 162); Heywood, *A sixt hundred of Epigrammes*, no. 86: 'Art thou in Newgate to stand to thy tacklyng? Nay: I am in Newgate to stand to my shaklying'; also *Misogonus* (II.iv.136).

1500, *Jack Sprot*, see n. on l. 568.

1504, *freete*, fret

1507, *Will*. Original, *Wit*. I give l. 1508 to Will. Instruction's tactics call for Wit to face Tediousness with javelin and shield, while Will is given the mobile role of taking him 'at certayne bayes.' Since the immediately following stage-direction is 'Let will trippe you downe', it would seem that the 'foyne behynde' (l. 1508) refers to this. In the first abortive encounter with Tediousness (IV.2), Will also attempts to get at the giant's legs: 'And I must have a legge of thee, if I can catche it' (l. 961). Further, the dialogue (between ll. 1502 and 1510) includes fighting taunts from each of the characters engaged. A contribution from Will rounds off the matter.

1512, *Oh!* Tediousness' single exclamation impresses one at first as perhaps the most inadequate doom-cry in the history of stage combat, but much may be made of 'Oh!' Redford gives the monster two additional 'ho's' (see *Wit and Science*, l. 998).

1518–19, *Take here … desyre*. Unlike Redford's and Merbury's plays, here Tediousness is killed and beheaded, it would seem, if not in full view of the audience, then at least on stage. The giant's costume may have included a false head.

1528, *blest*. H. and F. alter to *bliss*. Will could be referring to the victorious Wit or perhaps to all the witnesses of Wit's triumph.

1534, *redownds the gaine*. Cf. *Common Conditions* (l. 998), 'redownes to our profit.'

1536, sd Original, *Say all at once, Tediousness is slaine*, printed in BL, immediately follows l. 1536. It is clearly a stage-direction. H. retains it for Wit's speech; F. silently prints it as a stage-direction.

1537, *Act v Scene 6*. Continuing action. Science enters from her house.

1538, sd *Enter Science*. Only two characters are listed for this scene: 'Science, Witte.' However, as line 1556 makes clear, all Wit's combat allies are present; hence B.'s suggested 'Exeunt omnes' at the conclusion of the preceding scene is unnecessary.

1541, *fight*; so all editors. However, 'sight' may have been intended; the *f* can by no means be clearly distinguished from *s*.

1544, *O*. H. alters to *Our*.

1560, *have*. H. alters to *had*.

1564, FINIS. Below this is the same ornament that appears beneath 'The players names' on the verso of the title-page.

Bibliography and Index

Bibliography

LIST OF UNPRINTED MANUSCRIPT RECORDS

British Museum

MS Add. 15233 Poems and play fragments by Redford, Heywood, and others

MS Add. 27404 Chamber Accounts

MS Add. 29996 Poems by Redford and Thorne

MS Harl. 1080 ⎱ St. Paul's
MS Harl. 7041 ⎰ Almonry Registers

MS Royal 178 Book of Expenses

MS Lansdowne 6, no. 69 ⎱ Letters, Grindal to Cecil
MS Lansdowne 30, no. 5 ⎰

MS Lansdowne 21 Report on Dr Good

Guildhall Library

2859 ⎱ Visitation Books
2942 ⎰

9537/2 ⎱ Subsidy Payments
9537/3 ⎰

11816 ⎱ St. Paul's Estate Surveys
11816A ⎰

St Paul's Cathedral Library

WD 6 Common Place Book
WD 16 Almoner's Accounts
WD 25 Hackett's Researches
WD 32 Michael Shaller's Notebook
A/52/15 Almoner's Accounts 1526
A/53/20 Chamberlain's Receipts 1582
A/24/324 Indenture, Vicars Choral 1602
A/77/2059 Bond, Westcott 1564

Public Record Office

B 1643 Ancient Deed, Westekota
C/24/127 Chancery Suit, Westcott vs Clifton
E/139/334 Exchequer, Memoranda Roll
E/179/145/174 Lay Subsidy Roll

Somerset House, Prerogative Court of Canterbury

50 Alen, 18 Arundell, 121 Dorset, 1 Kidd, 95 Nevell, 3 Rutland, 14 Tirwhite, 31 Tirwhite, 60 Wood

Devon Record Office

Visitation Book, Oldham
Visitation Book, Vesey
Register, Vesey, Chanter no. 14.

City of Exeter Library

Westcott File

Parish Registers

St Mary the Virgin, Cheddon Fitzpaine, Somerset
SS Peter and Paul, South Petherton, Somerset

LIST OF PRINTED WORKS

GENERAL

Books

Arber, Edward *A Transcript of the Registers of the Company of Stationers of London* London 1879–94. 5 vols
Baldwin, T.W. *William Shakespeare's Five-Act Structure* Urbana 1947

Blom, Eric, ed. *Grove's Dictionary of Music and Musicians* Fifth Edition. London 1954. 9 vols

Clode, C.M. *The Early History of the Guild of Merchant Taylors* London 1888

– *Memorials of the Guild of Merchant Taylors* London 1875

Dasent, John Roche, ed. *Acts of the Privy Council of England* London 1890–1907. New Series, 32 vols

Duff, E. Gordon *A Century of the English Book Trade* London Bibliographical Society 1905

Fry, E.A., ed. *Calendar of Wills in the Court of the Archdeacon of Taunton, 1537–1799* 1912

Greg, W.W. *A Bibliography of The English Printed Drama* London, 1939–59. 4 vols

Handover, P.M. *The Second Cecil* London 1959

Heywood, John *A Dialogue of Proverbs* Ed. Rudolph E. Habenicht. Berkeley, California 1963

– *The Proverbs and Epigrams* (1562) Edited for the Spenser Society, London 1867; reprinted, New York 1967

Historical Manuscripts Commission. *Ninth Report, Pt 1* London 1883

Hogrefe, Pearl *The Sir Thomas More Circle* Urbana 1959

Index of Wills and Administrations relating to the County of Devon. Ed. J. John Beckerlegge. Devonshire Association for the Advancement of Science, Literature and Art 1950

Jenkins, Elizabeth *Elizabeth the Great* London 1958

London Marriage Licences, 1521–1869 Ed. Joseph Forster. London 1887

McKerrow, Ronald B. *Printers' and Publishers' Devices in England and Scotland, 1485–1640* London, Bibliographical Society 1949

– et al. *A Dictionary of Printers and Booksellers in England, Scotland and Ireland and of Foreign Printers of English Books, 1557–1640* London, Bibliographical Society 1910

Nichols, John, ed. *The Diary of Henry Machyn* London 1848

– ed. *The Chronicle of the Grey Friars of London* London 1852

Onions, C.T. *A Shakespeare Glossary* Oxford 1949

Partridge, Eric *A Dictionary of Slang and Unconventional English* London 1961. 2 vols

Rigg, J.M. *Calendar of State Papers Relative to English Affairs Preserved in Rome, Elizabeth 1558–1571* London 1916

Rosenberg, Eleanor *Leicester, Patron of Letters* New York 1955

Skeat, Walter W. and A.L. Mayhew *A Glossary of Tudor and Stuart Words* Oxford 1914

Stevenson, W.H. and H.E. Salter *The Early History of St John's College, Oxford* Oxford 1939

Stratman, Carl J. *Bibliography of Medieval Drama* Berkeley 1954

Tilley, Morris P. *A Dictionary of the Proverbs in England in the Sixteenth and Seventeenth Centuries* Ann Arbor 1950

Watson, Foster *Vives: On Education* Cambridge 1913

– *Vives and the Renascence Education of Women* London 1912

Whiting, B.J. *Proverbs in the Earlier English Drama* Cambridge, Massachusetts 1938

Whythorne, Thomas *Autobiography* Ed. James A. Osborn. Oxford 1961

Williams, Neville *Thomas Howard, Fourth Duke of Norfolk* London 1960

Woodward, W.H. *Desiderius Erasmus Concerning the Aim and Method of Education* Cambridge 1904

– *Studies in Education during the Age of the Renaissance, 1400–1600* Cambridge 1906

Articles

Leach, A.F. 'St Paul's School before Colet' *Archaeologia* 62 (1910) 191–238

McKerrow, Ronald B. 'Edward Allde as a Typical Trade Printer' *The Library*, Fourth Series x 2 (1929) 121–62

POLITICAL AND ECCLESIASTICAL HISTORY

Books

Birt, H.N. *The Elizabethan Religious Settlement* London 1907

Caraman, Philip *The Other Face* London 1960

Churton, Ralph *Life of Alexander Nowell* Oxford 1809

Cook, G.H. *Old St Paul's Cathedral* London 1955

– *English Collegiate Churches* London 1959

Dugdale, William *History of Saint Paul's Cathedral* (1658) Ed. H. Ellis. London 1818

– *Monasticon Anglicanum* London 1846

Edwards, Kathleen *The English Secular Cathedral in the Middle Ages* Manchester 1949; reprinted, New York 1967

Hackett, Maria *Correspondence and Evidences respecting The Ancient School Attached to Saint Paul's Cathedral* Third Edition. London 1832

– *A Brief Account of Cathedral and Collegiate Schools* London 1827

Hennessy, George *Novum Repertorium Ecclesiasticum Parochiale Londinense* London 1896

The Parish Church of Kingston St Mary [Taunton] Taunton 1948

Knowles, Dom. David *The Religious Orders in England* Cambridge 1959. 3 vols

Longman, William *A History of The Three Cathedrals Dedicated to St Paul in London* London 1873

Matthews, W.R. and W.M. Atkins, eds *A History of St Paul's Cathedral* London 1964

Meyer, A.O. *England and the Catholic Church under Queen Elizabeth* London 1916

Milman, H.H. *Annals of St Paul's Cathedral* London 1868

Oliver, George *Monasticon Dioecesis Exoniensis* Exeter 1846–54

– *Historic Collections relating to Monasteries in Devon* Exeter 1820

Pollen, J.H. *The English Catholics in the reign of Queen Elizabeth* London 1920

Simpson, W. Sparrow *Chapters in The History of Old St Paul's* London 1881

– *Gleanings From Old St Paul's* London 1889

– *S. Paul's Cathedral and Old City Life* London 1894

Sinclair, W.D. *Memorials of St Paul's Cathedral* London 1909

Stephan, John *The Ancient Religious Houses of Devon* Exeter 1935

Strype, John *Annals of the Reformation* London 1725–31. 4 vols

– *Life of Edmund Grindal* Oxford 1827

Summers, Vivian *Church of the Holy Cross, Crediton, Devon* Gloucester, nd

Thompson, Hamilton *The English Clergy* Oxford 1947

Articles

Pearson, J.B. 'The Church of Chulmleigh, North Devon' *Transactions of the Devon Association* 39 (1907) 208–15

Rose-Troup, Frances 'Lists relating to Persons Ejected from Religious Houses' *Devon and Cornwall Notes and Queries* 17 (1932) 285ff.

Sanders, Nicholas 'Report to Cardinal Moroni ... [1561]' Ed. J.H. Pollen *Miscellanea* 1. Catholic Record Society, London 1905

Simpson, W. Sparrow 'Charter and Statutes of the College of Minor Canons in St Paul's Cathedral, London' *Archaeologia* 43 (1871) 165–200

Walcott, M.E.C. 'Old St Paul's' *Transactions of the St Paul's Ecclesiological Society* 1 (1885) 177–87

TOPOGRAPHICAL

Books

Hearsey, John E.N. *Bridge, Church and Palace in Old London* London 1961

Hoskins, W.G. *Devon* London 1954

The Itinerary of John Leland in or about the years 1535–1543 Ed. Lucy
Toulmin Smith. London 1906–10. 5 vols

Reddaway, T.F. *The Rebuilding of London After the Great Fire* London
1940; reprinted 1951

Stow, John *A Survay of London* (1603) Ed. C.L. Kingsford. Oxford 1908.
2 vols

Westcote, Thomas *A View of Devonshire* Eds. G. Oliver and P. Jones. Exeter
1845

Wheatley, H.B. *London Past and Present* London 1891. 3 vols

Articles

Reichel, O.J. 'The "Domesday" Hundreds of Devon' *Transactions of the
Devon Association* 30 (1898) 391–432

– 'The Manor and Hundred of Crediton' *Transactions of the Devon Association* 54 (1923) 160–2

MUSIC AND POETRY

Books

Barclay, Alexander *The Castell of Labour* Ed. A.W. Pollard. Roxburghe
Club 1905

Berdan, J.M. *Early Tudor Poetry, 1485–1547* New York 1961

Bernard, J.E., Jr *The Prosody of the Tudor Interlude* New Haven 1939

Boyd, Morrison Comegys *Elizabethan Music and Musical Criticism*
Philadelphia 1962

Goodwin, James, ed. 'Six Ballads' *Early English Poetry, Ballads, and Popular Literature of the Middle Ages* Percy Society, London 1844

Hammond, E.P., ed. *English Verse Between Chaucer and Surrey* New York
1965

Hawes, Stephen *The Pastime of Pleasure*. Ed. W.E. Mead. Early English
Text Society. London 1928

Hazlitt, W. Carew *History of English Poetry* London 1871. 4 vols

Lewis, C.S. *The Allegory of Love* Oxford 1936

Lydgate, John *The Minor Poems* Ed. H.N. MacCracken. Early English Text
Society. London 1911–34. 2 vols

Nevill, William *The Castle of Pleasure* Ed. R.D. Cornelius. Early English
    Text Society. London 1931
Pattison, Bruce *Music and Poetry of the English Renaissance* London 1948
The Pilgrimage of the Life of Man Eds F.J. Furnivall and K.B. Locock. Early
    English Text Society. London 1899–1904
Reason and Sensuality Ed. E. Sieper. Early English Text Society. London
    1901–3
Reese, Gustave *Music in the Renaissance* London 1954
Rollins, Hyder Edward, ed. *Old English Ballads, 1553–1625* Cambridge
    1920
– *Index To The Ballad Entries (1557–1709) in the Stationers' Register*
    Chapel Hill 1924
– ed. *A Gorgeous Gallery of Gallant Inventions (1578)* Cambridge, Mas-
    sachusetts 1926
– ed. *The Paradise of Dainty Devices (1576–1606)* Cambridge, Mas-
    sachusetts 1927
– ed. *Tottel's Miscellany (1557- 1587)* Cambridge, Massachusetts 1929.
    2 vols
Rubel, Vere L. *Poetic Diction in the English Renaissance* New York 1941
Warton, Thomas *History of English Poetry* London 1774–81. 4 vols

Articles
Edwards, Alfred 'Crediton Musicians' *Transactions of the Devon Associa-
    tion* 14 (1882) 321–8
Petti, A.C. 'Peter Phillips, Composer and Organist, 1561–1628' *Recusant
    History* 4 (1957–8) 45–60

HISTORY OF THE DRAMA

Books
Adams, J.Q. *Shakespearean Playhouses* Boston 1917
Bevington, David M. *From 'Mankind' to Marlowe* Cambridge, Mas-
    sachusetts 1962
Boas, F.S. *University Drama in the Tudor Age* Oxford 1914
– *An Introduction to Tudor Drama* Oxford 1933
Bradbrook, M.C. *The Rise of the Common Player* London 1962
Brooke, C.F. Tucker *Tudor Drama* Boston 1911
Chambers, E.K. *The Medieval Stage* Oxford 1903. 2 vols
– *The Elizabethan Stage* Oxford 1923 4 vols
– *The English Folk-Play* Oxford 1933

Clemen, Wolfgang H. *English Tragedy before Shakespeare* Heidelberg
   1955; translated by T.S. Dorsch, London 1961
Collier, John Payne *The History of English Dramatic Poetry to the Time of
   Shakespeare and Annals of the Stage to the Restoration* London 1831.
   3 vols
Feuillerat, Albert 'Documents Relating to the Revels at Court in the time of
   King Edward vi and Queen Mary' *Materialien zur Kunde des älteren
   englischen Dramas* ed. W. Bang. Vol. xli Louvain 1914; reprinted 1963
– 'Documents Relating to the Office of the Revels in the time of Queen
   Elizabeth' *Materialien zur Kunde des älteren englischen Dramas* ed. W.
   Bang. Vol. xxi Louvain 1908; reprinted 1963
Fleay, F.G. *A Biographical Chronicle of the English Drama, 1559–1642*
   London 1891. 2 vols
– *A Chronicle History of the London Stage, 1559–1642* London 1890
Flecknoe, Richard *A Short Discourse of the English Stage* London 1664
Harbage, Alfred and Samuel Schoenbaum *Annals of English Drama,
   975–1700* London 1964
Hazlitt, W. Carew *The English Drama and Stage under the Tudor and
   Stuart Princes* London 1869; reprinted New York [1964?]
Hillebrand, Harold Newcomb *The Child Actors* Urbana 1926
Lawrence, W.J. *The Elizabethan Playhouse and Other Studies*. First Series,
   Stratford upon Avon 1912; Second Series, Philadelphia 1913
The Malone Society *Collections*, 2. Pt iii Oxford 1931
Murray, J.T. *The English Dramatic Companies, 1558–1642* London 1910;
   reprinted, New York 1963. 2 vols
Nichols, John *The Progresses and Public Processions of Queen Elizabeth*
   Second Edition. London 1823. 3 vols
Schelling, Feliz E. *Elizabethan Drama, 1558–1642* Boston 1908 2 vols
Smith, Irwin *Shakespeare's Blackfriars Theatre* New York 1964
Southern, Richard *The Staging of Plays before Shakespeare* London 1973
Stopes, C.C. *William Hunnis and the Revels of the Chapel Royal* Louvain
   1910
Wallace, C.W. *The Evolution of the English Drama up to Shakespeare, with
   a History of the First Blackfriars Theatre* Berlin 1912
– *The Children of the Chapel at Blackfriars, 1597–1603* 1908; reprinted,
   New York 1970
Wickham, Glynne *Early English Stages, 1300 to 1660* London 1963–72.
   3 vols
Wilson, F.P. *The English Drama 1485–1585* Ed. G.K. Hunter. Oxford 1969

Articles

Armstrong, W.A. 'The Audience of the Elizabethan Private Theatres'
Review of English Studies 10 (1959) 234–49
– *The Elizabethan Private Theatres: Facts and Problems* The Society for
Theatre Research Pamphlet. Series No. 6. London 1958
Ball, Roma 'The Choirboy Actors of St Paul's Cathedral' *Emporia State
Research Studies* 10 (1962) 5–16
Baskervill, C.R. 'Mummers' Wooing Plays in England' *Modern Philology*
21 (1924) 225–72
Bradbrook, M.C. '"Silk? Satin? Kersey? Rags?": The Choristers' Theatre
under Elizabeth and James' *Studies in English Literature* 1 (1961) 53–64
Brawner, J.P. 'Early Classical Narrative Plays by Sebastian Westcott and
Richard Mulcaster' *Modern Language Quarterly* 4 (1943) 455–64
'Dotted Crochet' 'The Children of St Paul's and the Plays they Acted' *The
Musical Times* 1 January 1907
Lennam, T.N.S. 'Sir Edward Dering's Collection of Playbooks, 1619–1624'
Shakespeare Quarterly 16 (1965) 145–53
Patterson, Morton 'The Stagecraft of the Revels Office During the Reign of
Elizabeth' *Studies in Elizabethan Theatre* (1961) 3–52
Sarlos, Robert K. 'Development and Operation of the First Blackfriars
Theatre' *Studies in Elizabethan Theatre* (1961) 139–78
Shapiro, Michael 'Three Notes on the Theatre at Paul's, c. 1569–1607'
Theatre Notebook XXIV (1970) 147–54
– 'Children's Troupes: Dramatic Illusion and Acting Style' *Comparative
Drama* III (1969) 42–53

COLLECTIONS AND SERIES OF PLAYS

Adams, J.Q., ed. *Chief Pre-Shakespearean Dramas* Cambridge, Massachusetts 1924
Amyot, Thomas, ed. *A Supplement to Dodsley's Old English Plays* London
1853. 4 vols
Bang, Willy, ed. *Materialien zur Kunde des älteren englischen Dramas*
Louvain and London 1902–
Bond, R. Warwick, ed. *Early Plays from the Italian* Oxford 1911
– ed. *The Complete Works of John Lyly* Oxford 1902. 3 vols
Farmer, John S., ed. *Five Anonymous Plays* Fourth Series. London 1908
– ed. *Six Anonymous Plays* Second Series. London 1906
– ed. *Recently Recovered 'Lost' Tudor Plays* London 1907

– ed. *The Dramatic Writings of Richard Wever and Thomas Ingelend*
London 1905
Hazlitt, W. Carew, ed. *Dodsley's Old English Plays* London 1874–6. 15 vols
Malone Society Reprints. Gen. Eds, W.W. Greg et al. Oxford 1907–
Manly, J.M., ed. *Specimens of the Pre-Shakespearean Drama* Boston
1897–1904. 2 vols
Tudor Facsimile Texts. Ed. J.S. Farmer. London 1907–14

PLAYS

Acolastus Ed. P.L. Carver. Early English Text Society 1937
All for Money Tudor Facsimile Texts 1910
Appius and Virginia Ed. R.B. McKerrow. Malone Society Reprint 1911
Cambises Tudor Facsimile Texts 1910
The Castle of Perseverance Eds F.J. Furnivall and A.W. Pollard. Early
English Text Society 1904
Clyomon and Clamydes Ed. W.W. Greg. Malone Society Reprint 1913
– Ed. Betty J. Littleton. Studies in English Literature 35. The Hague and
Paris 1968
Common Conditions Ed. C.F.T. Brooke. New Haven 1915
The Conflict of Conscience Eds Herbert Davis and F.P. Wilson. Malone
Society Reprint 1952
Damon and Pithias Ed. Arthur Brown. Malone Society Reprint 1957
The Disobedient Child Tudor Facsimile Texts 1908
Enough Is as Good as a Feast Ed. R. Mark Benbow. Regents Renaissance
Drama Series. Lincoln, Nebraska 1967
The Four Elements Tudor Facsimile Texts 1908
Gammer Gurton's Needle Tudor Facsimile Texts 1910
Gentleness and Nobility Ed. A.C. Partridge. Malone Society Reprint 1950
Horestes Tudor Facsimile Texts 1910
Impatient Poverty Tudor Facsimile Texts 1907
Jack Juggler Eds Eunice Lilian Smart and W.W. Greg. Malone Society
Reprint 1933
– Ed. W.H. Williams. Cambridge 1914
Jacob and Esau Ed. John Crow. Malone Society Reprint 1956
King Darius Tudor Facsimile Texts 1909
Liberality and Prodigality Ed. W.W. Greg. Malone Society Reprint 1913
The Longer Thou Livest Ed. R. Mark Benbow. Regents Renaissance Drama
Series. Lincoln, Nebraska 1967

Lusty Juventus Tudor Facsimile Texts 1907
Mankind Eds F.J. Furnivall and A.W. Pollard. Early English Text Society
  1904
A new and Pleasaunt enterlude intituled the marriage of witte and Science.
  Thomas Marshe London, nd
The Marriage of Wit and Science Ed. W.C. Hazlitt *Dodsley's Old English
  Plays* Volume II London 1874–6
– Ed. J.S. Farmer *Five Anonymous Plays* London 1908
– Tudor Facsimile Texts 1909
– Ed. Arthur Brown. Malone Society Reprint 1960 (1961)
A Contract of a Marriage between Wit and Wisdom Tudor Facsimile Texts
  1909
The Marriage of Wit and Wisdom Ed. J.O. Halliwell [-Phillips] London 1846
The Marriage between Wit and Widsom Ed. T.N.S. Lennam. Malone
  Society Reprint 1966 (1971)
Misogonus Ed. R. Warwick Bond *Early Plays from the Italian* Oxford 1911
Mundus et Infans Tudor Facsimile Texts 1909
Nature Tudor Facsimile Texts 1908
New Custom Tudor Facsimile Texts 1908
Nice Wanton Tudor Facsimile Texts 1909
Patient Grissell Eds R.B. McKerrow and W.W. Greg. Malone Society
  Reprint 1909
The Pedlar's Prophecy Ed. W.W. Greg. Malone Society Reprint 1914
Respublica Ed. W.W. Greg. Early English Text Society 1952
Sir Thomas More Ed. W.W. Greg. Malone Society Reprint 1911
The Most Virtuous and Godly Susanna Ed. B. Ifor Evans. Malone Society
  Reprint 1937
The Tide Tarrieth No Man Tudor Facsimile Texts 1910
The Trial of Treasure Tudor Facsimile Texts 1908
Tom Tyler and his Wife Eds G.C. Moore Smith and W.W. Greg. Malone
  Society Reprint 1910
Wealth and Health Ed. W.W. Greg. Malone Society Reprint 1907
The Moral Play of Wit and Science Ed. J.O. Halliwell [-Phillips] London
  1848
The Play of Wit and Science Tudor Facsimile Texts 1908
Wit and Science Ed. Thomas Amyot *A Supplement to Dodsley's Old English
  Plays* 1853
Wit and Science Ed. Arthur Brown. Malone Society Reprint 1951
Witty and Witless Tudor Facsimile Texts 1910
Youth Tudor Facsimile Texts 1908

STUDIES OF INDIVIDUAL PLAYS AND PLAYWRIGHTS

Books

Bolwell, R.G.W. *The Life and Works of John Heywood* New York 1921
Bradner, Leicester *The Life and Poems of Richard Edwards* New Haven 1927
Reed, A.W. *Early Tudor Drama* London 1926
– *The Canon of John Heywood's Plays* London 1918

Articles

'A Ballad Monger' *'The Marriage of Wit and Science*, an Interlude by John
  Redford' *Shakespeare Society Papers* 2 (1845) 76–8
Armstrong, W.A. 'The Background and Sources of Preston's *Cambises'*
  English Studies 31 (1950) 129–35
– 'The Authorship and Political Meaning of *Cambises' English Studies* 36
  (1955) 289–99
Brooke, C.F. Tucker 'On the Source of *Common Conditions' Modern
  Language Notes* 31 (1917) 474–8
Brown, Arthur 'Two Notes on John Redford' *Modern Language Review* 43
  (1948) 508–10
– 'Three Notes on Sebastian Westcott' *Modern Language Review* 44
  (1949) 229–32
– 'The Play of *Wit and Science* by John Redford' *Philological Quarterly* 28
  (1949) 429–42
– 'A Note on Sebastian Westcott and the Plays Presented by the Children of
  Paul's' *Modern Language Quarterly* 12 (1951) 134–6
– 'Sebastian Westcott at York' *Modern Language Review* 47 (1952) 49–50
Flood, W.H. Grattan 'Master Sebastian' *The Musical Antiquary* 3 (1913)
  149–57
Greg, W.W. 'The Date of *Wit and Wisdom' Philological Quarterly* 11
  (1932) 410
Habicht, Werner 'The *Wit*-Interludes and the Form of Pre-Shakespearean
  "Romantic Comedy"' *Renaissance Drama* 8 (1965) 73–88
Hillebrand, Harold Newcomb 'Sebastian Westcote, Dramatist and Master of
  the Children of Paul's' *Journal of English and Germanic Philology* 14
  (1915) 568–84
Lennam, T.N.S. 'Francis Merbury, 1555–1611' *Studies in Philology* 65
  (1968) 207–22

Mackenzie, W. Roy 'A Source for Medwall's *Nature' Publications of the Modern Language Association* 29 (1914) 189–99

Race, Sidney 'The Moral Play of *Wit and Science' Notes and Queries* 198 (1953) 96–9

– 'The Marriage of Wit and Wisdom' *Notes and Queries* 198 (1953) 18–20

Roberts, Charles W. 'The Authorship of Gammer Gurton's Needle' *Philological Quarterly* 19 (1940) 97–113

Sisson, C.J. 'A Note on Sebastian Westcott' *Review of English Studies* 19 (1943) 204–5

Tannenbaum, Samuel A. 'Comments on *The Marriage of Wit and Wisdom' Philological Quarterly* 9 (1930) 321–34

– 'Dr Tannenbaum Replies' *Philological Quarterly* 12 (1933) 88–9

– 'Editorial Notes on *Wit and Science' Philological Quarterly* 14 (1935) 307–26

Varma, R.S. 'Act and Scene Divisions in "The Marriage of Wit and Science"' *Notes and Queries*, New Series 10 (1963) 95–6

– 'Philosophical and Moral Ideas in *The Marriage of Wit and Science' Philological Quarterly* 44 (1965) 120–2

Withington, Robert 'Experience the Mother of Science' *Publications of the Modern Language Association* 57 (1942) 592

Index

This book
was designed by
WILLIAM RUETER
under the direction of
ALLAN FLEMING
and was printed by
University of
Toronto
Press